Contents at a Glance

Table of Contents

Part I   Getting Acquainted with Mountain Lion Basics

About the Author

Hi! I'm Yvonne Johnson, and I'm going to be your "instructor." I've been writing computer books and teaching computer classes since 1982, so you are in good hands. I have written more than 60 PC and Mac computer books and college texts for well-known publishers on practically every type of software that exists—from operating systems to desktop publishing, from word processing and spreadsheets to databases, from programming to graphic design and web design. Some of my most recent Mac books include *Using Mac OS X Lion* (Pearson Education), *Using Office 2011 for Mac* (Pearson Education), and *Introducing OS X Mountain Lion: What's New and What's Changed for Lion Users* (Pearson Education).

I actually started my computer-writing career when I established the first proprietary computer-training school in Kentucky. For the 12 years I owned the school, I wrote all the training manuals for all the software programs that we taught. After I sold the school, I continued to write computer training materials as a freelance writer, writing a large percentage of the curricula offered by a national computer-training company headquartered in Chicago and for a computer-training and consulting subsidiary of the *Washington Post* in New York City. Ultimately, I took a full-time position as Vice President of Curriculum Development for the *Washington Post* subsidiary.

So, as you can see, I've been at this for many years. I've amassed a great deal of teaching experience by delivering classroom computer training to thousands of employees of large and small businesses, military and government personnel, teachers, attorneys, secretaries, and, yes, even Microsoft software support engineers. One of the pitfalls of acquiring expertise in any field is the loss of the ability to communicate in simple terms, but I have never forgotten how to communicate with beginning learners because I am challenged on a daily basis to explain the mysteries of the computer to my husband, who will ever remain the Peter Pan of computers, the quintessential beginner. (His motto is, "Why should I memorize anything about computers when I can always ask you?" or as Peter Pan would say, "I'll never grow up!")

In addition to writing (and designing websites), I love to garden, play with my grandchildren, and entertain guests on our property in Franklin, Tennessee (which can be found on the *Vacation Rental by Owner* website, www.vrbo.com). If you should happen to book a vacation at our property, bring your book, and I will be happy to sign it for you!

Dedication

To "the new boy," Isaac Ross Johnson. May he survive his three older sisters!

Acknowledgments

From my perspective, the process of publishing a book is pretty much the same as it was when I wrote my first book in 1982. Basically, I crank out the chapters, and the publisher turns them into a real book. The team of people at Pearson who worked on this book was wonderful, as always, and I appreciate all their efforts, which made this book possible. First, I would like to thank Laura Norman, the acquisitions editor, who keeps me busy all the time; and Romny French, her intrepid editorial assistant. Many thanks also go to Mark Renfrow, the development editor; Chuck Hutchinson, the copy editor, and Tonya Simpson, the project editor. My special thanks go to my technical editor, Jennifer Ackerman-Kettell, whom I specifically requested because we have worked together on many books, and I have always found her to be thorough, meticulous, and informed. Finally, I want to thank Cindy Teeters for always making sure I get paid! I'm sure there are many additional people on the Pearson team that I don't even know about who worked behind the scenes to get this book into print, and I want to thank them as well.

Also, I would like to thank my husband for all his support and for good-naturedly letting me use his computer escapades as examples of what not to do. He is a wonderful father and grandfather and has been the love of my life since I was 16! Although he is the only husband I have ever had, I keep him in line ;-) by introducing him as "my first husband." To which he always rolls his eyes and mutters, "I must be made of steel."

We Want to Hear from You!

As the reader of this book, *you* are our most important critic and commentator. We value your opinion and want to know what we're doing right, what we could do better, what areas you'd like to see us publish in, and any other words of wisdom you're willing to pass our way.

We welcome your comments. You can email or write to let us know what you did or didn't like about this book—as well as what we can do to make our books better.

Please note that we cannot help you with technical problems related to the topic of this book.

When you write, please be sure to include this book's title and author as well as your name and email address. We will carefully review your comments and share them with the author and editors who worked on the book.

Email: feedback@quepublishing.com

Mail: Que Publishing
        ATTN: Reader Feedback
        800 East 96th Street
        Indianapolis, IN 46240 USA

Reader Services

Visit our website and register this book at quepublishing.com/register for convenient access to any updates, downloads, or errata that might be available for this book.

INTRODUCTION

Mountain Lion, the newest version of the Mac operating system, might be considered the offspring of two operating systems—OS X and iOS. OS X, pronounced *OS ten*, is the operating system that has been used on the Apple Macintosh computer since 2002. iOS, used first on the iPhone in 2007, was based on OS X and expanded to run the iPod touch and iPad. Collectively, the devices that run iOS are referred to as *iDevices*. Apple continued to develop and upgrade both operating systems along their own separate paths until one day the Apple developers said, "Hey, let's take the best things from both operating systems and make them work on all our products." In 2011, Apple released the first operating systems on the Mac and the iDevices that began to merge the two paths into what looks more like the same path.

With Mountain Lion, Apple has made a giant leap in making OS X more like iOS. In fact, many have called Mountain Lion the "iOSification of OS X." What this means to you is, if, for example, you have an iPhone, an iMac, and an iPad, all your devices function in almost the same way with just some minor differences. The underlying principles are the same. This makes it much easier for you to operate all your different devices.

Along with Apple's agenda to unify its devices, Apple also launched an initiative to make a user's data more important than the device that creates it. The technology that accomplishes this initiative is called the *iCloud*. iCloud synchronizes a user's data across all qualifying Apple devices. No single device is the keeper of data any more, but all devices store data on the iCloud. All roads lead to Rome, in other words. This means that you have access to your data from any device, and you don't have to worry about things such as keeping your iPhone contacts synchronized with your contacts on your Mac because the iCloud does this for you automatically.

The direction that Apple is taking with its hardware products and the implementation of the iCloud makes this an exciting time to be an "absolute beginner." *OS X Mountain Lion Absolute Beginner's Guide* is written from the standpoint that you are either a new Mac user or you are simply new to Mountain Lion, but assumes that you are certainly no beginner when it comes to computers. It assumes that you know many of the basic computer concepts such as how to start a computer, the difference between hardware and software, how to use a mouse, what the Internet is, and so on. What this book will help you do is learn the ins and outs of the Mountain Lion operating system and its many built-in applications.

The book covers how to use the essential features of the Mac operating system, such as the menus, windows, desktop, Dock, and so on; how to set hardware preferences and customize the software for the way you like to work; how to use the Finder to organize and access your files and folders; how to use the built-in applications, such as Safari, Contacts, Calendar, Notes, Reminders, Mail, Messages, FaceTime, and more; how to use the "leisure-time" applications, such as Game Center, DVD Player, QuickTime Player, iTunes, and Photo Booth; and finally, how to administer user accounts and keep your Mac running smoothly and securely. If you are an absolute beginner to Mountain Lion but not to the Mac, you will find that I've covered almost all the new features that Mountain Lion contains. These new features are scattered about in the chapters that are germane.

How This Book Is Organized

This book is organized into six main parts, as follows:

- **Part I, "Getting Acquainted with Mountain Lion Basics,"** discusses booting up and shutting down; using menus, the Dock, and windows; and understanding the iCloud.

- **Part II, "Customizing the Way Your Mac Works,"** shows you how to set preferences for your hardware, personalize the desktop, and customize the Dock.

- **Part III, "Working with Files, Folders, and Applications,"** talks about the Finder, Mountain Lion's file management application, and how to work with applications. This part covers how to use the Finder interface and its four different views; how to create folders of different types for file storage and special purposes; how to manipulate files (find, open, close, rename, copy, move, and so on); and how to launch applications, use the Autosave and Resume features, and install and upgrade applications.

- **Part IV, "Using Mountain Lion Apps,"** covers all the Productivity applications that are a part of Mountain Lion, including Safari, Contacts, Calendar, Notes, Reminders, Mail, Messages, FaceTime, TextEdit, Dashboard, and Preview.

- **Part V, "Entertaining Yourself,"** is the fun part of the book. This part covers the built-in applications that you can use to amuse and entertain yourself, including the new Game Center, DVD Player, QuickTime Player, iTunes, and Photo Booth.

- **Part VI, "Performing Administrative Routines,"** covers the topics that are essential to the successful and prolonged use of your Mac. These topics, though not as scintillating as twisting your nose up for a funny Photo Booth picture or as productive as cranking out emails and messages to your contacts, are not altogether without their own charm. You'll appreciate knowing how to share your computer with another user while maintaining each other's privacy, and you won't regret learning how to keep your Mac secure and back up your data.

Although the chapters in this book are organized in a logical sequence, you don't need to read the chapters sequentially. So feel free to jump right into the chapter that interests you most. If you need to read something that was discussed in another chapter to understand the current topic, there are cross-references to guide you to those discussions.

Conventions Used in This Book

The *Absolute Beginner's Guide* series uses conventions that should be easy enough to understand, but it never hurts to give more information than might be needed. The great thing about too much information is that you don't have to read it!

As you read through the pages, it helps to know precisely how I've presented specific types of information and what my viewpoint is. For example, there are usually three to four ways to do something. You might be able to make selections from the menu bar, click a button in the toolbar, use a shortcut menu, press a shortcut key combination, click a button in the Dock, use a swiping gesture, and so on. From my viewpoint, I don't think it's a good use of space to tell you every single way there is to accomplish the same thing, and it makes for tedious reading as well. I generally start with the menu commands and perhaps include one other way (or two other ways at the most).

Menu Commands

Many computer instructional books use a convention like this for menu commands: "Click **File**, **Open**." Often, however, an application window has many command sources available that could be confusing to you so I like to include the words *menu bar* in the instruction. This helps you know exactly where to look for the commands. So the instructions that I write usually say something like, "Click **File** in the menu bar and then click **Open**." This tells you immediately where to look for the first command.

Keyboard Shortcuts

A keyboard shortcut is just what it sounds like—keys that you press to accomplish a command quickly instead of using a longer method such as clicking through a menu structure. In this book, most keyboard shortcuts must be pressed together. If this is the case, the names of the keys are joined with a hyphen (-), as in Command-C, the shortcut for the copy command. To use the shortcut, you press the Command key and hold it down while you press the C key.

If the keyboard shortcut requires you to press the keys in succession without holding them down, the keys have no punctuation joining them. For example, FN FN is the keyboard shortcut that turns on the new Dictation tool.

Mouse and Trackpad Actions

In this book, I use the terms *click* and *right-click*. Click means to click the left side of the mouse, and, of course, right-click means to click the right side of the mouse. This is the way a right-handed user generally sets up his mouse. If you are a left-handed user, you may set your primary click on the right side of your mouse and the secondary click on the left side of your mouse—just the opposite of a right-handed user. If that is the case, you must make a mental adjustment when reading the terms *click* and *right-click*. Don't feel offended or slighted. It is so much easier and uses less space to say "right-click" instead of "click the secondary mouse button."

Many times in this book, I refer to swiping gestures on the Magic Mouse or Magic Trackpad. Swiping gestures can be up and down or left and right. These gestures may be done with one to four fingers, depending on how you have configured your mouse or trackpad. Instead of going into a lengthy discussion of the possibilities every time I mention a swiping gesture, I assume that you know how your hardware is set up and will use the appropriate number of fingers.

Special Elements

This book also includes a few special elements that provide additional information not included in the basic text. These elements are designed to supplement the text to make your learning faster, easier, and more efficient.

 TIP   A *tip* is a piece of advice—a little trick, actually—that helps you use your computer more effectively or maneuver around problems or limitations.

 NOTE   A *note* is designed to provide information that is generally useful but not specifically necessary for what you're doing at the moment. Some are like extended tips—interesting, but not essential.

 CAUTION   A *caution* tells you to beware of a potentially dangerous act or situation. In some cases, ignoring a caution could cause you significant problems—so pay attention to them!

Let Me Know What You Think

Writing a book on pre-released software is always problematic because the last version of software that an author uses is almost always different from the actual software that is released to the public. After the software is released, a very quick edit must be done and sometimes we miss some things that should be changed. I would be happy to hear from you if you find any of these oversights, or if you just have some questions or suggestions. You can email corrections or questions to me via feedback@quepublishing.com. When you send an email, please be sure to include this book's title and my name for reference.

1

IN THIS CHAPTER

- What happens after you flip the switch
- Shutting down versus sleeping
- Putting your computer on a schedule
- Knowing when to restart

BOOTING UP AND SHUTTING DOWN

What better place for the absolute beginner to start than turning your computer on and off? Of course, you don't need an entire chapter devoted exclusively to pressing a power button, but surely you realize there are other issues to be considered. This chapter gets into the real nitty-gritty of these issues. In fact, you'll likely be surprised to learn that there really is so much to it! After reading this chapter, you should be able to make some really informed decisions about how to set up your Mac and how to run it on a daily basis.

Turning on Your Mac

You can start your Mac, turn it on, or power up—the choice of terms is up to you—by pressing the power button. Immediately after you press this button, your Mac should boot up. "Boot up" is a pretty old computer term that means the "operating system"—in this case, OS X Mountain Lion—communicates with the hardware in such a way that the computer is ready for you to start entering your commands via the mouse and keyboard.

When a Mac boots up, the screen displays a gray linen-textured background with a silver Apple logo in the center. The next thing you see depends on whether automatic login is turned on or off. If it's turned on, the Mac automatically logs you in behind the scenes and displays the *desktop*. If automatic login is turned off, you see the login screen. The name and logo for every user who has an account on the Mac are shown on the login screen. To advance to the desktop, you must click your name or icon, type your password, and press Return.

Taking a Close Look at the Desktop

The desktop is called the desktop because it's your computer work surface—the virtual "top of your desk." That's about as far we can go with the analogy though. The characteristics of the desktop have no similarity to file trays, staplers, or anything else you might keep on your real desk.

The background for the Mountain Lion desktop is a starry graphic, as shown in Figure 1.1. Across the top of the screen is the menu bar. The left side of the bar contains the names of menus, and to the right of the last menu name, you see various icons. These icons are called *Menu Extras,* and they also display menus. Each Menu Extra displays a menu for a specific hardware device or feature, such as the Menu Extra for controlling the volume level or the one for controlling Bluetooth. Third-party applications, such as Twitter and Evernote, can add icons to this part of the menu bar as well.

Next on the menu bar you see the day of the week and the time. If you have multiple users on your Mac and you have turned on Fast User Switching, the next thing you see on the menu bar is your own name or your icon (because you are the user who is logged in). See "Working with Multiple User Logins" in Chapter 28, "Managing User Accounts," for information on how to use the Fast User Switching feature.

FIGURE 1.1

The default desktop for Mountain Lion is basically the same as Lion's except for the background graphic and the new Notification Center icon.

The next item in the menu bar is the Spotlight search icon, which is supposed to look like a magnifying glass (but some people think it looks like a Q). This icon does not display a menu, but opens a text box in which you can type a search phrase. The Spotlight search feature in the menu bar can search for practically anything anywhere on your computer. It can find files, applications, contacts, notes, reminders, and so on.

Finally, the last icon on the right is the Notification Center button. This button opens a panel on the right that lists notifications for such things as new email messages you have received, alarms you have set for appointments, and so on. To learn more about the Notifications Center, see "Using Notifications" in Chapter 7, "Personalizing the Desktop."

At the bottom of the desktop, you see the Dock—a reflective-looking shelf filled with colorful icons. For more information about this feature, see Chapter 3, "Using the Dock," and Chapter 8, "Customizing the Dock."

Putting Your Mac to Sleep or Shutting It Down

If you know you aren't going to use your Mac for the rest of the day or a lightning storm is expected, you might want to shut it down. This is just a personal decision, really. I never turn off any of my Macs at home unless I'm going to be gone for a week!

When you are not using your Mac during some point in the day, but you know you will be using it again very soon, I don't recommend turning off the computer. During the time you are not using it, you can just let it go to sleep.

When a Mac goes to sleep, it suspends all your open applications and files in memory, forces the screen to go black, and forces the hard drive to stop running. The Mac is still on while it's asleep, but it's drawing very little electricity. When you wake a Mac that is sleeping, everything that you had open when the Mac went to sleep reappears on your screen, and you are ready to go back to work with no delays.

Additionally, MacBooks with built-in flash storage can use the new Power Nap feature during the sleep mode. Power Nap keeps your data (mail, notes, reminders, messages, and so on) synchronized so you have the latest information when the Mac wakes up. It also can make Time Machine backups to Time Capsule and download OS X software updates that you can install when the Mac wakes up. Power Nap works whether you are running on AC or battery power. It works silently with no fan noises and without any lights coming on.

Using the Sleep Modes

The iMac and other desktop models have two sleep modes: one for the entire computer and one for just the screen. Laptops also have an additional sleep mode for just the hard drive.

By default, a Mac goes into the full computer sleep mode automatically if it is not being used for a period of 10 minutes. (This is the mode in which the screen goes black and the hard drive stops spinning.) A separate option that puts the screen only to sleep is also set by default for 10 minutes. The display sleep mode kicks in automatically after 10 minutes if no keyboard or mouse inputs are detected. When the screen is in sleep mode, it goes black, but the hard drive can still be working in the background. For example, if you are downloading an app from the App Store that you know is going to take quite awhile, you might decide to take a walk for some exercise while it is downloading. After 10 minutes of downloading, the display will turn black, but the download will continue.

Instead of waiting for your Mac to go into computer sleep on its own, you can put it into sleep mode manually. To do this, click the **Apple** menu and click **Sleep**.

To wake the Mac from the computer sleep mode or the display sleep mode, press any key or move the mouse.

Setting the Interval for Computer Sleep and Display Sleep

If the default times for the computer sleep mode or the display sleep mode are too long or too short, you can change them to whatever works for you. To change the time intervals, follow these steps:

1. Click the **System Preferences** icon in the Dock or open Launchpad and click the icon there.

 NOTE   Alternatively, you can click the **Apple** in the menu bar and click **System Preferences**.

2. Click **Energy Saver** in the Hardware group.

3. If the padlock is locked (see Figure 1.2), click it to unlock it. If you have administrative rights, your name appears in the message. Type your password and click **Unlock**. If you are not an administrative user, type the username of a user with administrative rights, type the password, and click **Unlock**. The padlock opens, allowing you to make changes.

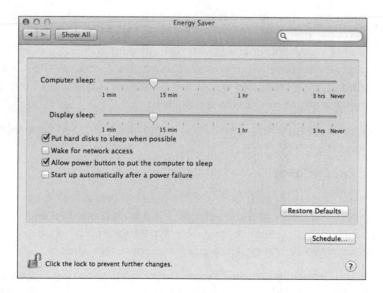

FIGURE 1.2

The Energy Saver window shown here is for an iMac. If you have a laptop, you will see different options.

4. Drag the slider for **Computer Sleep** to the right to increase the time or drag it to the left to decrease the time.

 TIP   If you have a laptop, you should set the Computer Sleep option on both the Battery and the Power Adapter tabs. On my laptop, I have a shorter interval for Battery Computer Sleep than for Power Adapter Computer Sleep, so I can conserve battery power whenever possible.

5. Drag the slider for **Display Sleep** to the right to increase the time or drag it to the left to decrease the time.

 NOTE   If you have the screen saver feature set to start before the display sleep feature, the screen saver will start first and the display sleep will still kick in at its regular time.

6. To prevent further changes, click the padlock to lock it.

7. Close the window when finished.

Scheduling Your Computer to Go to Sleep Automatically

If you have a fairly regimented routine that dictates exactly when you stop working on your computer, you can schedule Mountain Lion to put it to sleep for you automatically. Additionally, if you turn off your computer each day, and you have a regimented time when you start using the computer the next day, you can have Mountain Lion start your computer for you at a specified time. To schedule sleep time or a start time, follow these steps:

1. Click the **System Preferences** icon in the Dock or open Launchpad and click the icon there.

2. Click **Energy Saver**.

3. If the padlock is locked, click it to unlock it. If you have administrative rights, your name appears in the message. Type your password and click **Unlock**. If you are not an administrative user, type the username of a user with administrative rights, type the password, and click **Unlock**.

4. Click the **Schedule** button. Specify the options shown in Figure 1.3 and click **OK**.

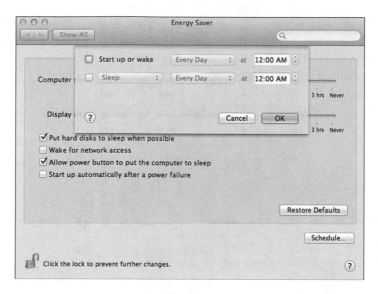

FIGURE 1.3

You can schedule sleep or start times if you have a pretty regular work routine.

5. To prevent further changes, click the padlock icon.

6. Close the window when finished.

Shutting Down the Computer

After you consider your options, I'm sure you will decide on a routine of shutting down the computer that works for you. You might decide to leave your Mac on for days at a time, as I do, or shut it down every day, or a little of both.

CAUTION   Always shut down your desktop computer if you plan to physically move it. Moving a computer while the hard disk is spinning could damage the disk. For a laptop, which is designed to be moved around, just close the case when you are moving it. This puts the laptop in sleep mode, which stops the hard drive from spinning.

Before shutting down the computer, you might want to make sure that all the other users (if there are any) are also ready to quit for the day. See Chapter 28 for special shutdown issues that pertain to Macs with multiple user accounts. If you are the only user of your Mac, or if all other users have logged out, follow these steps to shut down:

1. Click the **Apple** menu and click **Shut Down**. A dialog box, shown in Figure 1.4, asks if you are sure you want to shut down your computer now. If you do nothing from this point on, the computer will count down from 60 seconds and then shut down automatically.

FIGURE 1.4

The Shut Down dialog box remembers your setting for reopening windows.

2. During this 60-second grace period, you can always change your mind and click **Cancel**. Otherwise, you should decide if you want to enable or disable the option **Reopen Windows When Logging Back In**. This option allows you to resume your work right where you let off by reopening applications and files that you left open when you shut down.

 NOTE   Mountain Lion remembers what you choose for the reopen windows option and uses it the next time you shut down the computer.

3. If you are ready before the 60 seconds has counted down, you can click **Shut Down**, and Mountain Lion turns off the power for you at that moment.

 NOTE   If you are using third-party applications or an application that predates OS X Lion and have failed to save your work or close the application, you will see a prompt at this point warning you to save your work or close the application. Lion and Mountain Lion applications such as TextEdit or Pages do not have to be closed before shutting down the computer, and they save your files for you automatically.

Restarting Your Computer

Occasionally, you might need to restart your computer. For example, if you make a change to a preference that does not take effect until the next time you start your computer, you might want to restart immediately so the change will take effect right away. To restart your computer, follow these steps:

1. Click the **Apple** menu and click **Restart**. A dialog box, similar to the one shown in Figure 1.3, asks if you are sure you want to restart your computer now. If you do nothing, in 60 seconds the computer will shut down and then restart.

   TIP Before the end of this 60-second grace period, you can click **Cancel** if you change your mind.

2. Select or deselect **Reopen Windows When Logging Back In**.

3. When you are ready, you can click **Restart**, and Mountain Lion turns off the power for you and then restarts automatically.

   NOTE The same caution applies for restarting your computer as it does for shutting it down. If you have been using an application that predates OS X Lion (or a third-party application) and have failed to save your work or close the application, you will see a prompt warning you to save your work or close the application.

THE ABSOLUTE MINIMUM

- Everything you do on a Mac takes place on the desktop.

- Leaving your Mac running all the time doesn't hurt it if you put it in sleep mode.

- Never move your Mac while it is running (except for a laptop) because you could damage the hard drive. In the case of a laptop, be sure to close the case when you move it while it is still running.

- Don't forget that you can leave windows open when you shut down and Mountain Lion can reopen them for you when you log back in.

2

IN THIS CHAPTER

- Peeling away the multiple layers of menu characteristics
- Navigating the menu bar and dialog boxes like a pro
- Cutting through all the red tape with a shortcut menu

USING MENUS AND DIALOG BOXES

The primary method by which a user communicates with an application is through menus and dialog boxes.

In this chapter, we examine the two basic types of menus: the menu bar and the context menu. Additionally, we look at how to use the controls in dialog boxes and navigate a dialog box.

Using the Menu Bar

The menu bar displays the names of the menus for whatever application you are currently working in, and these menus generally contain *all* the commands available in that application. To execute a command using the menu bar, simply click the name of the menu that has the command you want to use. Then find and click the desired command.

 NOTE Most applications provide alternative methods for executing commands such as toolbars, keyboard shortcuts, mouse clicks, or trackpad gestures. Sometimes it's just easier to click a tool on a toolbar than to go digging through the menus until you find the command you need.

Examining the Elements of the Menu Bar

If you come from a PC background (and here a die-hard Mac user would offer you tons of sympathy), you are used to seeing individual menu bars in every open program window. On a Mac, no matter how many windows you have open, there is still only one menu bar at the top of the screen. The names of the menus in the menu bar come from the application that is in the current, active window. If you work in lots of windows at the same time, you could lose track of which window you were last working in if you are interrupted by something like a phone call. A quick glance at the menu bar, however, tells you which application has the focus because the menu bar always displays the name of the application as the first word on the left, as shown in Figure 2.1.

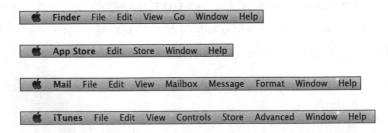

FIGURE 2.1

Compare the menu bars of the Finder, the App Store, Mail, and iTunes.

If you study Figure 2.1, you can see several similarities in the menus of the different applications. First of all, the menu bars have many menus in common, such as File, Edit, View, Window, and Help. Although the menu names are the same, the actual commands on these menus vary from application to application.

You also should notice that every menu bar displays the Apple icon on the far left side of the bar. This is not just a decoration! It's an actual menu, and it has the same commands on it for every menu bar. Figure 2.2 shows the commands on the Apple menu.

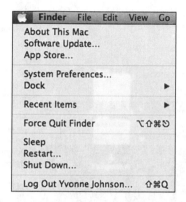

FIGURE 2.2

Except for the wording of the Force Quit command, the Apple menu commands never change regardless of the application that is open.

Examining the Elements of a Menu

When you click the name of a menu in the menu bar, a menu is displayed directly under that menu's name, as shown in Figure 2.3. Menus are a lot more complex than you might think, so let's look at all the elements and nuances of the menu shown in this figure.

The menu in Figure 2.3 shows examples of all the possible menu elements:

- **Submenu arrow**—If an option on a menu has a black arrow beside it that points to the right, it means the option is not really a command, but the name of a submenu. When you point to the option, the submenu slides out to the side and displays two or more related commands. (Notice that I wrote "point" to the menu option and not "click." Clicking closes the menu.) Submenus can be tricky sometimes. They close if you accidentally move the pointer to another option on the first menu while you are trying to click the command on the submenu.

- **Unavailable command**—An option that is "dimmed," that is, appears in light gray text instead of black, is not available because it is not relevant at the current time. For example, the Back command on the Go menu was not available at the time the menu was invoked because the user (that would be me!) had not "gone" anywhere yet, so there was nothing to go back to.

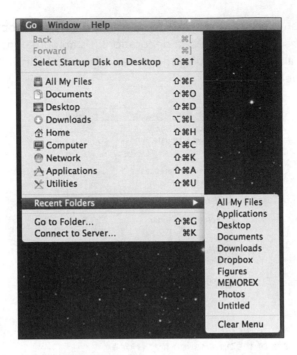

FIGURE 2.3

The Finder's Go menu has examples of all the menu elements.

- **Keyboard shortcut keys**—If a keyboard shortcut exists for a menu command, it is displayed to the right of the command. A keyboard shortcut performs a command instantly without opening a menu. Of course, you have to be able to read the hieroglyphics to be able to use one. Here's the key to the hieroglyphics:

  ⇧ = the Shift key

  ⌃ = the Control key

  ⌥ = the Alt/Option key

  ⌘ = the Command key

  To use a keyboard shortcut, first press and hold the "hieroglyphic keys" and then press the regular key. For example, to open All My Files in the Finder, press and hold the Shift and Command keys and then press the F key.

- **Ellipsis**—When you see an ellipsis after a menu command, it means that the command has to gather more information from you before it can do anything. Most of the time, this means that the menu is going to close and a dialog box is going to open in which you have to make some additional selections or enter some information in a text box. It's not always a dialog box that opens, however. Sometimes it's a window or an *Assistant* that opens. (An Assistant is a series of dialog boxes that guide you through a process.) In Mountain Lion, an ellipsis could mean that the menu closes and you have to do something directly in the application. For example, in the TextEdit application, when you select File, Rename…, the menu closes and the name of the document is selected in the title bar waiting for you to type the new name.

Using Dialog Boxes

A dialog box has different types of controls, such as check boxes, radio buttons, lists, input fields, pop-up buttons/menus, and so on. Figure 2.4 shows a dialog box with most of the different types of controls.

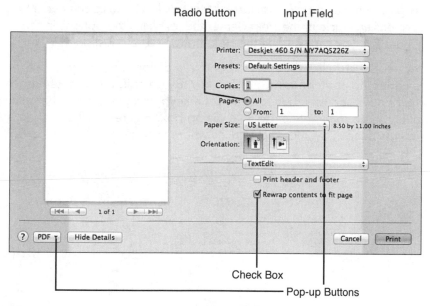

FIGURE 2.4

A dialog box collects all the necessary information to finally execute a command you have selected from a menu.

Using the controls in dialog boxes is fairly intuitive, but a couple of controls bear further explaining. Here are some things you should know about some of the controls:

- **Radio buttons**—These controls are generally in a group, and you can select only one of the options in the group.

- **Input fields**—If an input field has default text in it, you can change the text by editing it or by deleting it and retyping. When a dialog box opens and the content of a text field is already selected for you, you can simply type the text you want and the selected text will be replaced.

- **Pop-up menus**—This type of control comes in two flavors. If the control has two triangles (one pointing up and the other pointing down), the selection that is currently displayed is the default. When you click this control, it displays a pop-up menu with a check mark beside the selection. You can select any other option on the menu if you like. The second type of pop-up control has only one downward-pointing triangle on it. This control really has nothing selected for you already and in most cases is not a required option. In Figure 2.4, the PDF control is an example of this type. You would not select an option from the PDF pop-up menu if you are only printing the file. This menu allows you to save a file in PDF format.

The majority of dialog boxes have at least two buttons: a button to cancel everything you might have changed and close the dialog box and a button to execute all the settings in the dialog box and close it. Most dialog boxes also have a Help button that opens an article in the Help Center that explains the options in the dialog box. In Figure 2.4, you can see that the Help button has a question mark on it.

Most people just click their way around in a dialog box, but you can move from one control to another using the Tab key. By default, the Tab key moves only to text boxes and lists, but you can set a keyboard preference that allows the Tab key to go to every control in a dialog box. Figure 2.5 shows the Keyboard Shortcuts pane in System Preferences where you can set this option.

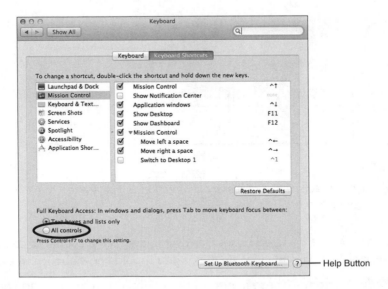

FIGURE 2.5

To display the pane shown in this figure, open System Preferences, click Keyboard, and click the Keyboard Shortcuts tab.

Using Context Menus

A context menu is probably referred to more often as a *shortcut menu*, or if you are coming from the PC world, as a *right-click menu*. A context menu contains only those options that could apply to a specific circumstance. As an example, if you point to a file in the Finder and display the context menu, you will see commands that could be executed on a file. (See Figure 2.6.) If you had to rely solely on the menus in the menu bar, you would have to go to at least two different menus to find some of the commands that are listed on the shortcut menu, and you would see a lot of commands that did not apply in the process. So you might say a context menu really "cuts to the chase." Everything else about a context menu— the dimmed options, submenus, ellipses, and so on—is just like a regular menu.

FIGURE 2.6

This shortcut menu displays only commands that can be executed on a file.

To display a context menu, you can point to an item on the screen and click the secondary mouse button. If you are using a trackpad, you can point to the item and then hold two fingers on the trackpad while you click the trackpad. If you want to use a keyboard combination, hold down the Control key while you click the primary mouse button or the trackpad.

In some circumstances, no context menu is available. For example, if you right-click a blank space in the menu bar, no shortcut menu opens.

CAUTION If you have a two-button mouse that has never had the default settings changed, both the left and right buttons function as primary buttons. If you right-click the mouse, the shortcut menu will not appear. Refer to Chapter 6, "Using and Controlling Your Hardware," to find out how to set the preferences for a mouse.

Using Menu Extras

The Menu Extras located on the right side of the menu bar, also called *menulets*, do not display menu names. Instead a menulet uses an icon. A menulet displays a short menu for a specific feature, such as Bluetooth. Not all menulets are displayed by default, but Figure 2.7 shows all the icons it is possible to display for Mountain Lion features.

FIGURE 2.7

Menulets from left to right are Accessibility, Time Machine, Display, Bluetooth, Networks, Volume, and Keyboard.

Third-party applications that you install may also place a Menu Extra icon on the menu bar. One popular application called Dropbox is an example.

To use a menulet, click the icon to display the menu. Menulet menus look like regular menus and function in the same way, so there is nothing new to learn about how to use them. To learn more about how to display, rearrange, or delete menulets, refer to Chapter 7, "Personalizing the Desktop."

THE ABSOLUTE MINIMUM

- Becoming familiar with what an application's commands are and where they are located in the menu bar system is worth the time it takes.

- You can always tell what application has focus by looking at the menu bar because it displays the name of the application.

- You can move to every control in a dialog box by pressing the Tab key if you enable a setting in the Keyboard Shortcuts preferences.

- It never hurts to try to open a context menu. If there is one, it is displayed. If there isn't one, nothing happens.

- The icons on the right side of the menu bar display menus for specific features, such as volume control, Bluetooth status, battery status, and so on.

IN THIS CHAPTER

- Examining the flashiest part of the desktop
- Identifying the "immutable" Dock icons and the ones that are more malleable
- Using Dock icons to launch applications and open folders

3

USING THE DOCK

The Dock is a very important part of the desktop, and you will use it often. This chapter is short and sweet; it contains all the basic things you need to know about how to use this essential tool. So give this chapter a quick read, and you'll be well on your way to becoming a proficient Mountain Lion user.

 NOTE Even though you can get along just fine if you learned only the information in this chapter, it will also be worth your while to read the chapter on how to customize the Dock. (That's Chapter 8, "Customizing the Dock.")

Examining the Parts of the Dock

The Dock is divided into two sections by a dotted line, as shown in Figure 3.1. The left side of the line has icons for applications, and the right side of the line has icons for files and folders. As you learn to use the various applications on your Mac, you will see that the right side of the Dock also can display other icons temporarily in certain situations. For example, if you open an email and then minimize it, a temporary icon for the email message is displayed on the right side of the separator. You learn about this in detail in Chapter 12, "Working with Applications."

 TIP   If you point to an icon, you can see the name of the application or folder it represents.

FIGURE 3.1

The line that divides the two sides of the Dock is called the separator.

The first icon in the Dock is for the Finder application, the application that shows you where all your files are stored and allows you to perform operations on your files and folders such as move, copy, rename, and so on. The Finder icon cannot be removed from the Dock or even moved to a different location on the Dock. The last icon on the Dock is the Trash icon. Like the Finder icon, the Trash icon cannot be removed or moved to a different location on the Dock.

The Dock does not contain an icon for every single application that is installed on your Mac. The initial selection of icons that appear in the Dock is determined by Apple, but really, everything between the Finder icon and the Trash icon is fair game. In other words, you can put any additional applications on the left side of the Dock; you can put any file or folder you want on the right side of the Dock; you can arrange them in any order (except for moving Finder or Trash, of course); and you can even delete any of the icons you don't want between the Finder and Trash icons. For information about adding, deleting, or rearranging Dock icons, see Chapter 8.

Launching Applications from the Dock

Clicking one of the icons on the left side of the Dock launches the application represented by the icon. Most of the default icons launch full-blown applications such as Safari, the web browsing application; Contacts, the address book; Mail, the email application; Calendar, the appointment-scheduling application; and so on. A few of the default icons on the Dock launch applications that are more like utilities. For example, one icon on the Dock launches Mission Control, a utility that shows all your open windows at once and helps you navigate them. Another launches the System Preferences, a window where you can set personal, hardware, Internet, wireless, system, and user account preferences. The icon that has a rocket ship on it launches the application called Launchpad. This utility displays icons for the applications installed on your Mac, and, as its name implies, you use it to launch applications. (It's good for launching applications that are not represented on the Dock.)

 NOTE   To learn more about the Launchpad and launching applications in general, see Chapter 12.

When you launch an application, a glowing blue bubble appears under the application's icon on the Dock. If you have really been paying attention, you might have a question right about now: What about an application launched from the Launchpad that doesn't have an icon on the Dock? That's a good question, and the answer is that Mountain Lion places a temporary icon on the Dock for the application (on the left side of the separator line, of course). While an application is running, its temporary icon in the Dock has the blue bubble under it, and when you close the application, the temporary icon in the Dock disappears.

Opening Folders on the Dock

As I've already mentioned, the right side of the Dock is for icons that represent folders or files. By default, only two folder icons appear here: the Downloads icon and the Trash icon. If you add your own folders to the right side of the Dock, they will function just like the Downloads folder as described next.

Opening the Downloads Folder

The Downloads folder, which is the default location for all files you download from the Web, is a special kind of icon for a folder called a *stack*. It's called a stack because the icon is really a stack of icons—one icon for each file in the folder (hypothetically). Each icon is a preview of the file, and because the last file you downloaded is always displayed on the top of the stack, the icon changes.

When you click a stack icon, the individual items in the folder are displayed right on the desktop. They may be displayed as a fan (see Figure 3.2), a grid (see Figure 3.3), or a list (see Figure 3.4). By default, the display for stacks is set to Automatic so Mountain Lion can decide the best way to display the items depending on the number of items in the folder.

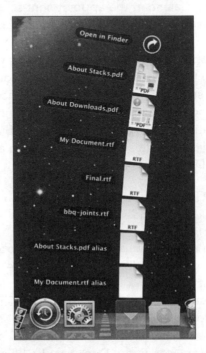

FIGURE 3.2

The fan view. Notice that you can open the folder in Finder.

FIGURE 3.3

The grid view.

FIGURE 3.4

The list view.

To open an individual item displayed by the stack, just click the item. If the stack displays items in a fan, however, you must click the icon for the item to open it. Clicking the name of the item just closes the fan. After displaying the items in a stack, if you don't really want to open one of them, you can press Esc or click on a blank area of the desktop.

Opening the Trash Folder

The Trash icon contains the contents of the Trash folder, but it does not operate like a stack icon. When you click the Trash icon, the Finder opens and displays the Trash folder as shown in Figure 3.5. If you have never deleted anything, the trash can looks empty on the Dock icon, but when you delete something, the trash can looks like it has crumpled paper in it.

Files in the Trash folder are just "waiting to be taken out," but before you empty the trash for good, you can go through the trash and remove any files that you might want back again. For more information about deleting and retrieving files and folders, see Chapter 11, "Working with Files and Folders in the Finder."

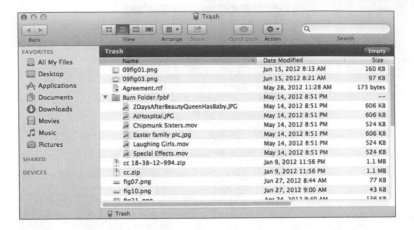

FIGURE 3.5

Clicking the Trash icon opens the Trash folder in the Finder window.

THE ABSOLUTE MINIMUM

- The Dock looks and works just fine as it is, but I tell you how you can customize the dock in Chapter 8, so don't miss that chapter.

- You can launch applications from the Launchpad if you don't have an icon for the app on the Dock.

- A stack icon can display its contents as a fan, grid, or list.

- You can add folders to the Dock so that the files you use the most are more accessible.

- You can see the files that are in the Trash folder and even retrieve them from the Trash and put them back where they were.

4

IN THIS CHAPTER

- Minimizing windows in three different ways
- Making a window take up as little room on the screen as possible
- Making a window take up as much room on the screen as possible
- Keeping track of all your windows with Mission Control
- Segregating your work with individual desktops

WORKING WITH WINDOWS

The window is such an essential and basic element of the computer experience, for both Mac and PC users, that everyone probably knows what a window is; however, things that have become too common are often taken for granted. This chapter goes beyond the obvious to explore some of the special features of windows and digs a little deeper into the common details. This is *not* an exercise in trivial pursuit, but a journey that will make you a better, faster, more efficient computer user.

Performing Common Window Functions

The common window functions include the following: close, minimize, zoom, switch to full-screen, resize, move, and scroll. Most of these are functions that anyone who has ever used a computer probably knows how to do, but just to be thorough, here's a short summary of how to perform each function:

- **Close**—Click the red Close button in the upper-left corner of the window. The window closes.

- **Minimize**—Click the yellow Minimize button in the upper-left corner of the window. The window closes on the screen but remains open as an icon on the right side of the Dock.

- **Zoom**—Click the green Zoom button in the upper-left corner of the window. The window zooms to its previous size. If the previous size was smaller than the current size, the window gets smaller. If the previous size was larger than the current size, the window gets larger.

- **Switch to Full-Screen**—Click the Full-Screen button in the upper-right corner. To switch back, point to the top of the screen to redisplay the menu bar, and click the Full-Screen button on the far right side. Note that not all applications can display in full-screen mode. Those that cannot do not have a Full-Screen button.

- **Resize**—Point to any edge of the window or to a corner and drag the window to the size you want.

- **Move**—Drag the window by its title bar and drop it in the new location.

- **Scroll**—If the content of a window exceeds the size of the window, you have to scroll vertically or horizontally to see the hidden content. By default, if content is hidden, vertical or horizontal scrollbars are displayed on the right and bottom borders of the window, respectively. You also can scroll content in the window using the up- or down-arrow keys on the keyboard, using a wheel on a mouse, or using a gesture on a trackpad.

Taking a Closer Look at Windows

At a minimum, a window has a title bar at the top and borders on the other three sides. Some windows have a status bar at the bottom that may or may not be visible. Different applications may have additional components that have the capability to show or hide. Some windows have sidebars, for example; the Finder has a path bar; Mail has a favorites bar; and so on. To show or hide a window component, you may be able to find an option on the View menu. In some applications, however, you might have to set application preferences to show or hide particular components.

Now, as promised, this section digs a little deeper into the details of windows. You may find some useful techniques you weren't aware of here.

Closing Windows

In most cases, closing a window closes the file, but not the application. You can prove this to yourself by launching an application and then closing the window. You should still see the glowing blue bubble under the application's icon in the Dock, which indicates the application is still running. There are a few exceptions to this rule. Contacts and App Store are two applications that close when you close their windows.

In some applications, such as TextEdit, for example, if you have several windows open, you can close all of them at once by clicking **File** and clicking **Close All Windows**. If you have minimized windows in the application, they will remain open.

Minimizing Windows

You can set a preference that allows you to minimize a window by double-clicking its title bar. To set the preference, click the **System Preferences** icon in the Dock and click **Dock**. Figure 4.1 shows the option.

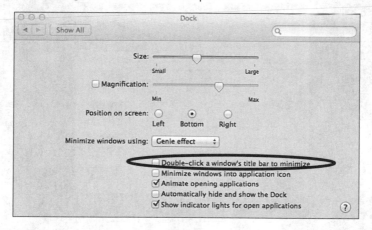

FIGURE 4.1

Select the option that is circled to add another method of minimizing a window.

By default, minimizing a window creates an icon on the right side of the Dock. Each minimized window in the Dock has an *app badge* on it to help identify it, as shown in Figure 4.2.

App Badges

FIGURE 4.2

The icon for each minimized window is a preview of the file, but it may be too small to tell what the file contains.

If you have several of the same type of file minimized on the Dock, it's difficult to tell by looking which icon represents which file. You could point to each icon to see the name of the file above the icon, or you could right-click the application's icon on the left side of the Dock and click **Show All Windows**. All open windows for the application are displayed; the minimized windows are displayed below the line as thumbnails and the nonminimized windows are displayed above the line, as shown in Figure 4.3. In this mode, the minimized previews are larger, and you can usually tell by looking which window is which. Then you can click the window you want to work in (or press **Esc** to exit this mode).

FIGURE 4.3

Minimized windows are displayed as thumbnails.

As an alternative to minimizing windows to the right side of the Dock, you can minimize windows to the application icon on the left side of the Dock. To enable this action, open System Preferences and click **Dock**. Click **Minimize Windows into Application Icon**. (Look back at Figure 4.1.) After you set this preference, when you minimize a window, it appears to zoom into the application icon on the Dock where its preview icon is hidden. This option uses less space on the Dock but also makes it impossible to see at a glance if any windows are minimized.

Resizing Windows

Every window has a limit to how small you can make it, and this minimum size varies by application. Normally, when you are resizing a window and you point to a window border, the cursor changes to a two-headed arrow. If you have reached the limit of how narrow the window can be, when you point the cursor at either side border, the cursor changes to a single-headed arrow, indicating the only direction in which you can move the border. The same is true when you have reached the limit of how tall a window can be.

Moving Windows

When moving windows around on the desktop, you are not limited by the edges of the screen. You actually can move a window beyond the edge so that part of the window is hidden. You might want to do this when you want to keep the window open but out of your way until you are ready to use it. This gives you more space on the screen. Of course, you can't move the entire window beyond the edge.

As you know, you move a window by dragging its title bar. One application in the OS X suite can be moved around by dragging *any* area of the open window. This application is Contacts. No other application has this capability.

Scrolling Windows

In Mountain Lion, you can set several preferences that control the way scrollbars work. These preferences are located on the General pane of System Preferences. If you like a clean look, you can set the Show Scroll Bars option to show scrollbars only when you are scrolling. With the When Scrolling option, Mountain Lion detects your intentions and displays the scrollbars only when it knows you want to scroll. Most people choose the Always options. Always displaying scrollbars when they are needed is a visual cue that there is more to see than the window is currently displaying. The option Automatically Based on Mouse or Trackpad means the scrollbars are visible only when you are using a mouse as an input device or when you are using a trackpad as an input device. Because most people are using one or the other, this option is not much different from the Always option. The Click in the Scroll Bar To option in the General pane enables you to jump to the next page when you click in the scrollbar or jump to the spot that's clicked.

Using Full Screen Mode

The Full Screen mode enlarges a window so that it occupies the whole screen. It also hides all extraneous elements, such as the menu bar, toolbars, and the Dock. If a window can go into the Full Screen mode, it has a Full Screen button in the upper-right corner, like the one shown in Figure 4.4. Most windows can go into the Full Screen mode, but one that doesn't is the Finder.

FIGURE 4.4

Look for this button in the upper-right corner of a window to see if it can go into Full Screen mode.

To switch to the Full Screen mode, click the **Full Screen** button. To switch back to the previous window size, point to the top edge of the screen to display the menu bar and click the button on the far-right side of the menu bar. See Figure 4.5.

FIGURE 4.5

This button is hidden so you have to display the menu bar to see it.

While you are working in Full Screen mode, you can access the menu bar or the toolbars (if there are any) simply by pointing to the top edge of the screen. When you are finished using the menus or the toolbar, they hide again. To access the Dock, point to the bottom edge of the screen.

If you have several full-screen windows open, you can move back and forth between them by using a two-finger swipe on a Magic Mouse or a Magic Trackpad. (Of course, you must have your mouse or trackpad preferences set for this gesture. See Chapter 6, "Using and Controlling Your Hardware.")

Switching Between Windows

If you are a hardcore multitasker, you might have several files open in several different applications at once. This results in lots of overlapping windows, with some stacked on top of each other as well. How can you keep track of all your windows and switch between them?

If you can see any part of a window, you can click the visible part, and that window becomes the active window. If you can't see any part of the window, you can click the window's application icon in the Dock, and one of its windows comes to the front. If it's not the window you want, you can click **Window** in the menu bar and select the window you want from that menu. If all this sounds like too much trouble, just use Mission Control. That's what it's there for!

Using Mission Control to Navigate Windows

The Mission Control feature makes the multitasker's life much easier. Its whole purpose is to give you an overview of all the windows you have open on the desktop, all your desktops, and all your full-screen windows. Figure 4.6 shows a desktop full of windows, and Figure 4.7 shows how those windows look in Mission Control.

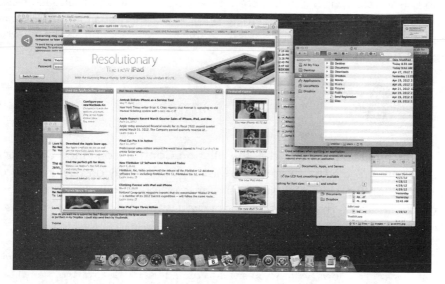

FIGURE 4.6

This desktop is cluttered with lots of open windows.

FIGURE 4.7

Mission Control shows exactly what applications and files are open.

In Figure 4.7, notice the row at the top of the screen. It contains a thumbnail for the Dashboard (which is considered a desktop), a thumbnail for each desktop (see the next topic to learn how to create one), and a thumbnail for an application open in full screen. All other open windows are grouped by application below the row of thumbnails.

 NOTE   In Mission Control, the groups of application windows (under the top row of thumbnails) do not include any minimized windows.

To launch Mission Control, click the **Mission Control** icon in the Dock (or in the Launchpad). You also can press the Mission Control key on your keyboard (**F3**) or swipe up on the Magic Trackpad with three or four fingers (depending on how you configure it). Then click the window you want to go to or press **Esc** to exit Mission Control.

 TIP   To use Mission Control to switch between full-screen windows, you can press **F3** to open Mission Control and then click the thumbnail of the full-screen window you want to go to in the top row.

Creating Separate Spaces for Applications

Another way Mission Control helps you organize a large number of windows is to create separate desktops for them. (A desktop, which is really nothing more than a work area, is also called a *space*.) After you create a new desktop, you assign the applications you want to run in that space. When assigning applications, you can select from three options:

- **All Desktops**—If you select this option, when you launch the application, it opens in all your desktop spaces simultaneously. Everything you do in the application is exactly the same on every desktop because each desktop is just a different view of the same window.

- **This Desktop**—If you select this option, the application can run in only this desktop, but you can assign it to other desktops using the same option. So if you have an application assigned to two desktops, when you launch that application, it is displayed in both desktops simultaneously. If you assign an application to only one desktop, no matter what desktop you are working in, if you launch that application, it will switch you to the desktop to which it is assigned.

- **None**—None is the default setting for every application. An application with a None assignment is not assigned to any one desktop but can open in any desktop. When it is open in a desktop, however, it cannot be seen from another desktop.

To further illustrate these options, suppose you create a desktop for your personal applications and one for your business applications. The personal desktop might have these applications assigned to it: Messages, all your games, and Safari. The business desktop might have these applications assigned to it: Word, Excel, and Safari. When you launch Messages, it would be displayed in only the personal desktop, and when you launch Word, it would be displayed in only the business desktop. When you launch Safari, however, it would be displayed in both desktops simultaneously. (Remember that only one instance of Safari is running and each desktop has the same view of it. So don't think you can do different things in Safari on each desktop.)

This is what your workflow would be like with the two desktops: You open Word and then open a document that contains your resume and begin to edit the document. Then you decide to send a message to someone. You click the Message icon in the Dock, and you are automatically switched from your business desktop to the personal desktop. While on your personal desktop, you decide to start a game of Solitaire. You also open an application that is not assigned to any desktop, such as Mail. Then you open Safari to check your favorite site for news.

After a while, you decide it's time to get back to work, so you click the Word icon to continue working on your resume. Back in your business desktop where you had only the Word window open, you now also have the Safari window open. You close the Safari window and start working on your resume. Your personal desktop still has the windows open for Message, Solitaire, and Mail, but not Safari because you closed it in the business desktop. You can't see any of the personal windows, so they are not in your way, but you also cannot see your Mail without returning to the personal desktop. You realize that you should assign Mail to All Desktops because you want to be able to check mail no matter where you are. (You could assign Mail individually to both your existing desktops, but if there is a chance you will create more desktops, the All Desktops option is the better choice.)

 NOTE For the purpose of the preceding explanation, I referred to the desktops as "personal" and "business." I don't want to give you the wrong impression here. You cannot name the desktops. They are named Desktop 1, Desktop 2, and so on.

So now that you know how things work, here are the steps to follow for creating a desktop and assigning applications to it:

1. Open Mission Control.

2. Point to the upper-right corner of the screen until you see a plus, as shown in Figure 4.8.

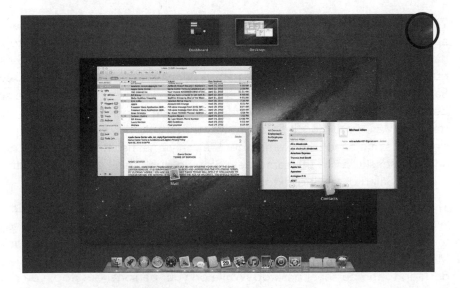

FIGURE 4.8

The plus shows up only when you point to the area that is circled.

3. Click the plus. Mission Control adds a desktop to the row of thumbnails in the top row and numbers it with the next consecutive number.

4. Click the new desktop, and it opens while simultaneously closing Mission Control.

5. Right-click the icon in the Dock for an application you want to assign.

 TIP If the application doesn't have an icon in the Dock, launch the application from the Launchpad so it does have an icon in the Dock. See Chapter 12, "Working with Applications."

6. Click **Options** and select **All Desktops**, **This Desktop,** or **None**, as shown in Figure 4.9.

FIGURE 4.9

Right-click the icon of the application you want to assign to a desktop.

7. To assign more applications, repeat steps 5 and 6.

When you have more than one desktop, launching Mission Control gives you an overview of the windows for the current desktop only. To see an orderly overview of the windows on a different desktop, you must switch to that desktop and then launch Mission Control. To switch from one desktop to another, launch Mission Control and click the desktop you want to go to. If you have a Magic Trackpad, swipe left or right with three fingers to scroll left or right through the desktop spaces. (You also can configure the trackpad to scroll horizontally with a four-finger swipe.)

 TIP You also could switch to a desktop by clicking a Dock icon for an application that is open only in that desktop.

You can delete any desktop you have created, but you cannot delete the default desktop (Desktop 1). To delete a desktop, open Mission Control and point to the desktop you want to delete until you see a Close button appear in the upper-left corner. Then click the **Close** button. All desktops to the right of the deleted desktop (if there are any) are renumbered.

NOTE   If windows are open on the desktop that you want to delete, don't worry; you won't lose anything when you delete the desktop. The windows just move to the default desktop.

THE ABSOLUTE MINIMUM

- The common window functions include minimizing, zooming, resizing, moving, and closing.

- Mission Control displays a row at the top of the screen that contains a thumbnail for the Dashboard, a thumbnail for each desktop, and a thumbnail for each application open in full screen. All other open windows are grouped by application below the row of thumbnails.

- Mission Control can create individual desktops to help you separate your work so you can have more control over open windows.

5

USING iCLOUD

Using iCloud can make your life so much easier in so many ways! If you have more than one Apple qualifying device, you can keep them synchronized like never before. (Here "qualifying device" means an iPhone, iPad, or iPod touch that runs on iOS 5 or a Mac that runs on Lion or Mountain Lion.) Even if you have only one Apple device, the iCloud is a perfect way to access your data from anyone's computer or back up and restore your data.

This chapter answers lots of questions about the iCloud: What is it? What does it do? Why do I want it? How can I get it? How does it work? How can I see what's on the iCloud? How can I get more of it?

What Is the iCloud?

iCloud is Apple's cloud computing technology. The term *cloud computing* conjures up images of giant hard drives in the sky, but the term originally comes from illustrations that depict the Internet as a cloud in computer network diagrams. So, in essence, cloud computing is a reference to using the Internet as a means of delivering computing and storage capacity as a service to a large number of users.

To use cloud computing, you must entrust your data to the service that provides the computer network (in this case, Apple), and the service provider has to store that data somewhere. Because every Apple iCloud account includes a free webmail address (that doesn't bombard you with advertising) and 5 gigabytes (GB) of free storage space, Apple needs an almost unfathomable amount of data storage space for hundreds of millions of potential users. To support the iCloud, Apple has invested at least $1 billion in one of the world's largest data centers and is in the process of building even more data centers in other locations.

What Does It Do?

The iCloud stores certain types of data that you generate from your Apple devices. This data includes email, notes, reminders, calendars, messages, photos, music, Safari bookmarks, web pages you have open in Safari in real time, certain types of applications, and certain types of data files.

As the iCloud stores data that you have generated from a device, it also pushes that data to the other qualifying devices you have. For example, suppose you have an iPhone and a Mac. If you take a photo with your iPhone, the photo is stored on the iCloud, and then the iCloud downloads it to iPhoto on your Mac. The downloading process is referred to as *pushing* because it happens automatically. You don't have to go to your Mac and tell it to download anything from the iCloud. Now suppose you loaded some photos from your camera into iPhoto on your Mac. Those photos go automatically to the iCloud and then automatically to your iPhone.

 NOTE   Although iCloud use on a PC is beyond the scope of this book, you might be interested to know that if you have a PC running Windows Vista (Service Pack 2) or Windows 7, you can use iCloud for Outlook 2007 and Outlook 2010.

Why Do I Want It?

Life is complicated at best. So much to remember and do—so little time! How can you keep up with everything? iCloud can help! Now all the applications you use to organize your life—Notes, Reminders, Calendar, and Mail—can be synchronized across all your devices. This means that you can carry the most up-to-date details of your personal and business life wherever you go if you have an iPhone, iPad, or iPod touch. You can make changes while you're on the go—check items off your reminder list, add notes as you think of them, send emails—and the iCloud will push that information back to your Mac automatically.

iCloud saves you time by eliminating the need to enter the same information on all your devices or even take the time to cable your devices together and synchronize them. iCloud performs all its functions several times a day without a single keystroke or screen tap from you! It's the ultimate organizing tool that runs on autopilot. This is why you want it!

How Can I Get It?

To take advantage of iCloud, you must have an Apple ID. Then it's just a simple matter of turning on iCloud. If you already had a paid MobileMe account with Apple, you already have an Apple ID. If you didn't, you can get one free when you turn on the iCloud services. (See "Turning on iCloud" later in this chapter.)

 NOTE   If you had a MobileMe account, you had until June 30, 2012, to move it over to an iCloud account, and Apple gave MobileMe members plenty of reminders about doing this. So, it is very likely that you have already moved your account to iCloud if you had one.

How Does It Work?

Of course, all this automatic storage and synchronization doesn't just happen by magic. There are a couple of things you have to put in place to make all this work. After that, though, everything else is pretty much magic. First and foremost, you must have iCloud enabled on your devices. Second, your devices need to have a WiFi Internet connection to be able to send data to iCloud and synchronize the data with your other devices.

Turning On iCloud

When you turn on a new Mac for the first time, the Setup Assistant guides you through a short process of setting up your computer. At that time, it requests your Apple ID so it can turn on iCloud for you. If you did not turn on iCloud during setup, you can turn it on at any time by following these steps:

1. Click the **System Preferences** icon in the Dock or open Launchpad and click the icon there.

2. Click **iCloud**. The window shown in Figure 5.1 opens.

FIGURE 5.1

iCloud requires an Apple ID.

3. If you have an Apple ID, enter it and your password; then click **Sign In**.

 TIP If you don't have an Apple ID, click **Create an Apple ID**. Select your location, enter your birth date, and click **Next**. Continue entering information and following the prompts.

4. Enter an administrative name and password in the dialog box (shown in Figure 5.2) and click **Modify Configuration**. The two options in the iCloud window are selected for you by default.

FIGURE 5.2

You see this dialog box only when you turn on iCloud for the first time or if you have signed out of iCloud and you want to turn it on again.

5. Click **Next**. All services that can be turned on are enabled.

6. Close the System Preferences window.

At this point, you have turned on iCloud, but you still need to take some additional steps to be able to synchronize your iTunes purchases. Follow these steps to turn on iTunes synchronization:

1. Launch iTunes by clicking its icon on the Dock or in the Launchpad.

2. Click **iTunes** (in the menu bar), **Preferences**, **Store**. The dialog box shown in Figure 5.3 opens.

3. Click each of the options for Automatic Downloads that you want to keep synchronized (Music, Apps, and Books). Selecting any of these options means that iTunes will download all files to all devices. This option does not, however, take care of previously purchased files. To download these files, sign into the iTunes store and click the link in the sidebar for Purchases. There you can see everything you've purchased before and decide which ones you want to download to the current computer.

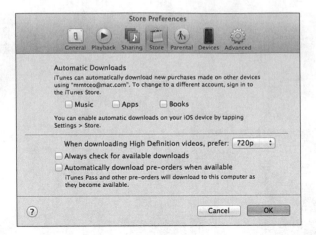

FIGURE 5.3

The Automatic Downloads option is for all subsequent downloads and does not download previous purchases.

NOTE The only books iTunes will keep in sync are those you purchase through iTunes for the iBooks app.

4. Click **OK**.

NOTE If you have a different Apple ID for iTunes than you do for your iCloud account, you cannot merge the two Apple IDs, but you can continue to use both of the IDs for their separate purposes. In other words, you can use one Apple ID for store purchases and use your iCloud Apple ID for your mail, contacts, calendars, and other services.

Accessing iCloud Data Without Your Apple Devices

Even if you don't have access to your Mac, your iPhone, your iPad, or your iPod touch, if you can get on the Internet, you can access your information. Just go to icloud.com and log in to your account. Figure 5.4 shows my iCloud account.

From your iCloud account online, you can use any of the applications you are synchronizing. You can read and send email, look up or edit a contact, and so on. Additionally, if one of your devices is lost or stolen, you can find out where it is by clicking the **Find My iPhone** icon on the home screen. (Even if you don't have an iPhone, this is the icon you see when you want to find one of your devices.)

FIGURE 5.4

The Find My iPhone icon on the iCloud home page gives you access to finding all your devices, not just an iPhone.

 NOTE   If you do not have an Apple ID with a me.com email address, you cannot synchronize email.

iCloud uses GPS to locate your device on a map for you. If the map shows your current location, your device is probably just covered up by something. If that's the case, you can make the device play a sound so you can find it. Or if the location is somewhere else, and it is a location you recognize and trust, you might want to send a message to your device for whoever finds it. If you feel the location of your device is not secure, you can lock the device remotely, or, in dire circumstances, you can even wipe the device remotely. Of course, your device must be turned on and connected to a WiFi source for this to work.

Stopping iCloud Services

If you want to stop synchronizing a particular application, you can open the iCloud System Preferences window and uncheck the application. When you do that, the data for that application will be deleted from your Mac.

If you want to stop using iCloud on your Mac completely, you can open the iCloud System Preferences window and click **Sign Out**. This deletes all iCloud data on your Mac but doesn't delete the data on the iCloud.

How Can I See What's on the iCloud?

In general, you know what's on the iCloud. It's the content of your Mail, Notes, Reminders, and so on, but you also can get more specific information about your data, such as the amount of space each type of data is using and the amount of storage space you have left in your account. Just open the iCloud preferences (in System Preferences) and click the **Manage** button to open the dialog box shown in Figure 5.5.

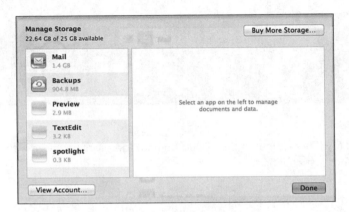

FIGURE 5.5

The apps on the left have created data that are stored on iCloud.

In Figure 5.5, you can see that the sidebar does not list every kind of data that you can synchronize. Only those applications that count against your space are displayed. For example, your purchased music, movies, apps, books, and TV shows, as well as your Photo Stream, don't count against your storage.

How Can I Get More of It?

At some point, you may start getting close to the limit of your free 5GB of storage space. Before you buy more space, you can try to reduce the space you are using. For example, you can delete your unneeded emails and then erase the deleted items in the Trash.

NOTE   If you had a MobileMe account that you moved to your iCloud account, Apple gave you the same amount of storage space you originally paid for in the MobileMe account (20GB or 40GB) and added the free 5GB to it. The 20GB or 40GB of storage was complimentary until September 30, 2012, at which time it became a yearly recurring charge to your account.

Because iCloud is set up differently from MobileMe, it is very likely that previous MobileMe members do not need to continue paying for the extra space and can downgrade their storage to the free 5GB.

If you do need to purchase more space (or reduce your amount of additional space), follow these steps:

1. Click the **System Preferences** icon in the Dock or open Launchpad and click the icon there.

2. Click **iCloud** and click **Manage**.

3. Click **Buy More Storage**. The screen shown in Figure 5.6 opens.

FIGURE 5.6

Apple charges the credit card on file with your Apple ID for the extra storage.

4. Select the amount of space you want, click **Next**, and follow the prompts.

   Or

   If you want to downgrade your storage amount, click **Downgrade Options** instead and select the amount you want.

5. When finished, close the System Preferences window.

THE ABSOLUTE MINIMUM

- You can get an Apple ID free, and it comes with a me.com email address (if you want one) and 5GB of free storage.

- Even though you can associate your Apple ID with an existing email address, you cannot synchronize your email unless you have a me.com email address.

- See and use your iCloud data from any computer anywhere by logging in to icloud.com.

- The 5GB of free storage space is probably sufficient for most users because purchased music, movies, apps, books, and TV shows, and Photo Stream don't count against your storage.

- You can purchase an extra 20 or 50GB of storage space at any time.

IN THIS CHAPTER

- Getting the automatic response you want when you insert a CD or DVD
- Connecting external drives and disconnecting them the right way so you don't lose any data
- Making your screen more readable
- Determining how the function keys should work
- Mapping the keyboard so you can type in another language
- Making the secondary mouse button work
- Installing printers and selecting a default printer
- Turning off obnoxious music that suddenly starts playing on the Internet (or anywhere)

6

USING AND CONTROLLING YOUR HARDWARE

Making your hardware work like it's supposed to or the way *you* want it to can make all the difference in your computer experience. Instead of being frustrated or thinking there's something wrong with one of your components, after reading this chapter, you can be in control. You will know what's going on and why, and you'll be able to change the way things work if you want to.

Setting Hardware Preferences

One of the keys to making your hardware work the way you want it to is setting the preferences correctly. You can find the hardware preferences on the second line of the System Preferences window, as shown in Figure 6.1.

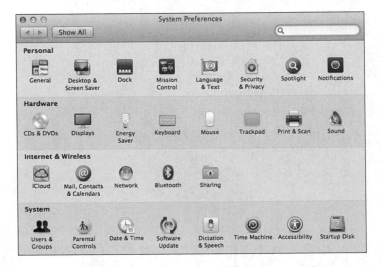

FIGURE 6.1

Hardware components are listed on the second line of the System Preferences main screen.

To open the System Preferences window, click the **System Preferences** icon in the Dock or open Launchpad and click the icon there. To set the preferences for any one of the hardware items listed on the second line, just click the icon, and make your selections. To return to the main System Preferences screen, click **Show All**. Then you can select another item (in any category).

In the remainder of this chapter, you learn how to use the Mac's hardware components. Additionally, you examine some of the important preferences you should set for the components, so you will be looking at the System Preferences window quite a bit.

Using the CD/DVD SuperDrive

The SuperDrive that comes with all new Macs, except MacBook Air, is a built-in optical drive that reads and writes DVDs (even Double Layer) and CDs. It operates at super-fast speeds ranging from 8 to 24 times normal speed.

Inserting and Ejecting Discs

To insert a CD or DVD, first wake up your Mac if necessary and then gently push the disc into the slot until you feel the disc being pulled in. The SuperDrive grabs the disc and seats it properly in the drive. To eject a disc, press the **Eject** button on the keyboard. (Look for a button with a triangle and a line under it.)

Two other ways to eject a disc are also available as explained here. Both of the methods depend on preferences set for the Finder. (See Chapter 9, "Getting Acquainted with the Finder.")

- **Method 1**—If you have set the Finder preference to show CDs and DVDs on the desktop, you can right-click the icon and click **Eject**. Alternatively, you can drag the icon to the Trash in the Dock. This technique might seem a little scary, but you will be relieved to see that when you drag the icon there, the Trash icon changes to an eject symbol.

- **Method 2**—If you have set the Finder preference to show CDs and DVDs in the sidebar, you can click the eject symbol that appears to the right of the name, as shown in Figure 6.2.

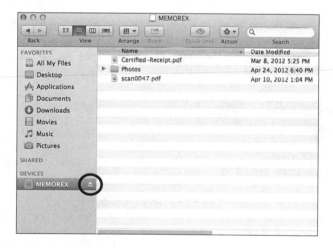

FIGURE 6.2

The Eject button is circled.

Setting Preferences for CDs and DVDs

What happens after you insert a CD or DVD is entirely up to you. Just open the System Preferences, click **CDs & DVDs** in the Hardware row, and decide what you want to happen for each type of disc. If you want to do something different every time, select the option Ask What To Do. Figure 6.3 shows what will happen if you make no changes to the default preferences.

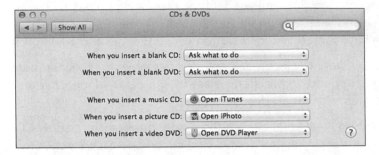

FIGURE 6.3

The default preferences for CDs and DVDs are probably the ones you really want, so you don't need to change anything on this screen.

Using External Drives

An external drive is any storage device connected to the Mac via USB, FireWire, or Thunderbolt cable. For example, the drive could be a flash drive, an additional DVD drive, an external hard drive (perhaps one that you use for Time Machine), and so on.

 NOTE   For more information about Time Machine, see Chapter 29, "Maintaining and Securing Your Mac."

Connecting an External Drive

To connect an external drive of any type, simply plug the cable or connector for the drive into the correct type of port. That's it. The Mac recognizes the drive right away, and it's ready for you to use.

Ejecting an External Drive

The steps to eject an external drive are similar to the steps for ejecting a disc from the SuperDrive, except you can't use the eject key on the keyboard. If you have set the Finder preference to show external drives on the desktop, you can right-click the icon for the drive and click **Eject**. Alternatively, you can drag the icon to the Trash icon in the Dock. If you have set the Finder preference to show external drives in the sidebar, you can click the eject symbol that appears to the right of the name.

CAUTION   Never simply unplug an external drive from your Mac without properly ejecting it first. Data could be lost.

Controlling the Brightness and Resolution of the Screen

To set the brightness or resolution of the screen, open the System Preferences and click **Display**. If necessary, click the **Display** tab. To set brightness, slide the **Brightness** slider to the left to make the screen darker or to the right to make the screen brighter. If you are using a laptop, your Brightness option is a check box for Automatically Adjust Brightness. This option allows the screen to adjust to the ambient light.

TIP   Alternatively, you can use two keys on your keyboard to brighten or darken the screen. The F1 key darkens the screen, and the F2 key brightens the screen. If you are using an older keyboard, look for keys with a large sunburst and a small sunburst on them.

The screen resolution determines how large text and images appear on your screen. You have several screen resolutions to choose from. Screen resolution is expressed by the number of pixels in the width and the height of the screen. Lower screen resolutions show less detail at a larger size, and higher resolutions show more detail at a smaller size. For example, if you select a resolution of 800 × 600, text and objects will appear much larger on your screen than if you selected a resolution of 1440 × 900. Generally, most users prefer to set a high resolution for the screen and use other methods of zooming in when they need to enlarge text or objects.

To set the resolution, on the Display tab, click the resolution in the list that you want to try. The new resolution takes effect immediately, and the System Preferences window remains open so you can try a different one if you want to. If you like the resolution you have selected, click **Show All** to return to the main System Preferences screen or close the window.

Setting Up the Keyboard

In the olden days, when I first started teaching people how to use computers, I had to spend a lot of time teaching them the difference between a computer keyboard and a typewriter keyboard. Thankfully, I don't have to do that any more, but I do want to warn you that I'm also not going to teach you the differences between the different keyboards that Apple has produced over the years. I'm going to assume that you are using the latest keyboard. If you aren't, some of the keys mentioned in this chapter may not work for you. You might have to hunt for the correct keys on your keyboard.

Controlling the Behavior of the Function Keys

Many function keys (those are the keys with F1, F2, F3, and so on, on them) have standard as well as special functions. For example, the standard function of the F12 key is to display the Dashboard. The special function, which is pictured on the key, is to turn up the volume. By default, the key performs the special function when you press it. To make the function key perform the standard function, you must first press the **Fn** key and hold it while you press the function key. Figure 6.4 shows the option that controls this feature. If you prefer to press the Fn key for the special functions instead, you can check the option circled in the figure.

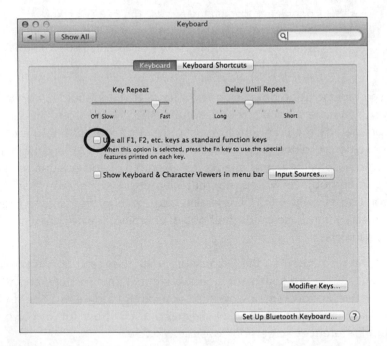

FIGURE 6.4

You can decide if you want to press the Fn key with the standard functions or with the special functions.

Lighting Up the Keys on a Laptop

If you have a MacBook, you have special, backlit keys that can light up in the dark. The preference for this feature, also located on the Keyboard tab of the Keyboard preferences, is Adjust Keyboard Brightness in Low Light. Additionally, you can set an inactivity interval at which time the illumination will turn off. When the illumination goes off, though, if the ambient light is still low, just touching the keyboard turns the keyboard illumination back on.

 TIP To make the keyboard illumination brighter, press **F6**. To make it dimmer, press **F5**.

Setting Up Keyboards for Different Languages

If you frequently need to type documents in a language that doesn't use the same letters as the English language (such as Chinese), you should select an input source for that language. The input source maps the letters of that language to your existing keyboard. (You might think the keyboard language preference is located in the Keyboard preferences, but it's really located in the Language preferences on the first row of the System Preferences.)

To select a different language for the keyboard, follow these steps:

1. Open **System Preferences**.

2. Click the **Language & Text** icon and then click **Input Sources**.

3. In the sidebar, click the check box for each additional language that you want to be able to use.

4. For your own convenience, I recommend you select **Show Input Menu in Menu Bar**. The menulet displays the flag of the current language's country.

5. To return to the main System Preferences screen, click **Show All** or, if finished, just close the window.

Now, to type in the new language, click the flag in the menu bar, select the flag for the language you want to use, and begin typing. Uh oh! How do you know which keys on your keyboard produce the letters for the language? If you are not as familiar with the language's keyboard as you are for the English keyboard, you can view the keyboard layout by clicking the flag icon again and clicking **Show Keyboard Viewer**.

Operating the Mouse or Trackpad

All new model Macs come with the Apple Magic Mouse—except, of course, the Mac Mini, the MacBook Pro, and the MacBook Air. The Mac Mini comes with no mouse, and the MacBook Pro and MacBook Air come with a built-in, multitouch trackpad.

Setting Magic Mouse Preferences

The wireless Magic Mouse has no visible buttons, but it has an area for a right click and a left click so you can set the primary and secondary buttons. Initially, though, both sides of the mouse are set as primary buttons. The Magic Mouse must be paired to your Mac via Bluetooth before you can set the preferences for it.

To pair the Magic Mouse with your Mac, be sure the mouse has good batteries and then turn on the mouse using the switch on the underside. A green light begins flashing. When the Mac recognizes the mouse, a window opens briefly on the screen to tell you it's connected, and the green light illuminates continuously. If the mouse doesn't pair immediately, open System Preferences and select **Bluetooth**. Select the mouse in the list, click the button with the gear icon, and click **Connect**.

To set the preferences for the Magic Mouse, follow these steps:

1. Open **System Preferences** and click **Mouse**.

2. Click **Point & Click**, if necessary. Figure 6.5 shows the Point & Click Preferences pane.

3. For Scroll Direction, Natural is selected by default. Some people have difficulty with this direction of scrolling because it is the opposite of the way scrolling used to work in earlier versions of OS X. If you have difficulty with the natural direction, deselect this option.

4. If this is the first time you have configured the Magic Mouse, the option for Secondary Click is not selected. This means that clicking the left or right side of the mouse performs the same function. Most people want to be able to open a context menu with a secondary mouse click. Click the check box for the option, and then select which side of the mouse should be the secondary click side if you want to use the two sides of the mouse for different functions.

5. The Smart Zoom option is selected by default. It allows you to double-tap (not double-click) with one finger to zoom in on text or graphics in applications such as Safari and Preview.

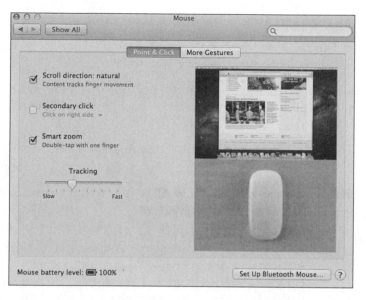

FIGURE 6.5

To help you understand the options in this window, a video demonstrates each gesture when you hover the mouse over the option.

6. Using the slider, set the speed for Tracking. This setting determines how fast the mouse pointer moves on the screen.

7. Click the **More Gestures** tab.

8. Click the pop-up button for **Swipe between Pages** and select the option you want (one finger, two fingers, or both). Because two fingers are used for scrolling between full-screen apps (the next option), you might want to leave this option set on one finger.

9. The other two options on this pane are selected by default, and I recommend you keep the defaults so you get the most out of your Magic Mouse!

10. To return to the main System Preferences screen, click **Show All** or, if finished, just close the window.

Setting Trackpad Preferences

Although the multitouch trackpad has many possible gestures, you might not want to use all of them. You can select the gestures you want to use in the Trackpad Preferences window. To set options for the trackpad, follow these steps:

1. Open **System Preferences** and click **Trackpad** in the Hardware row.

2. Set the speed for tracking, double-clicking, and scrolling.

3. Select **Tap to Click** if you want to tap on the trackpad to select an item. This is equivalent to clicking on the bottom of the trackpad.

4. To open a shortcut menu with a trackpad gesture, under One Finger, select **Secondary Click** and select a trackpad zone or select **Secondary Click** under Two Fingers.

5. Select each gesture you want to use for three and four fingers. A video demonstrates the gestures for you when you point to an option.

6. When you are finished, click **Show All** to return to the main System Preferences screen or close the window.

 NOTE If you like using the multitouch gestures of the built-in trackpad on the MacBook Pro and the MacBook Air, you can get the same features on a wireless Magic Trackpad and use the trackpad with your iMac or other desktop model. Like the Magic Mouse, it must be paired via Bluetooth before you can set the preferences for it.

Installing and Managing Printers

In most cases, you can connect a new printer to a Mac, and Mountain Lion lists it for you immediately in the list of printers on your Mac. The reason is that Mountain Lion comes with the printer drivers (the software) for most common printers.

Manually Installing a Printer

If you have plugged in your printer to your Mac and tried to print a document but did not see the name of your printer in the list of printers, try this:

1. Open **System Preferences** and click **Print & Scan**. Figure 6.6 shows the window.

2. Click the **Add** button (circled in Figure 6.6).

3. If you see your printer listed, select it and then click the **Add** button. If you don't see your printer listed, refer to the printer's documentation for further instructions.

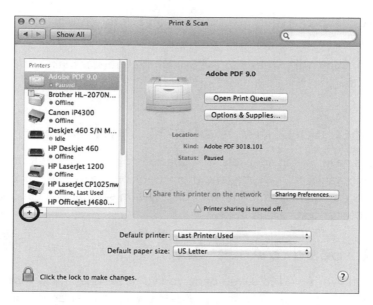

FIGURE 6.6

All the printers you have ever installed on your Mac are displayed in the sidebar (whether or not they are currently plugged into your Mac).

 NOTE   Mountain Lion automatically downloads printer driver upgrades for the printers you have installed as they become available.

Setting a Default Printer

The default printer is the printer that Mountain Lion suggests you use when you send a file to print. If the default printer is the one you want, you can set the other print options and click the **Print** button. If you want to use a different printer, all you have to do is click the **Printer** pop-up button and select another printer from the pop-up menu.

 NOTE   Instead of designating a specific printer as the default, you also can select the option **Last Printer Used**.

To set the default printer, follow these steps:

1. Open **System Preferences** and click **Print & Scan**.

2. Click the pop-up button on the **Default Printer** option and select the printer you want.

3. Click **Show All** to return to the System Preferences main screen or close the window.

Controlling Speaker Volume and Sound Alerts

All Macs have built-in speakers. The speakers play the sound from music CDs, the audio tracks of DVDs, the audio of videos on the Internet, and so on. The speakers also announce the time or play system sounds, such as sound effects when you perform certain tasks.

Using the Keyboard to Adjust Sound

Have you ever surfed to a web page you've never been on before and it suddenly started playing some music that you didn't want to hear or you didn't want someone else to hear (such as your boss or the client you were talking to on the phone)? A quick way to shut off that music is to press the **F10** key (or **Fn-F10**, if you've changed the setting for how the function keys work).

To turn down the volume, you can press **F11** (**Fn-F11**), and to turn up the volume, you can press **F12** (**Fn-F12**). Both F11 and F12 also turn on the speakers after they have been turned off. (If you are using an older keyboard, the function keys may be different. Look for three keys that have a speaker icon on them. You should be able to figure out which key does what.)

Another way to adjust your volume is to use the Volume menulet, which appears on the menu bar by default. To use the menulet, click the speaker icon to display a volume slider. Slide it up to increase the volume and slide it down to decrease the volume or turn it off completely.

Setting Alerts and Interface Sounds

Alerts and interface sounds give you audio feedback. To set preferences for these sounds, follow these steps:

1. Open **System Preferences** and click **Sound** in the Hardware row.

2. Click the **Sound Effects** tab if necessary.

3. Click an alert sound in the list to hear it play. When you find the one you want, click to select it. This will be the sound that plays when you try to do something that is not allowed or the computer needs more information from you.

4. Set the volume of the alert by dragging the slider for **Alert Volume**.

5. The Play User Interface Sound Effects option is selected by default, and I recommend you keep this setting. The option causes a sound to play to give you audio feedback that something has happened. For example, when you drag an item to the Trash, the interface sound you hear sounds like something hitting the bottom of a trash can. If you drag an icon off the Dock, the interface sound you hear sounds like someone blowing out a candle. These sounds validate that you have done something correctly or help alert you to things that you might not even be aware of. For example, it's very easy to accidentally drag an icon off the Dock. The puffing sound tells you that you did something you didn't notice when you were doing it.

6. Click **Show All** to return to the main System Preferences screen or, if finished, close the window.

Enabling Dictation

You can use the new Dictation tool anywhere in Mountain Lion that you would ordinarily type text. Before using this tool, you must enable it by opening System Preferences and clicking **Dictation & Speech**. On the Dictation tab, click **On**.

 NOTE Before you decide whether you want to use Dictation, read the privacy information that Apple provides by clicking the **About Dictation and Privacy** button. The words you dictate are actually sent to Apple to be converted into text. Additional personal information about you is also sent to Apple to "help the dictation feature understand you better and recognize what you say." Apple does not link this data to any other data that Apple might have about you that you have supplied to use other Apple services.

More specific instructions for using the Dictation tool are given in appropriate chapters, such as Chapter 14, "Using Contacts," Chapter 15, "Using Calendar," and Chapter 16, "Using Notes."

THE ABSOLUTE MINIMUM

- Never remove an external drive without properly ejecting it first.

- The larger the screen resolution numbers, the smaller and more detailed are the images and text on the screen.

- Many function keys perform two functions, but you must use the Fn key with the function key to perform the second function.

- By default, the secondary mouse button is not set to operate, so you'll probably want to change that, especially if you want to use shortcut menus!

- Mountain Lion keeps your printer drivers up-to-date for you automatically.

- Use the F10 (or Fn-F10 key) to quickly turn off your computer's sound.

PERSONALIZING THE DESKTOP

If you walk into practically anyone's office today and look at the desk, you'll probably see a framed picture or two, maybe a small potted plant, and any manner of personal items. Everyone likes to personalize his or her space. The same is true of the Mac desktop, and Mountain Lion gives you lots of latitude when it comes to personalizing. You can change the picture in the background, add or delete icons on the desktop and arrange them however you want, use a screen saver, and so on. This chapter shows you how to do all this and more.

Changing the Background

The desktop background can be a single static graphic, a solid color, or a series of graphics that change periodically. Mountain Lion offers you a rich assortment of photographs, abstract graphics, textures, and colors to choose from. Each graphic file is perfectly sized to fill the entire screen.

You also can select your own graphic files from iPhoto and your Pictures folder. Presumably these files are photos, but they don't have to be. Because your photos may not be as high a quality as what Apple supplies, Mountain Lion gives you some alternatives on how to display them instead of displaying them full screen.

To change the desktop picture, follow these steps:

1. Right-click an empty spot on the desktop to open the shortcut menu and click **Change Desktop Background**. The Desktop & Screen Saver preferences window opens to the Desktop pane, as shown in Figure 7.1.

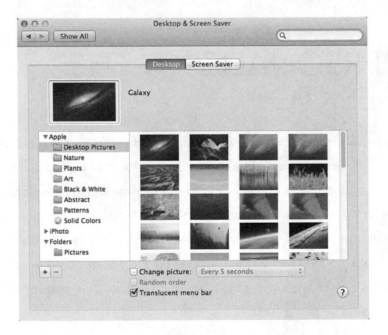

FIGURE 7.1

The current desktop graphic is shown above the list on the left.

 NOTE The sidebar lists three categories: Apple, iPhoto (only if you have iPhoto installed), and Folders. Click the triangle to the left of a category to hide or display the items under it.

2. If you prefer to use some of your own photos for the background instead of the Apple-supplied graphics, skip this step and go to step 3.

   To use an Apple background, click a folder under Apple in the sidebar and then click the graphic (or solid color) you want to use in the right pane. (If you select the Solid Color folder, and you want to use a color not supplied in the right pane, click **Custom Color** and select a color from any tab in the Color Inspector. Whatever choice you make changes the background immediately, and you can see it behind the System Preferences window.)

3. To use one of your own photos, select an item under iPhoto (All Photos, Events, an album, and so on) or select the Pictures folder under Folders. Select the photo you want to use from the right pane and specify the way you want it to be displayed. The default setting is Fill Screen, but if your photos don't look good blown up, you can choose another option. A better choice might be Center. With this option, Mountain Lion fills the screen if the photo has a high enough resolution or, if it doesn't, just centers it in the middle of the screen with a solid color background (and, of course, you can select the color by clicking the color sample on the right).

    TIP   To create a slideshow effect with all the photos in the selected source in iPhoto or the Pictures folder, choose **Change Picture** and then specify a time interval. (The default 5-second interval is a little too often for me!) Choose **Random Order** if you don't want to get bored.

4. Close the window when finished.

Personally, I don't like a cluttered-looking desktop. Because I generally have quite a few icons on my desktop, I like to use a background that is not too busy so the icons don't get lost in the graphics.

Using a Screen Saver

A *screen saver* is a type of computer program that was initially designed to prevent phosphor burn-in on cathode ray tube (CRT) and plasma monitors. With the advent of liquid crystal display (LCD) monitors, screen savers are really not necessary, but they are still available on all computers. I think they are more of an entertainment feature now. (I know my husband loves it when his screen saver comes on because it plays his photographs of the Mediterranean.) You also can use a screen saver to lock the screen if you assign a password to it. Follow these steps to select and use a screen saver:

1. Open **System Preferences** and click **Desktop & Screen Saver.**

2. Click the **Screen Saver** tab, if necessary, to display the pane shown in Figure 7.2. The graphics that you can see in the sidebar represent slideshow-type screen savers. If you scroll down, you will also find a group of regular screen savers.

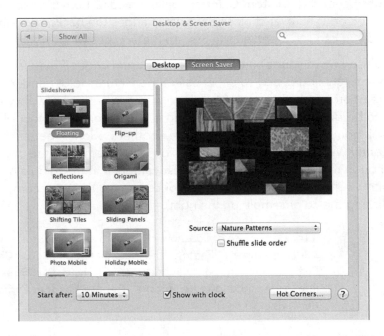

FIGURE 7.2

A preview of the screen saver plays in the pane on the right.

3. Select a slideshow or a regular screen saver in the sidebar. If you select a slideshow screen saver, you can select a source, as shown in Figure 7.2. Apple provides you with several interesting sources, but you also can select your own photos by selecting **Choose Folder** for Source and selecting one of your folders that contains the photos you want to use. (If you select Photo Stream as the source, the screen saver displays your most recent photos.)

4. Click **Show with Clock** if you want to display the time. (The time doesn't show up in the preview.)

5. For the **Start After** option, specify the amount of time of inactivity that the screen saver will wait before starting.

6. Close the window when finished.

TIP If you use a slideshow screen saver, when the photos are displayed, you can use the right- or left-arrow keys to scroll manually forward or backward through the photos.

Displaying and Using Icons on the Desktop

The desktop can display icons for various devices, files, and folders, including the following: hard drives, CD and DVD drives, iPods, external disks, connected servers, individual user files, disk image files (DMGs), individual user folders, and *aliases* for files or folders. (An alias is not an actual file or a folder, but merely a pointer to the actual file or folder. Clicking an alias on the desktop opens the file or folder no matter where it is really stored. See Chapter 11, "Working with Files and Folders in the Finder," to learn more about aliases.)

Displaying Device and Server Icons

Just because you *can* display an icon on the desktop doesn't mean you should. On one hand, I don't recommend that you display the hard drive icon because doing so just puts it in harm's way. On the other hand, I like to display icons for external disks, CDs, DVDs, and iPods because I can easily eject them by dragging their icons to the Trash.

 NOTE A CD or DVD icon does not appear on the desktop unless the computer has a disc in it.

If you want to see icons for your devices and servers on the desktop, follow these steps:

1. Click **Finder** in the Dock.

2. Click **Finder** in the menu bar and then click **Preferences**.

3. Click the **General** tab, if necessary. Click each of the items that you want to see on the desktop. Figure 7.3 shows the options I recommend, but keep in mind that I don't connect to any servers.

4. Close the window when finished.

FIGURE 7.3

In the General pane, you can select the items you want to show on the desktop.

Storing Files, Folders, and Aliases on the Desktop

The desktop is actually a folder, and like any other folder, it can hold files, subfolders, and aliases. You can move or copy existing files and folders (as well as aliases) to the desktop, save a file directly to the desktop, and create a folder on the desktop.

To create a folder on the desktop, right-click a blank area on the desktop and click **New Folder**. Type a name for the folder and press **Return**. To delete a folder, right-click the folder and click **Move to Trash**, or simply drag the folder icon to the Trash icon on the Dock and drop it there. For information about moving and copying files and folders, see Chapter 11.

Arranging Icons on the Desktop

If you start to accumulate icons on the desktop, you might want to group certain ones together or place the icons in certain locations on the screen. You can move icons to other locations simply by dragging them.

NOTE If you try to drag an icon to a different location and it snaps back to the original location, it means that the icons have been arranged with the Sort By command and cannot move out of their sorted order.

After you have dragged the icons where you want them, you can line them up with each other vertically and horizontally by using the Clean Up command on the desktop's shortcut menu. This command aligns the icons by making them snap to an invisible grid.

Instead of arranging the icons manually, you can let Mountain Lion do it for you by using the Clean Up By command, also available on the desktop's shortcut menu. The Clean Up By command aligns icons to the invisible grid but places them in the sorted order of your choice vertically on the right side of the screen. As you can see in Figure 7.4, your choices for sorting are Name, Kind, Date Modified, Date Created, Size, and Label. After arranging the icons with this command, you can still move the icons freely around the desktop.

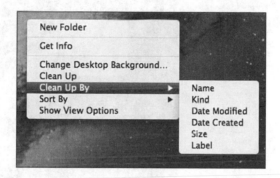

FIGURE 7.4

The Clean Up By command aligns your icons and sorts them at the same time.

After you sort icons with the Sort By command, they not only stay in their sorted arrangement, but any new icons that are added to the desktop move into the correct position in the sorted order. The Sort By command has all the options of the Clean Up By command plus three more: None, Date Last Opened, and Date Added. If you select None for Sort By, the icons stay where you put them when you arrange them manually by dragging them.

Customizing the Icons on the Desktop

You can make a number of modifications to icons on the desktop. You can change their size and spacing, the location of the label, the size of the text, and so on. To make changes to the icons, follow these steps:

1. Right-click the desktop and click **Show View Options**. The Desktop window opens. If you don't see the word *Desktop* in the title bar, you have a Finder window open. Close the Finder window or click the desktop first and try this step again.

2. Make any changes that you want. I like to see additional information for the file and folder icons, so I check **Show Item Info**. The info displayed for a file is the size of the file, and the info displayed for a folder is the number of items in the folder. (See Figure 7.5.)

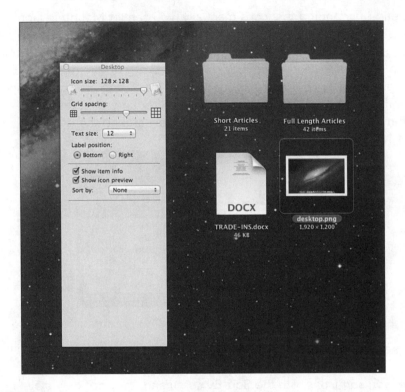

FIGURE 7.5

The Desktop view options determine how the icons look.

3. Close the window when finished.

Configuring Notifications

The Notification Center is a new feature in Mountain Lion that collects and displays alerts for emails, tweets, game challenges, appointments, reminders, updates from the App Store, and so on. It is a panel on the far right side of the screen that remains hidden unless you display it. When you display it, the desktop slides over to the left to reveal it. While the Notification Center panel is hidden, alerts and banners are displayed as they come in on the right side of the screen.

For each application that you set up to receive notifications, you can determine how you want the alerts to look when they come in. The alert can be a vanishing banner that is displayed momentarily at the top of the right side of the screen, or it can be a persistent dialog box (an alert) that remains at the top right until you acknowledge it. (See Figure 7.6.) If you don't want to see either the banner or the alert, you can choose None as the alert style.

Persistent Dialog Box Style Alert

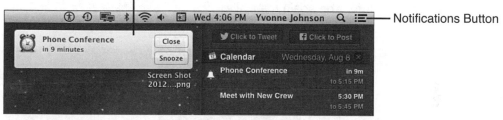

Notifications Button

FIGURE 7.6

You can respond to an appointment notification by clicking Close or Snooze.

Opening and Closing the Notification Center

To open or close the Notification Center panel, click the **Notifications** button. It's the last button on the far right side of the menu bar shown in Figure 7.6. If you have turned off the Show Notifications switch (see the next topic), the Notifications button is dimmed. (See Figure 7.7.)

In the Notification Center, each application has its own title bar, and the alerts from that application are displayed beneath its title bar. By default, the Notification Center displays only the last five alerts received in each application. If, for some reason, you want to delete all the current notifications in an application, you can just close the category by clicking the **Close** button on the right side of the application's title bar. The next new notification you get from the application reestablishes the title bar, but the previous alerts are not redisplayed.

When you have the Notification Center open, you can take action on your notifications. For example, you can click a message notification, and the message opens in Messages where you can respond to it. After you take action on a notification in the Notification Center, the notification disappears.

Showing or Hiding Notifications

If you are very involved with messaging, tweeting, emailing, and gaming, alerts for these items can become very distracting when you are trying to concentrate on something. If you turn the Show Alerts and Banners switch to Off, the alerts go directly into the Notification Center without displaying either the vanishing banner or the persistent dialog box. Then you can look at your alerts when doing so is convenient for you. To reveal the Show Alerts and Banners switch, open the Notification Center panel and click in the panel just below the menu bar. The control shown in Figure 7.7 appears at the top of the panel. (You might have to scroll up to see it.) Click **Off** in the control, and it changes to On and vice versa. The Show Alerts and Banners switch automatically turns itself back on the next day, or you can turn it on again manually.

FIGURE 7.7

When Alerts and Banners are turned off, the Notifications button is dimmed.

Setting Preferences for Notifications

By default, all applications that can send you alerts are enabled, so your first order of business is deciding whether you really want notifications for all these applications. Next, you need to decide how the alert should look for each application. Do you want to use the vanishing banner or the persistent dialog box? To set the preferences for notifications, follow these steps:

1. Click the **Notifications** button in the menu bar and then click the button in the bottom-right corner of the panel. (It can be difficult to see.) Alternatively, you can open System Preferences and click **Notifications**.

2. Select the first application in the list on the left side. By default, this is the Sharing Widget for Twitter. You can select or deselect the option to show the widget in the Notification Center.

3. Select an application, such as Calendar, FaceTime, Game Center, and so on as shown in Figure 7.8.

FIGURE 7.8

All OS X applications that can send notifications are listed in the sidebar.

4. If you do not want notifications for this application, click to remove the check for the **Show in Notification Center** check box and repeat step 3. If you want to receive notifications for the application, continue to step 5.

 NOTE When you uncheck the Show in Notification Center check box, the application moves to the bottom of the list under the heading Not in Notification Center. Later, if you want to start receiving notifications from the application, you can select it and check the Show in Notification Center check box.

5. Select the alert style you want to use for the application. If you select None, the application shows neither a vanishing banner nor a persistent dialog box. It shows the notification only in the Notification Center.

 NOTE If you set all applications to None, the Notification Center functions as it does when the Show Notifications switch is set to Off. Of course, it's easier to turn off the switch than it is to reset the alert style for every application!

6. Select the maximum number of alerts to display in the Notification Center. (Your choices are 1, 5, and 20.)

CAUTION   Give careful consideration to how you work with notifications when selecting this number. If you select None as the alert type for some applications, or you turn off alerts and banners frequently, you could miss some notifications. For example, if you get 10 notifications for an application before you look at them, and your number of Recent Items is set to 5, you will miss the first 5 notifications.

7. Decide whether or not you want to see a badge with the number of notifications and if you want to hear a sound when the notifications come in; then set these options.

8. Drag the applications in the list on the left into the order you want them to be listed in the Notification Center.

9. Close the window when finished.

Modifying the Menu Bar

You can't change the names or order of the menus displayed on the left side of the menu bar, but you can control many of the icons and indicators displayed on the right side. They include the Menu Extras (a.k.a. menulets) and the date and time. Additionally, if you have multiple users on your Mac, you can decide whether or not you want to see the usernames in the menu bar. See Chapter 28, "Managing User Accounts," to find out more about this setting.

Adding and Deleting Menu Extras

Most Menu Extras make their way to the menu bar via the System Preferences window. For example, on the Bluetooth pane, the option to make the Bluetooth menulet available is Show Bluetooth Status in the Menu Bar; on the Sound pane, the option to make the volume control appear on the menu bar is Show Volume in Menu Bar. So if you want to display a particular menulet in the menu bar, you can check the option for it in the appropriate pane in System Preferences. When the menulet appears in the menu bar, you can drag it to a different location (on the right side only) by holding down the Command key as you drag it.

If you want to remove a menulet from the menu bar, you can go back and uncheck the item in the System Preferences pane. Alternatively, you can hold down the Command key as you drag the icon off the menu bar.

Showing or Hiding the Date and Time

By default, Mountain Lion shows the day of the week and the time in the menu bar. You can change the format of the date and time or hide it completely as follows:

1. Open System Preferences and then click **Date & Time**.

2. If necessary, click the **Clock** tab, which is shown in Figure 7.9.

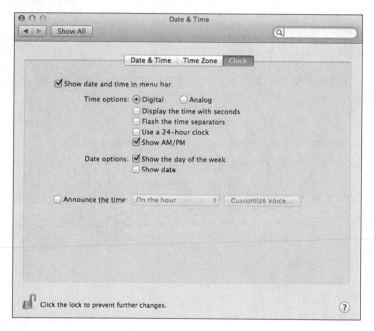

FIGURE 7.9

If you do not have the Calendar icon in the Dock, which always displays the date, you might want to select Show Date so you can see it in the menu bar.

3. Uncheck **Show Date and Time in Menu Bar** if you don't want to see this information in the menu bar.

   If you do want to see the date and time in the menu bar, select the Time Options you want and then select the Date Options you want.

 TIP If you would like to hear the time announced, click **Announce the Time** and select a frequency from the pop-up menu.

4. Close the window when finished.

THE ABSOLUTE MINIMUM

- You can personalize the desktop by using one of your own photos for the background.

- Screen savers are no longer essential, but feel free to use them for your own entertainment.

- The desktop is actually a folder, and it displays icons for files and subfolders that are stored in it.

- All applications that can send notifications are enabled by default, but you can disable the ones you don't want.

- Use the Show Alerts and Banners switch to temporarily turn off notifications.

- Go to System Preferences to add menulets on the right side of the menu bar for features you want to monitor the status of or access quickly.

IN THIS CHAPTER

- Taking the Dock preferences out for a trial run
- Configuring the Dock with the icons you want most
- Changing the appearance of stack icons

8

CUSTOMIZING THE DOCK

The Dock is a key component of the desktop—one that you use continually. In Chapter 3, "Using the Dock," you learned about the two sides of the Dock, what the icons do, and generally how to use the Dock. In this chapter, you learn how to take the Dock up a notch or two. You find out how to tweak the Dock in every possible way.

Setting the Preferences for the Dock

Even if you don't know what the default preferences for the Dock are, you probably have experienced the fact that they work just fine. Don't settle for "just fine," though. Make the Dock work just perfectly for you. Make sure it's in the best position for the way you work, that it's the right size, that it has the right icons, and so on. To do that, you need to look at the preferences for the Dock and see if there is anything you want to change. Follow these steps to explore the preferences for the Dock:

1. Click the **System Preferences** icon in the Dock or open Launchpad and click the icon there. Alternatively, click the **Apple** menu in the menu bar, point to **Dock**, and click **Dock Preferences**.

2. Click **Dock** (located in the first row). Figure 8.1 shows the default settings for the Dock.

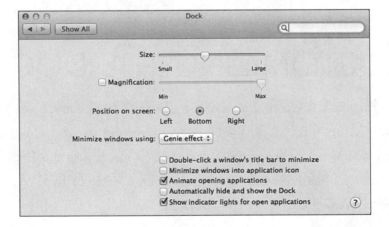

FIGURE 8.1

The default preferences for the Dock place the Dock at the bottom of the screen.

3. Slide the **Size** slider all the way to the right and notice how large the icons get and how wide the Dock gets. Now slide it all the way to the left and notice how small the icons get and how much smaller the width of the Dock is. Now adjust the slider to the size you want. Keep in mind that you can add more icons to the Dock while you are working (minimized windows, for example), and this will make the Dock wider. When the Dock reaches its full width, adding more icons in the Dock makes the icons smaller.

TIP Try this shortcut for sizing the Dock: Point to the separator. The pointer changes to a two-headed arrow. Drag up (for larger) or down (for smaller).

4. Check the **Magnification** check box and then point to any icon in the Dock to see the effects. (See Figure 8.2.) Try the minimum and maximum settings of this feature and then decide whether you really want to use it. It's a good feature to use if you have set a very small size for the Dock.

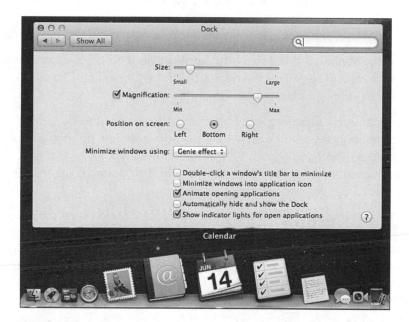

FIGURE 8.2

Magnification enlarges the icons closest to the pointer.

5. Click the **Left** radio button on the **Position on Screen** option and notice where the Dock goes. Now try the one for **Right**. Decide where you think the Dock best suits your purposes and click that radio button. For example, if you want to use the full height of the screen for your application windows, you could position the Dock on the left or right.

 TIP You also can change the position of the Dock by clicking the **Apple** menu in the menu bar and pointing to **Dock**. Then click **Position on Left**, **Position on Bottom**, or **Position on Right**.

6. In preparation for testing the effects of the Minimize Windows Using option, open any window. Notice that the default for this option is Genie Effect. Now minimize the window you just opened and notice how the window mimics a genie returning to its bottle. Click the minimized window to open it again and then select **Scale Effect**. Minimize the window again and notice the difference in the effect. Select the one you like better.

7. Click that minimized window again to open it and then check the box for **Double-click a Window's Title Bar to Minimize**. Now test the option by double-clicking the window's title bar. There's no harm in leaving this option selected. It just provides you with another way to minimize a window.

8. Select **Minimize Windows into Application Icon** if you don't want to see minimized windows on the right side of the Dock. See Chapter 4, "Working with Windows," for a discussion of this topic.

9. The Animate Opening Applications option is selected by default. Application icons bounce up and down while the application is opening if this option is selected. Additionally, if an application needs your attention because there is a problem or it needs input from you, its icon bounces up and down on the Dock to get your attention.

10. The Automatically Hide and Show the Dock option hides the Dock and shows it only when you point to the border where it resides. You also can turn Dock hiding on and off using the Apple menu in the menu bar. Click **Apple**, point to the **Dock** menu, and click **Turn Hiding On** or **Turn Hiding Off** (as the case may be).

 NOTE   Applications that don't have a full-screen mode benefit from the extra screen real estate of hiding the Dock.

11. The last option for the Dock is Show Indicator Lights for Open Applications. This option controls the display of the glowing blue bubbles you see under icons in the Dock if the applications are open. The bubble provides valuable information, so I recommend you go ahead and use this option.

12. When finished, close the window.

Examining Icons in the Dock

The default configuration of the Dock has a good assortment of icons for the applications that you will probably use frequently, but you don't have to keep this configuration. The only things set in stone on the Dock are the Finder and the Trash. Neither icon can be removed from the Dock or moved to a new position.

As for the rest of the icons, you can rearrange them or remove them. You also can add different icons to the Dock. Just remember that the left side of the Dock holds only application icons and the right side of the Dock holds only file and folder icons.

Removing Icons from the Dock

After using your Mac for a while, you will begin to notice the icons you use and the ones you don't use. Leaving icons on the Dock you don't use very much is perfectly fine unless you need more room for other icons.

To remove an icon from the Dock, just drag it off. You'll see a little puff of smoke and hear a "poof" sound when the icon is removed. If you remove an icon accidentally, there's no command that will quickly undo your mistake. Don't worry though; you haven't actually deleted the application, file, or folder. The icons in the Dock are just links. You can add an icon back to the Dock very easily.

Adding Application Icons to the Dock

To add an application icon to the Dock, click the Launchpad in the Dock and scroll to the page that contains the application icon you want to put on the Dock. Drag it to the Dock and don't let go until the icons that are in the way move aside.

 NOTE   When you are dragging an icon to the Dock from Launchpad, it looks as though the icon is being deleted from Launchpad, but as soon as you place the icon on the Dock, the icon also pops back in its place on the Launchpad screen.

If the application icon you are trying to drag to the Dock just won't let you drop it, you are trying to put the icon on the wrong side of the Dock. You cannot place an application icon to the right of the separator.

Oops! What do you do if the icon you removed from the Dock is the Launchpad icon? In this case, you open the Finder and click **Applications** in the sidebar. Then you drag the Launchpad file (found in the right pane) to the Dock.

Another way to add an application to the Dock is to launch the application and then right-click its temporary icon in the Dock to open the shortcut menu. Click Options, Keep in Dock.

Adding File or Folder Icons to the Dock

To add a file or folder icon to the right side of the Dock, locate the file or folder in the Finder (or on the desktop if it happens to be there) and drag it to the right side of the Dock. You may remember that folder icons in the Dock are called stacks. Chapter 3 describes what happens when you click a stack on the Dock.

Rearranging Icons on the Dock

At any time, you can rearrange the icons on the Dock. To change an icon's location, just drag it to the new spot. Remember that you cannot move the Finder icon or the Trash icon, and, of course, you cannot drag icons across the separator.

Customizing Folder Icons

A folder icon on the right side of the Dock is called a stack because it looks like a stack of icons. The stack displays a preview icon for each item in the folder, but because the icons are stacked on top of each other like a deck of cards, only the top icon shows. Folder icons can also look like folders. The two different appearances are shown in Figure 8.3.

FIGURE 8.3

The example on the left is a stack, and the example on the right is a folder.

To select the icon appearance you want to use, right-click the icon and click either Folder or Stack, as you prefer. (See Figure 8.4.)

If you would like to change the boring graphic of the standard blue folder, you can choose from several apps available in the Mac App Store to add graphics to a folder. Based on the reviews, it looks as though the app called Folders Factory (not to be confused with Folder Factory) is the most highly rated by users. Figure 8.5 shows you what the app can do.

FIGURE 8.4

You can change the appearance of a folder icon by selecting an option from its shortcut menu.

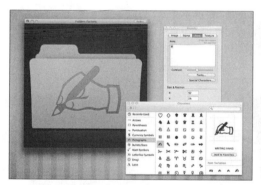

FIGURE 8.5

The Folders Factory app can change the appearance of a folder icon by using your own graphics.

THE ABSOLUTE MINIMUM

- You can drag icons to and from the Dock on both sides of the separator.

- The icons in the Dock are just links to the real applications, files, or folders.

- You can change the appearance of a folder icon so it looks like a stack or it looks like a folder.

9

IN THIS CHAPTER

- Identifying your default folders and finding where they're located
- Using all the components of the Finder window
- Populating the Finder sidebar with the sources that are most important to you
- Examining all four of the Finder views and setting a default view for the one you like best
- Creating a custom view for individual folders
- Opening more than one Finder window

GETTING ACQUAINTED WITH THE FINDER

Although the Finder is an application, it's not "just" another application like Mail or Safari. You could live without Mail and Safari, as well as many other applications that come with Mountain Lion, but you cannot live without the Finder. It's integral to everything you do on the Mac.

Because the Finder is such an important part of the operating system, you need to learn as much about it as you can. This chapter gives you a solid introduction to the interface, and the next two chapters that explain how to work in the Finder will round out your education.

Getting Started with the Finder

Every time you start your Mac, the Finder application opens automatically and remains open until you shut down the computer. You can't even close it; its little blue bubble is always glowing on the Dock.

Well, what exactly is the Finder? It's the interface between you and all your file storage devices—your hard drive, the SuperDrive, any external drives you may have, and even the iCloud.

When you want direct access to a file on one of your storage devices, you just launch the Finder application and do your thing—rename the file, move it, delete it, and so on. The Finder also provides indirect access to your files. When you need to access a file while working in another application, it's the Finder that really provides the application with access to the file. For example, if you are working in TextEdit, and you want to open a file, TextEdit taps Finder on the shoulder and says, "Hey, can you make the file storage devices available so my user can open a file?" Then TextEdit displays a dialog box for you to use to find your file, courtesy of the Finder.

Examining the File Structure

Before going much further in our discussion of the Finder, we have to understand how your files are stored on a storage device. The file structure of a drive is comparable to a file cabinet. The case that holds all the file drawers in the cabinet is comparable to the drive itself (whether it is an internal hard drive, an external hard drive, a CD, a DVD, or a flash drive). The file drawers in the file cabinet are comparable to folders in the Finder; the manila file folders in the file drawers are comparable to subfolders in the Finder, and the individual documents in the file folders are comparable to computer files, such as word processing documents or spreadsheets.

 NOTE   Although *subfolder* is a term used to describe a folder within a folder, there really is no difference between a folder and a subfolder. You can just call all these elements *folders* if you want to.

Exploring the Default Folders

Although you undoubtedly will create your own folders, the operating system creates some default folders for you. Your primary folder, the one that holds all your other folders, is referred to as your *home folder*, but it's not named "home." When you set up your computer initially, your Mac suggests a name for your home folder based on your username, but you might have changed it to something else—your first name or your nickname. Whatever the name is, I'm sure you know which folder is your home folder. The home folder contains the following folders by default:

- **Desktop**—You might be surprised to learn that the desktop is actually a folder (especially if you haven't read Chapter 7, "Personalizing the Desktop"). Initially, it has no file in it, but if you save files to the desktop or move files or folders to the desktop, you are actually putting files and folders into the Desktop folder.

- **Documents**—This folder is the one most Mac applications suggest as the file location when you save a file. You don't have to use it, but it's the default.

- **Downloads**—This folder is the default location for any files you download from the Internet.

- **Movies, Music, Pictures**—These folders are the defaults used by such applications as QuickTime Player, iMovie, iTunes, iPhoto, and Photo Booth.

- **Public**—This folder can contain any files you want to share with people on your network or with other user accounts on your Mac. Anything you put in this folder can be accessed without a password, can be viewed or copied, but cannot be changed or deleted.

 NOTE   Every user on your Mac has this same set of folders in his or her home folder. This is how Mountain Lion keeps each user's work and preferences separate. The Applications folder, however, is not in the user's home folder. All users have access to it and can, therefore, run all programs unless restricted by Parental Controls or unless a user installs a program somewhere in his or her own home folder.

Exploring the Finder Window

Clicking the Finder icon in the Dock opens the Finder window. By default, the Finder is set to open All My Files, shown in Figure 9.1. This means every time you open the Finder, you will see All My Files. As the name implies, the All My Files feature lists all your user files on your system as well as on the iCloud. The files are categorized by type—Images, PDF Documents, Documents, and so on. If you create a document of a new type, say a spreadsheet, a new category called Spreadsheets appears for All My Files.

FIGURE 9.1

The Icon view of the Finder represents each file with a preview icon.

I personally prefer to see my Documents folder every time I open the Finder, so I have changed the setting for the default folder to Documents. To select a folder of your choice as the default, click **Finder** in the Finder menu bar, click **Preferences**, and then click the **General** tab. Click the pop-up button for **New Finder Windows Show**, select the folder you want, and close the Preferences window.

Like all windows, the Finder window has a title bar at the top and borders on the remaining three sides. The title bar displays the name of the source selected in the sidebar or in the right pane. Under the title bar is the toolbar. Figure 9.2 shows the buttons.

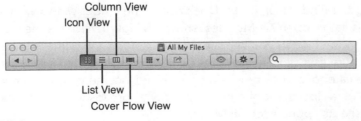

FIGURE 9.2

This is the default Finder toolbar, but you can customize the toolbar.

TIP   You can rearrange, add, or delete buttons in the toolbar by right-clicking the toolbar and clicking **Customize Toolbar**.

The Finder window is divided into two panes. The pane on the left is called the *sidebar*, and it contains a list of file sources categorized under three headings: Favorites, Shared, and Devices. The sources may be folders, devices, servers, external drives, and so on. The pane on the right shows the content of the source selected in the sidebar. For example, if you select Applications in the sidebar, the pane on the right shows the applications installed on your system. If you select another folder, its content is displayed in the right pane replacing what was previously displayed. Use the **Back** button in the toolbar to view the previous window. Then click the **Forward** button to go forward again.

You can display or hide the items under each category in the sidebar by pointing to the category name and then clicking **Hide**. (The Hide option is visible only when you point to the category.) To redisplay the items, point to the category name again and click **Show**.

By default, two components of the Finder window are not visible: the path bar and status bar. The status bar displays valuable information about the number and size of files or folders selected in the sidebar or right pane, and the path bar displays the path of the item selected in the sidebar or right pane, as shown in Figure 9.3. To display either bar, click **View** in the menu bar and click **Show Path Bar** or **Show Status Bar**. When both bars are displayed, the status bar is located at the bottom of the window, and the path bar is above it.

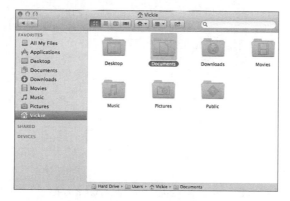

FIGURE 9.3

The Miscellaneous folder is selected in the right pane, and the path shown in the path bar is Hard Drive -> Users -> Vickie's Home Folder -> Documents -> Miscellaneous.

Configuring the Sidebar

In the Finder Preferences window, you can determine the sources you want to list in the sidebar. Figure 9.4 shows the sources you can make visible in the sidebar for each category. When you decide what items you want to see in the sidebar, check the items you want and uncheck the items you don't want. Before you actually know what you'll need and won't need, it doesn't hurt to display everything in the Favorites and Shared categories. Even though Figure 9.4 shows all items checked, I suggest you display only External Disks and CDs, DVDs, and iPods in the Devices category. There's no point in making your Mac or the hard drive accessible because you will rarely need to do anything with the files on them. Alternatively, you can check all the options and then hide the devices in the sidebar as explained previously.

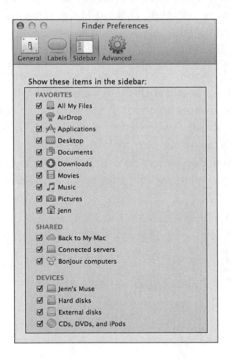

FIGURE 9.4

Click Finder, Preferences, and then click the Sidebar tab to display this page.

NOTE   All the sources in the Favorites category, with the exception of All My Files and Applications, are actually default folders stored in the home folder. This is your clue that even though the file structure is hierarchical, the Finder does not show a hierarchical list of folders. (You might be expecting a hierarchical list if you recently switched from a PC. The Windows Explorer application, which performs the same function as the Finder, uses hierarchical listings.)

After you make your selections and close the Finder Preferences window, you will see the items you have selected listed in the sidebar. You can rearrange the items in each category by dragging and dropping them within the category, and you also can rearrange the order of the categories by dragging them. (Don't forget you also can hide items in a category.)

At any time, you can go back into the Preferences window and change the default items you want to show in the sidebar. For example, if, on that rare occasion, you need to access the hard disk, you can open the Sidebar Preferences window, check the **Hard Disks** option under devices, do whatever it is you have to do, and then uncheck Hard Disks when you are finished. Alternatively, you can just drag an item off the sidebar by holding down the **Command** key as you drag it. (Every item on the sidebar is just a pointer to the real item, so don't worry that you are deleting anything.)

In addition to the sources you select for Favorites, you can add your own files or folders to the Favorites category right in the Finder window. To add a file or folder to the sidebar, follow these steps:

1. Click the **Finder** icon in the Dock if the Finder window is not open or if it's hidden under another window on the desktop.

2. Navigate to the file or folder you want to add so it is visible in the right pane.

3. Drag the file or folder in the right pane to the Favorites category in the sidebar, dropping it where you want it.

TIP   If you delete any item that you have added to the sidebar and you want to put it back on the sidebar again, repeat the preceding steps.

Using Finder Views

The Finder has four different views you can use to see the files and folders on your Mac: Icon, List, Column, and Cover Flow. Each view has a different look and presents somewhat different information about the files and folders. To select the view you want to use, click the appropriate button in the toolbar (refer to Figure 9.2).

Using the Icon View

The Icon view uses icons in the right pane to represent files and folders. Figure 9.3 shows the Icon view for the Documents folder. You can drag the icons in this view to any location. For example, you might want to drag files that you plan to delete soon to the bottom of the pane. When you drag icons to new locations, existing icons do not move aside for you, but after you get all the icons moved to their new locations, you can align the icons neatly by right-clicking the folder window and clicking **Clean Up**.

 NOTE   If you are viewing All My Files in the Icon view in the Finder, or if you have selected a Sort By or Arrange By viewing option, you can't drag the icons at all.

One nice Icon view feature is the capability to preview certain types of files using the file's icon. Some types of files, such as PDF, DOC, DOCX files, and .PAGES, display a set of back and forward arrows on the file icons when you point to them. To preview the content of the file, first make the icons more readable by using the slider in the status bar to make the icons larger; then click the buttons to go forward or backward. Other files, such as music and video files, display a play button. Clicking the button plays the music or the video.

 NOTE   The Cover Flow and Column views also have this preview feature.

Using the List View

Figure 9.5 shows the List view. As you can see, the List view gives you the following information about each file: Name, Date Modified, Size, Kind, and Date Added. If you can't see all these columns, you can make the Finder window wider. You also can add or remove columns by right-clicking a column heading and checking or unchecking a column heading listed in the context menu.

 NOTE   If you are looking at All My Files in the List view, the information given for each file is Name, Kind, and Last Opened.

Disclosure Triangle

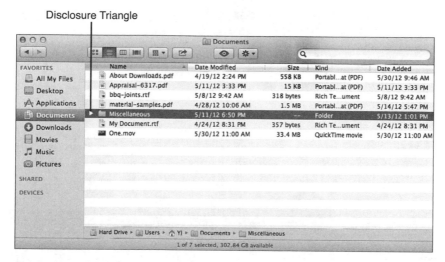

FIGURE 9.5

You can resize each column of information in the List view to make it wider or narrower.

If you prefer a different order for the columns of information, you can rearrange the columns by dragging the column headings to a new location, except for the Name column. It can't be moved.

Sometimes the columns may be too wide or too narrow for your liking. If that's the case, you can change the width of columns. Point to the right side of a column title until you see a double-headed arrow and then drag to the left or right.

In the List view, if a folder has files or folders in it, a disclosure triangle appears to the left of its name and icon. Clicking the triangle displays or hides the items in the folder.

By default, files are sorted in the List view in alphabetical order by Name. Click any column heading, and you sort all the items in the view by that column. Click the column heading again to sort in the opposite direction.

Using the Column View

Figure 9.6 shows the Column view. In this view, you use columns instead of disclosure triangles to drill down into the content of a folder. The first column shows the content of the source selected in the sidebar. If you select a folder in the first column, the second column displays the content of the folder. If you select a folder in the second column, the third column displays the content of the folder in the second column, and so on, until finally a file is selected instead of a folder. Then the last column displays the content of the file if it is a viewable file. Otherwise, the last column displays a representative icon.

FIGURE 9.6

The Column view helps you keep track of where you are as you move up and down in hierarchical folders.

Using the Cover Flow View

The Cover Flow view is shown in Figure 9.7. It uses the List view in the bottom pane and a graphic view in the top pane. As you can see in the figure, the item you select in the List view at the bottom of the pane is displayed as a preview in the top pane.

FIGURE 9.7

The Cover Flow view combines the List view at the bottom with a graphic representation at the top.

The key feature of the Cover Flow view is the preview at the top, so it behooves you to make the graphic area larger. Point to the bottom of the graphic pane; when the pointer changes to a hand, drag the pane downward.

If one is visible (as seen in Figure 9.7), use the horizontal scrollbar toward the bottom of the graphic pane to scroll through the items in the graphic pane. (You will see a scrollbar if Always is selected on the General tab of System Preferences.) Alternatively, you can scroll with a swiping motion on a Magic Mouse or Magic Trackpad or by using the left- and right-arrow keys on the keyboard. As you scroll through the items, the top and bottom panes are synchronized; that is, the item previewed in the top pane is the item selected in the bottom pane, and vice versa.

 TIP   When you're trying to find a particular file, you can size the top pane to preview files in a readable size and even use the pop-up buttons to page through those documents.

Changing the Item Arrangement in Any View

The button in the toolbar identified in Figure 9.8 enables you to quickly sort the items displayed in the right pane of the Finder. Figure 9.8 shows the sorting options available on this button's pop-up menu. This button is available in the toolbar in all views, and it displays the same menu options for all sources in the sidebar except the Applications folder, which has fewer options.

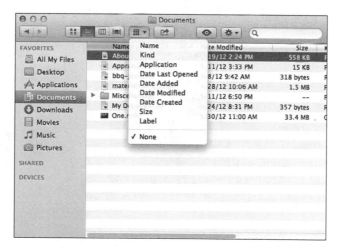

FIGURE 9.8

Use this button to change the arrangement of items in any view.

 NOTE   When you sort items in the List view using this button, you cannot rearrange the columns by dragging the headers.

Customizing the Finder Views for Specific Folders

Each of the four views has many options for customizing. For example, in the Icon view, you can change the default size of the icons and the background color. In the List view, you can select the default columns of information you want to see. In the Columns view, you can turn off the last column that shows the file preview. In the Cover Flow view, you can change the Sort By order in the bottom of the pane. You can apply any of these customizations to a specific folder so that whenever you open that folder in the customized view, it always uses your custom settings.

To set options for any one of the Finder views, follow these steps:

1. Click the **Finder** icon in the Dock and select the folder you want to display in the customized view.

2. Click the view button in the toolbar for the view you want to customize for that folder.

3. Click **View** in the menu bar and click **Show View Options**. Figure 9.9 shows the options for the List view.

4. Select the options that you want, and then close the window.

FIGURE 9.9

Each time you open the Documents folder in the List view, it is displayed using the options you select in this window.

Using Your Preferred View

If you have a view that you prefer to use most of the time, you can make the Finder use this view every time it opens. Follow these steps to set the default view of the Finder:

1. Click the **Finder** icon in the Dock.

2. Click the view button in the toolbar for the view you want to make the default.

3. Click **View** in the menu bar and click **Show View Options**.

4. Click **Always Open in <Name of View> View**. At this point, you have set the view for only the selected folder.

5. Set other options in the window as desired.

6. Click **Use as Defaults** to make the view and all the options the defaults for all folders.

7. Close the window.

 NOTE   The default view preferences that you set do not override the preferences you set for individual folders.

Opening Multiple Finder Windows

By default, the Finder operates in only one window at a time, but if you want to open a new window every time you open a folder in the Finder, you can set an option to do that. This might be a good practice if you copy or move files between folders frequently. To set the multiple window behavior as a default, follow these steps:

1. Click **Finder** in the menu bar and click **Preferences**.

2. Click the **General** tab, if necessary.

3. Check the box for **Always Open Folders in a New Window**.

4. Close the Preferences window.

Instead of setting the behavior to open a new window every time you open a folder, you can just manually open a new Finder window when you want one by clicking **File, New Finder Window**.

THE ABSOLUTE MINIMUM

- The Finder, which gives you access to all your files, is always running and cannot be closed.

- Every user on a Mac starts out with the same default folders.

- The Finder sidebar, which lists folders and devices on your system, can be customized to list the sources you use the most.

- The Finder has four distinct views that you can use to view your files and folders: Icon, List, Column, and Cover Flow.

CREATING FOLDERS IN THE FINDER

In the Finder, you can create three different types of folders: a regular folder that can hold files and other folders, a *Smart Folder* with dynamic content that changes based on user-supplied criteria, and a burn folder that holds pointers to files you want to burn to a CD or DVD. In this chapter, I tell you how to create all three types and how to use them.

Creating "Regular" Folders

When you know you are going to create several files that all relate to each other or to the same topic, you might want to create a folder for the files in advance. For example, if you get a new client, you might want to create a folder with that client's name even before you start creating any files that relate to the client. In another scenario, you might find that you already have files that are somehow related that you want to group together in a folder. In either case, you can create a folder in the Finder with very few steps.

To create a folder before you even have any files to put in it, follow these steps:

1. Open the Finder window and change to the Column view.

 NOTE   You can create a new folder in any view, but I like to use the Column view because it helps you keep track of where you are in the hierarchy of folders.

2. Click the folder that should hold the new folder.

3. Click **File** in the menu bar and then click **New Folder**. A new folder appears in the column to the right with the name *Untitled Folder*. The name is highlighted, waiting for you to type the name you want to give the folder.

 TIP   In lieu of step 3, you can use the keyboard shortcut **Command-Shift-N**.

4. Type the name you want to give the folder and press **Return**. If several files or folders are in the same location as the new folder, the folder moves to a new place in the list based on how the list is sorted.

 TIP   If you create folders on a fairly regular basis, you might want to add the New Folder button to the toolbar. Click **View** in the Finder menu bar, or right-click the toolbar and then click **Customize Toolbar**. Drag the New Folder button onto the toolbar and click **Done**.

Now let's talk about how you can create a folder for existing files. One way, of course, would be to create a folder and then move the existing files into the folder. That's a perfectly good method, and we'll talk about moving files in the next chapter, but there is another way to create a folder without going to quite so much trouble. Here are the steps:

1. Open the Finder window. If the files and folders you want to gather into one folder are scattered all over, use the List view and select your home folder in the sidebar.

2. Select the files and/or folders that should go into the new folder. After selecting the first file or folder, press the **Command** key as you click each additional file or folder you want to include.

3. Right-click any one of the selected files or folders and click **New Folder with Selection**, as shown in Figure 10.1. The new folder is created, and the default name of the folder (New Folder with Items) is selected. The location of the new folder depends on where the files and folders were located. If they were all located in the same folder, the new folder becomes a subfolder of that folder. If the files and folders were scattered everywhere, the new folder becomes a subfolder of your home folder.

4. Type a name for the folder and press **Return**.

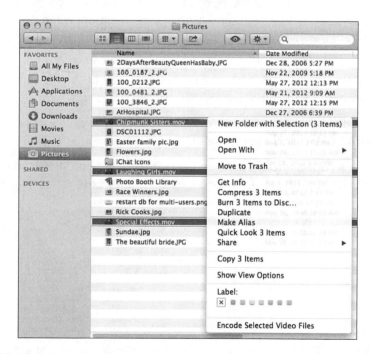

FIGURE 10.1

You can create a folder from existing files.

Creating and Using Smart Folders

A Smart Folder is not really a folder at all—not in a physical sense. It's a virtual folder that gathers its content of files and folders together every time you open it. The content of the Smart Folder is based on search criteria that you define. Each time you open the folder, the Finder looks for all the files and folders on your system that meet your criteria and lists them as if they were located in the virtual folder. As you add and delete files on your system, the content of the Smart Folder changes if any of the new or deleted files meet the criteria.

To create a Smart Folder, follow these steps:

1. Open the Finder window.

2. If you want the search to be limited to a specific folder, open it first.

3. Click in the **Spotlight** search box and type a criterion such as **agreement**. An appropriate pop-up menu opens with options for you to choose from, such as Filename Contains "Agreement." Select the option in the pop-up menu you want. Files anywhere on the Mac that meet the criterion appear immediately in the right pane.

4. To narrow the search to the folder you selected in step 2, click the name of the folder in the Search bar (just to the right of "This Mac").

5. To add another criterion, click the button with the plus (under the Spotlight search box) to add another search criterion line.

6. Select an option from the Kind pop-up menu and complete the new criterion using the appropriate additional pop-up menus or text boxes. (See Figure 10.2.)

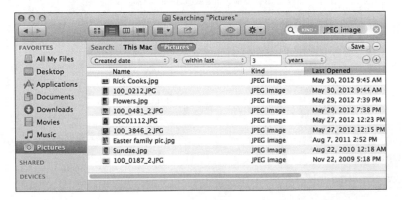

FIGURE 10.2

You can add as many criteria as needed to identify the files you want in your Smart Folder.

7. Repeat steps 5 and 6 for additional criteria.

8. Click **Save**. The dialog box shown in Figure 10.3 opens.

Specify a name and location for your Smart Folder

Save As: Searching "Pictures".savedSearch

Where: Saved Searches

☑ Add To Sidebar

Cancel   Save

FIGURE 10.3

Add to Sidebar is not selected by default the first time you create a Smart Folder. Take advantage of it so you can find your Smart folders easily!

9. Type a name for the Smart Folder and click **Save**. The Smart Folder will be saved in the Saved Searches folder by default, unless you select a different location. The Smart Folder will appear in the sidebar unless you uncheck the **Add to Sidebar** option.

CAUTION   If you do not want to see the Smart Folder in the sidebar, I highly recommend you select another location for Where; otherwise, finding the Smart Folder will be very difficult and potentially dangerous. It is stored in a folder that users generally should not access.

TIP   As an alternative, you can start the process of creating a Smart Folder by pressing **Option-Command-N** or by clicking **File** in the menu bar and clicking **New Smart Folder**.

To open a Smart Folder, select it in the Finder sidebar. The right pane shows the files that meet all the criteria.

Creating and Using Burn Folders

A burn folder is a special folder that you can create to help you burn files and folders to a CD or DVD. It is certainly possible to burn files and folders to a disc without creating a burn folder, so the question arises, "Why would you want to create one?" The answer is that you can use a burn folder over and over again, which makes it much easier to burn multiple copies of a disc.

A burn folder does not contain actual files. You can drag files into the burn folder or copy and paste them, but Mountain Lion creates an alias for each file—a link to the actual file—instead of making a real copy of the original. Every time you use the burn folder to burn a disc, the most up-to-date files are burned on the disc. So, for example, if you are constantly editing files and then backing them up to a disc, a burn folder is your perfect solution.

To create a burn folder, follow these steps:

1. Open the Finder and open the location where you want to create the burn folder. Click **File** in the menu bar and then click **New Burn Folder**.

 TIP   If you plan to use the burn folder frequently, you might want to create it on the desktop. Instead of opening the Finder as instructed in step 1, right-click a blank spot on the desktop and click **New Burn Folder**.

2. Type a name for the folder and press **Return**.

3. Copy or drag the files and folders that you want to burn on a disc into the new burn folder. (See Chapter 11, "Working with Files and Folders in the Finder," for information on how to copy files.)

After you have all the files and folders you want in a burn folder, you are ready to burn the disc. Follow these steps:

1. Double-click the burn folder in the Finder (or on the desktop if you stored it there). The burn folder has a black banner at the top and a Burn button. See Figure 10.4.

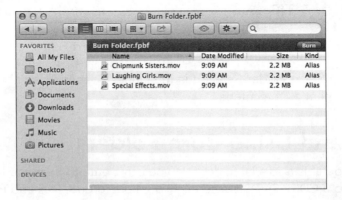

FIGURE 10.4

The burn folder has a Burn button that starts the process.

2. Click the **Burn** button. The Finder does a quick check to be sure the original files and folders are still where the aliases are pointing. If any files are missing, you see a dialog box like the one shown in Figure 10.5. You can click the **Skip** button to continue.

FIGURE 10.5

If any items in the burn folder point to files that can no longer be found, you can still burn the disc.

3. You are prompted to insert a blank disc. You can insert a blank disc before you even do step 1, but if you wait until this point, the dialog box that prompts you to insert the disc also tells you how much space you will need on the disc. Insert the disc, and the prompt eventually closes automatically, but a new dialog box opens.

4. The disc is given the name of the burn folder by default. If you want to name it something else, type the new name in the **Disc Name** field.

5. Click **Burn**. Don't work on any of the files that you are burning to the disc. The last step in the burn process is the verification. If the disc is verified as reliable, you're finished. If it can't be verified, you'll probably need to use a different disc and try again.

THE ABSOLUTE MINIMUM

- You can create a new folder with nothing in it, or you can create a folder that automatically holds existing files or folders you have selected.

- Smart Folders do not really contain files or folders. They are virtual folders with dynamic content.

- Burn folders contain only aliases, not the real files that you burn to a disc.

IN THIS CHAPTER

- Creating shortcuts to files that are deeply buried in the file structure
- Searching for files using data about the file or in the file
- Taking a "Quick Look" at a file's content without actually opening the file
- Applying colors to filenames
- Renaming, copying, moving, and deleting files
- Sharing a file in a message or a tweet, with other users wirelessly, and with Flickr
- Burning files to a disc

11

WORKING WITH FILES AND FOLDERS IN THE FINDER

The two chapters previous to this one have very useful information—information that you need to know—but it's all information that supports the activities in *this* chapter. The Finder isn't like iPhoto. You don't open the Finder to admire your files. You open the Finder so you can *do* things such as preview, rename, open, copy, move, or delete a file. This chapter explains "where you really live" in the Finder.

Opening Folders and Files in the Finder

One way to open a folder is to double-click it in the Finder. This action causes the folder to open in the right pane, and you can see the files and folders it contains. If you have set the preference to open a new window every time you open a folder, as discussed in Chapter 9, "Getting Acquainted with the Finder," double-clicking a folder displays the content of the folder in a new window.

 TIP   When using only one window, you can go back to a previous folder and then forward again by using the Back and Forward buttons in the toolbar.

When it comes to opening files, you already know that you can launch an application and then open any files that application has created for you. But did you also know that you can open a file from the Finder? Just double-click the file in the Finder, and its default application automatically launches, opening the file simultaneously.

 NOTE   If the default application that usually creates or works with the file is not on your system, you have the option to open the file with another application that can read the file if there is one. If there is no application that can read the file, you just can't open it on your Mac.

Another way to open a file outside its application, so to speak, is to click an *alias* that has been created for the file. An alias is a pointer to a file. It can reside anywhere on the system and be moved anywhere, and it will still point to the original file. Sometimes Mountain Lion creates an alias for you, as in the case of a burn folder. (See Chapter 10, "Creating Folders in the Finder.") Use the following steps to create your own aliases:

1. Open the Finder and select the file or folder in the right pane for which you want to create an alias.

2. Right-click the file and click **Make Alias**. The alias appears in the right pane, and the text of the name is selected. The name is the same as the original file with *alias* appended to the end of the file's extension.

3. Type a new name for the alias if you want to and then press **Return**.

4. To move the icon to the desktop or to any other location, see the "Copying and Moving Files" section later in this chapter.

NOTE If you move the original file to a different location, the alias will not work anymore.

Finding Files and Folders

If you have a relatively small number of files and folders on your computer, you may be able to find your own files by simply perusing the Finder window and using some of the viewing techniques discussed in Chapter 9. If you have a large number of files and folders, you might need a little help. Don't worry. Finding files and folders is "job one" for the Finder!

Searching with Spotlight

Finder's search tool, Spotlight, is located on the far right side of the toolbar. To use this tool to find a file or folder, follow these steps:

1. Open the Finder window.

2. If you want the search to be limited to a specific folder, open it now.

3. Click in the Spotlight search box and type something about the file you remember, such as part of the name, a phrase in the content, a date, and so on. An appropriate pop-up menu opens with options for you to choose from, such as Filename Contains. Select the option in the pop-up menu that applies to what you typed. The text you typed in the Spotlight box is encapsulated as shown in Figure 11.1. (Apple refers to this as a *search token*.) Files anywhere on the Mac that meet the criterion appear immediately in the right pane of the Finder.

 NOTE If you don't select an option from the pop-up menu, and you press Return instead, all files that meet the criterion in any way are displayed in the right pane. So, for instance, if you type **agree** and press Return, you get all files that have the word *agree* in the name as well as in the content of the file.

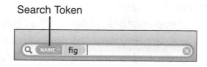

Search Token

FIGURE 11.1

The capsule in the Spotlight search box is called a search token.

4. Repeat step 3 to add more search tokens if needed.

5. To narrow the search to the folder you selected in step 2, click the name of the folder in the Search bar (just to the right of "This Mac").

6. To add a more precise criterion, click the button with the plus (under the Spotlight search box) and select an option from the Kind pop-up menu. Complete the new criterion using the appropriate additional pop-up menus or text boxes. You can repeat this step to add more criteria.

After the Finder presents all the files and folders that meet your criteria, you should be able to find the exact one you are looking for, but under certain circumstances you still might not be sure exactly which one is the one you want. If you are searching for a folder, probably all you have to do is open the folder to know if it's the one. If it's a file you're searching for, you might need to see the content to be sure it's the one you want. Opening every single file to check the contents, however, could be quite a pain, but the Finder has a feature to help you here, too. It's called Quick Look.

Examining Files with Quick Look

The Quick Look feature shows you a preview of a file without actually opening the file. Just select the file you want to preview and click the **Quick Look** button in the Finder toolbar (the button that looks like an eye). If you prefer keyboard shortcuts, you can press the **spacebar** instead. To close the Quick Look window, click the **Quick Look** button again or press the **spacebar** again.

Quick Look also can preview a group of files. Simply select all the files you want to preview and open Quick Look as just described. You can cycle through the previews of each file by clicking the **Next** and **Previous** buttons, or you can press the **spacebar** to advance to the next preview. Additionally, you can use Quick Look to advance the files automatically. Just click the **Full Screen** button and then click the **Play** button, as shown in Figure 11.2. This technique can be used to create a quick, ad hoc slideshow. You also can see all the files at once by clicking the **Grid** button in the Full Screen mode.

Sometimes you might want to use Quick Look to preview a folder. You might guess that Quick Look previews all the files in the folder, but it doesn't. What Quick Look shows you is a larger image of the blue folder icon. Although this seems like a useless endeavor, the preview shows you one piece of critical information about the folder: its size. You could use this technique to find out if a folder's content will actually fit on a CD or DVD you want to burn.

FIGURE 11.2

When in Full Screen mode as shown here, use the Full Screen button to return to the regular-size window or click the Close button to exit Quick Look.

Using Color Labels to Help Identify Files

Applying a colored label to a file is a good way to help identify a file when you are using the eyeball method to search for your files. To apply a color label to a file, follow these steps:

1. Select the file; then click the **Action** button in the Finder's toolbar to open the Action menu shown in Figure 11.3.

2. Under the Label option, click the color you want to apply. When you point to each colored block, the name of the label is displayed (Red, Orange, Yellow, and so on).

  TIP These color names are not too helpful, but you can change them to more meaningful names. Open the Finder preferences and click the **Labels** tab. Select the text beside the label, type the name you want to assign, and press **Return**. Close the Preferences window when finished.

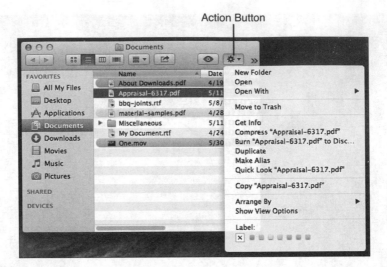

FIGURE 11.3

Apply a color label to a filename using the Action menu.

If you apply different color labels to several files, it's likely that at some time you will want to sort the files by color. You can do this in the List view if you add the Label column to the view. Right-click any column heading and click **Label**. After you add the column to the view, you can click the column heading to sort on that column. To remove the label color, right-click the file and click the **x** under Label.

Renaming Files and Folders

You want to change the name of a file or folder? It's too long? Too short? Misspelled? Inappropriate? No problem. To rename a file or folder, select it in the Finder and press **Return**. The filename is selected. Type the new name, press **Return**, and then watch out! Depending on the new name, the file or folder could jump to a new location if the files are sorted in the Finder view in alphabetical order by name. For example, if you change the name of the file from Agreement.docx to Willoughby Agreement.docx, the file will jump down toward the bottom of the list.

When renaming files, observe these rules:

- Never change the name of your home folder. Recovering from this error is not easy; data could be and most likely *will be* lost.

- Never change the names of the system folders found on the hard drive.

- Never change the name or file extension of an application file.

NOTE If you have set the Finder preference to show *file extensions* (the characters to the right of the dot in the complete filename), when you select a file and press **Return**, the file extension is not included in the automatic text selection. This is Mountain Lion's way of reminding you that you should not change a file's extension.

Copying and Moving Files

When you copy a file, you make an exact duplicate of the file. If you copy the file to a new location, the file also has the exact same name. If, however, you copy the file to the same folder, the Finder has to alter the name because no two files can have the same name if they reside in the same folder. So if you make a copy of a file in the same folder, Finder appends *copy* to the end of the new filename (just before the dot and the extension). A second copy in the same folder would have *copy 2* appended to the new filename, and so on.

When you move a file, the file goes from one storage location to another. The name of the file doesn't change during the move.

Copying Files Using Shortcuts

Most of the time when I copy files, I like to use keyboard shortcuts or shortcut menus. Additionally, I like to use the List view when I'm selecting the files. This view is especially good to use if you need to select files that reside in different folders. You can select your home folder in the sidebar, and this gives you access to all files in all locations. You may develop your own preferred method of copying files, but here are the steps I like to use:

1. Open the Finder and switch to the List view if necessary.

2. Select the file (or multiple files) to copy. (If selecting multiple files, Command-click to select each file.)

3. Press **Command-C** to copy or right-click the file(s) and click the **Copy** command. (Depending on how many files you have selected, the command may say something like Copy Agreement.docx or Copy 3 Items.)

4. Double-click the target location so it is the only folder open in the right pane.

5. Press **Command-V** to paste.

TIP   If you want to paste using the shortcut menu command, switch to the Icon view and then right-click a blank area in the view. Click the **Paste Item(s)** command. (There is no "blank" area to click in the List view, so that's why you have to switch views.)

6.   Repeat steps 4 and 5 if you want to copy the same files to multiple locations.

Copying or Moving Files and Folders by Dragging

The method of dragging a file from one Finder window to another is also a good way to copy files and folders. It's also the only way to move them. These are the steps I use when I'm using the dragging method:

1.   Open the Finder window and click **File**, **New Finder Window**.

2.   Set the view in one window to List and the other to Icon. For the same reasons stated previously, I like to use the List view for the Finder window where I select the file(s), and the Icon view for the Finder window where I drop the files. (The Icon view gives you a better target area.)

3.   In the List view window, select the file (or files) you want to copy or move.

4.   Begin dragging the selection and then press the **Option** key to copy or the **Command** key to move. If you are copying, a green circle with a plus in it is displayed. If you are dragging more than one file, the number of files you are dragging appears in a red circle.

5.   Drop the file(s) in the right pane of the Icon view window.

NOTE   If you forget to press either the Option key or Command key while you are dragging files, the files may be copied, or they may be moved, depending on the source and destination of the files. If you drag *from* and *to* a location on the *same* disc, the Finder moves the files. If you drag *from* one disc *to* another disc, the Finder copies the files.

Sharing Files

Mountain Lion provides the traditional ways to share files with other users (through email and messages) and adds a few new ways: Twitter, Facebook, Flickr, and Vimeo. Mountain Lion makes it easy to share files instantly with these social networking sites. All you have to do is give Mountain Lion your account information for each service, and then when you are ready to share a file, Mountain Lion connects to your account automatically. To do that, follow these steps:

1. Click the **System Preferences** icon in the Dock or click **Launchpad** and click the icon there.

2. Click **Mail, Contacts & Calendars**.

3. In the list on the right, click the type of account you want to set up. A dialog box opens to collect your account information. The dialog box for a Flickr account is shown in Figure 11.4.

FIGURE 11.4

You must already have an account set up in Flickr before you can supply the information in this dialog box.

4. Fill out the information and click **Sign In**. Your account is added to the list on the left, and your account information is displayed on the right.

5. To set up another type of account, click the **Add** button and repeat step 4.

 NOTE At this time you cannot set up multiple accounts for the same service.

Sharing Files in the Finder

When you are using the Finder, you can share a file by selecting it and clicking the new **Share** button in the toolbar. Alternatively, you can right-click the file and click **Share**. Appropriate options for sharing are displayed based on the type of file you have selected. For example, in Figure 11.5, the selected file is a movie file, so one of the options for sharing is Vimeo. Click the Share option you want to use and continue with any steps required by the option. For example, if you select **Email** as the Sharing option, a new email message is created for you automatically with the file attached. Then, at a minimum, you have to fill out the To address and click Send. If you share a photo to Facebook, you can add it to one of your albums.

 NOTE If you select a social network sharing option for which you don't have an account, you are presented with a dialog box that allows you to set up a new account.

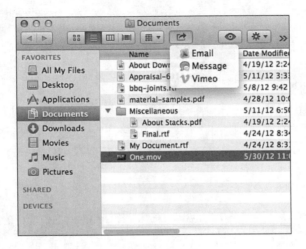

FIGURE 11.5

Vimeo is a Share option because the selected file is a movie.

Sending Files by AirDrop

AirDrop is a method of sending and receiving files wirelessly between qualifying Macs that are in range of each other (as in the same building). To be a qualifying Mac, it must be running Lion or Mountain Lion, and it must be new enough to use AirDrop. This section doesn't go into all possible models that qualify, but suffice it to say that if you can use AirDrop, you will see a command for it in the Finder's Go menu.

To send a file between two qualified Macs, follow these steps:

1. Open the Finder and select the file you want to send.

2. Click the **AirDrop** icon in the sidebar. AirDrop automatically discovers all the other WiFi-enabled Macs running AirDrop that are near your computer and displays them in the right pane. (This process can take a few seconds.) If the owner of that computer is one of your contacts, his or her name appears in the right pane. Also, if you have the owner's photo and Apple ID in your Contacts list, that information also is displayed.

3. Drag the file to the name of the person you want to send the file to and confirm that you want to send it. When the recipient accepts the transfer, the file is transmitted to the his or her Download folder. The file is encrypted during transfer, and Mountain Lion creates a temporary firewall between your computer and the receiving computer during the transfer so no one else can access your computer during the connection.

4. Close the Finder window when finished.

 TIP   To cancel receiving a file during transfer, click the **Downloads** icon in the Dock and click the **X** that appears on the file that is being downloaded.

Moving Files to the Trash a.k.a. Deleting Files

The quickest and easiest way to delete a file or folder is to select it and press **Command-Delete**. As an alternative, you also can drag the file or folder to the Trash icon in the Dock. If you drag to the Trash icon, be sure you see the word *Trash* before you drop the file or folder. Otherwise, you will have successfully moved the file or folder to the desktop or onto the Dock instead of deleting it.

If you use the menu commands to delete a file, don't look for a Delete command. The command is Move to Trash. You can find this command on the Edit menu in the Finder's menu bar and on context menus.

You shouldn't really think of a file or folder as deleted just because you've put it in the trash. It really is still on the computer until you "empty the trash." Before then, you can open the Trash folder and get a file or folder back. To empty the trash for good, click **Finder** in the menu bar and click **Empty Trash** or **Secure Empty Trash**. If you prefer to see what's in the Trash before emptying it, click the Trash icon in the Dock and then click the Empty button.

CAUTION When you choose Empty Trash, you are giving your Mac permission to use the space those files occupy for other data. Until new data is written to that spot, however, the old data is still there and could potentially be recovered by third-party software. Selecting **Secure Empty Trash** tells your Mac to write over the existing data immediately. Therefore, this method of emptying the trash takes a little longer, but it is much more secure. You can select this method as the default on the Advanced tab in the Finder Preferences window.

To retrieve a file from the trash, follow these steps:

1. Click the **Trash** icon in the Dock. The Finder window opens displaying all the items in the Trash.

2. If you can find the file you want to retrieve easily, select it and press **Command-Delete,** or click **File** in the menu bar and then click **Put Back**. Finder puts the file back in its original location. If it has to, it will even put back the folder the file was in if the folder has been deleted too.

TIP If you can't find the file in Trash, perform a Spotlight search in the Trash folder. After the results are displayed, verify that the file is the one you want by using Quick Look.

Burning Files to a Disc

If you want to make a backup of your files or prepare a disc to give to someone, you can burn the files to a writeable CD or DVD. Before making your disc, check the capacity of the disc and make sure the total size of all the files you want to put on the disc does not exceed the capacity of the disc.

Follow these steps to burn files to a disc:

1. Select the files and folders you want to burn to a CD or DVD.

2. Click **File, Burn <x> Items to Disc**.

3. You are prompted to insert a blank disc. You can insert a blank disc before you even do step 1, but if you wait until this point, the dialog box that prompts you to insert the disc also tells you how much space you will need on the disc. Insert the disc, and the prompt eventually closes automatically and a new dialog box opens.

4. Type the name you want to give the disc in the **Disc Name** field.

5. Click **Burn**. When the files are written to the disc, the Finder verifies the disc to be sure it is reliable. If the disc can't be verified, try again with a different disc.

THE ABSOLUTE MINIMUM

- Double-click a file or folder in the Finder to open it.

- To quickly see the content of a file in the Finder, select the file and press the spacebar.

- No two files can have the same name if they reside in the same folder.

- You can copy or move files by dragging them. Press the Option key while you drag to copy and the Command key while you drag to move.

- Deleting a file moves it to the Trash folder, and using the Secure Empty Trash command overwrites the file's data so it cannot be recovered in any way.

IN THIS CHAPTER

- Launching applications four different ways
- Arranging applications in the Launchpad
- Closing applications without having to save your work
- Downloading and installing applications from the App Store
- Updating your applications

12

WORKING WITH APPLICATIONS

An application is a program used by a computer—the software *yin* to the hardware *yang*. One is nothing without the other. Everything that happens on your computer is the result of an instruction from an application. And where do you fit into the picture? You are the driving force, of course—the one who dispenses the application's instructions. In this chapter, we'll look at some of the instructions that all applications have in common, such as launching, closing, quitting, and resuming. Additionally, I'll help you expand your role by telling you how to obtain and install even more applications.

Launching Applications

Launching an application starts the application and makes all its features available for your use. As explained in Chapter 3, "Using the Dock," when you launch an application, the application icon appears in the Dock (if it doesn't happen to be in the Dock already), and a glowing blue bubble appears under the application's icon.

You can use any of several techniques for launching applications. You can launch an application by

- Clicking its icon in the Applications folder in the Finder

- Clicking its icon in the Dock (if there is one)

- Double-clicking a file that was created by the application in the Finder

- Clicking Launchpad and clicking the application's icon there

Using Launchpad

Launchpad was introduced in OS X Lion, and it took its design from iOS (used in the iPhone, iPad, and iPod). For example, when you look at your iPhone, you see icons for all your apps, and you can swipe from page to page to view all of them. When you click the **Launchpad** icon (a rocket on a silver disc) on the Dock, all your applications are displayed in Full Screen mode, as shown in Figure 12.1.

 TIP You can open Launchpad using the Magic Trackpad by pinching three fingers and your thumb on the pad.

Each application has an icon, and the name of the application is displayed under the icon. When you click the application icon in Launchpad, the application launches. Some icons represent folders. Clicking a folder icon opens the folder to display the applications that are in it. You can click the icon for the application you want to launch, or you can close the folder by clicking in the Launchpad window anywhere outside the folder.

 CAUTION The complete names of some applications are too long to be displayed in Launchpad, but you cannot change the names. As you know, if you have read Chapter 11, "Working with Files and Folders in the Finder," you should never change the name of an application file.

These dots
indicate pages.

FIGURE 12.1

Launchpad looks similar to the iDevice interface that displays all your apps.

Launchpad is not just one screen. It can have as many pages as you want. In Figure 12.1, the dots at the bottom of the screen are page indicators. To go to another page, you can just click one of these dots. Additionally, you can go to different pages by pressing the right- or left-arrow keys or using the appropriate horizontal swiping gesture if you have a Magic Mouse or Trackpad. (Gestures are set up in the Preferences windows.)

To close the Launchpad, click the **Launchpad** icon in the Dock again, press **Esc**, or click anywhere in the background. Launchpad always opens to the last page you viewed. If you had a folder open when you closed Launchpad, Launchpad reopens to that folder.

Arranging Icons in the Launchpad

If the Mac initial arrangement of icons in Launchpad doesn't work for you, you can rearrange the icons to suit yourself. You can move icons to different pages and also create folders for them. Using different pages and folders enables you to group applications. For example, you can have all your graphic applications on one screen and all your games on another screen.

To move application icons, open the Launchpad and drag the icons. You can drag icons to a new location on the same page or to another page. To drag an icon off the page and drop it on another page, drag the icon to the appropriate edge of the screen (right edge to go to the next page, left edge to go to the previous page) and hold it there until the other page appears. Then continue dragging the icon to the location where you want to put it on that page (if there are other icons on the page already). When you are finished rearranging, just click the screen. Note that if there is no existing page to the left or right, Launchpad creates one for you when you drag the icon.

Working with Folders in the Launchpad

Figure 12.2 shows the default folder named Other that Mountain Lion creates for you. This folder contains a group of miscellaneous applications and utilities. If you use any of these applications on a regular basis, you might want to drag the application icons out of the folder so you can get to them more easily. If you don't want icons to be grouped in a folder at all, drag icons out of the folder until the folder disappears. (The folder disappears when only one icon is left.)

FIGURE 12.2

Use Launchpad folders to group similar or miscellaneous applications.

If you have applications that you want to group together in a folder, you can create and name your own folder. Just follow these steps:

1. Open Launchpad, drag the first icon you want to place in a folder, and drop it on a second icon you want to place in the folder. The two icons appear together in a dark gray band, as shown in Figure 12.3. Mountain Lion gives the folder an appropriate name, such as Productivity, Video, Puzzle Games, and so on.

 NOTE Unlike the Finder, Launchpad can have folders with the same names.

FIGURE 12.3

Launchpad names folders for you automatically, but you can change the names if you want.

2. To rename the folder, click the name, type a new name, and press **Return**.

3. Click anywhere outside the dark gray band to close the folder.

4. Drag the next icon to the new folder icon. Repeat for each application you want to put in the folder.

Searching for Applications in Launchpad

After you have rearranged icons, put them on different pages, and grouped them in folders, you might find the search feature in Launchpad useful. To find any application, just type a few letters of its name. Your typing immediately appears in the Spotlight search box and applications that match the text appear under the box. Figure 12.4 shows what comes up when you type **co** in Launchpad. Notice that any application with *co* anywhere in its name appears in the search results. Click the icon for the application you want to launch.

FIGURE 12.4

The Search feature in Launchpad is a new addition in Mountain Lion.

Adding and Deleting Icons in Launchpad

Installing a new application from the App Store automatically adds an icon to the Launchpad. If you install an application from another source, and it doesn't place an icon in the Launchpad for you (probably a rare occurrence), you can add the icon for the application yourself. Open the Applications folder in the Finder and drag the application icon to the Launchpad icon in the Dock.

Some icons displayed in Launchpad cannot be deleted, such as Contacts, Mail, iTunes, Photo Booth, TextEdit, and other applications that are part of Mountain Lion. You may or may not be able to delete other icons, mainly for applications that you have installed yourself, from Launchpad. Deleting an application icon in Launchpad is tantamount to deleting the application file in the Applications folder. So when you delete an icon in Launchpad, you're not just deleting an alias; you're removing the application from your system.

 NOTE   If you delete an application you have purchased from the App Store, you can reinstall it any time. See "Installing Apps from the Mac App Store" later in this chapter.

You can easily see which applications in Launchpad can be deleted by opening Launchpad and pressing the **Option** key. While you are holding down the Option key, the icons start to wiggle, and any application that can be deleted has an **X** in the upper-left corner of the icon. (You also can point to an icon and hold down the mouse button on the icon to make the icons start to wiggle.) To delete an icon, click the **X** button and then confirm that you want to delete the application in the dialog box that opens.

Closing Applications

In pre-Lion versions of the operating system, the glowing blue bubbles on the Dock (mentioned at the beginning of this chapter) helped you to know what applications you should close before shutting down the computer. Starting with Lion, you no longer have to save all your work and close your applications before shutting down. Lion introduced three features that made this step unnecessary: Autosave, Versions, and Resume.

 NOTE Not all third-party applications make use of the Autosave, Versions, and Resume features. If they don't, Mountain Lion warns you that you need to save your work before closing the application.

Using Autosave

The Autosave feature automatically saves your file continually as you are working as well as when you close either the file or the application, so you never have to worry about losing any data. If you prefer to be prompted to save your changes before closing a file, a new preference on the General page (Ask to Keep Changes When Closing Documents) enables this pre-Lion behavior. To learn more about how this feature works in a specific program, see Chapter 21, "Using TextEdit."

Using Resume

The Resume feature has two functions. One function focuses in narrowly on closing and opening individual applications, and the other has a global focus that controls what happens when you shut down and reboot the computer.

The narrow focus of the Resume feature enables an application to open all your work that you left open the last time you closed the application. Resume doesn't just reopen the files you were working on last; it reopens the files and all auxiliary windows, palettes, toolbars, and so on that were open before. It even places the pointer in the file right where it was when you closed the application. The preference for this behavior, Close Windows When Quitting an Application, which is enabled by default, is set in the General System Preferences window. If you change this option, it takes effect the next time you start the computer.

The global focus of the Resume feature allows all applications and files that were open when you shut down the computer to reopen when you reboot. You control this behavior in the dialog box that opens when you shut down or restart your computer, as shown in Figure 12.5. The Reopen Windows option is not selected by default. If you check the box, the next time you start the computer, all applications and files that were open when you shut down the computer reopen.

FIGURE 12.5

Mountain Lion remembers the setting you make for the Reopen Windows option and uses it the next time you shut down or restart your computer.

Quitting Applications

With the exception of the Finder, you can quit any application in a number of different ways. You can

- Click the name of the application in the menu bar and click **Quit**
- Right-click the application's icon in the Dock and click **Quit**
- Press **Command-Q** while you are in the application

Sometimes an application gets hung up and stops working. If you see the Spinning Beach Ball of Death (SBBOD) for a very long time, your application is hung up. In this case, none of the techniques described previously to quit the application will work, and you have to use the Force Quit technique.

In all likelihood, when you have to force quit an application, you will lose data. It might be a little or a lot, depending on the application and the last time the file was saved. Even if you are using an application that has Autosave built in, you will lose the data you have entered between the last Autosave and the hang-up.

To force an application to quit, follow these steps:

1. Right-click the application's icon in the Dock and click **Force Quit** or press **Command-Option-Esc**. The Force Quit Applications window opens, and it lists all running applications.

     NOTE   The Apple menu also has a Force Quit option, but you cannot access the Apple menu within the unresponsive application. You would have to switch to another application such as the Finder and then access the Apple menu.

2. Select the unresponsive application in the window and click **Force Quit**. A dialog box opens asking you to verify that you want to force the application to quit.

3. Click **Force Quit**. A dialog box opens, and you can either send a report to Apple or just ignore the incident. If you click Report, a report will be sent to Apple via the Internet. Apple uses these reports to improve its applications, so sending them is a good idea.

4. Close the Force Quit window.

Installing Applications

Your most trusted source for obtaining and installing applications for your Mac is the App Store—not to be confused with the iTunes App Store, which is used to obtain apps for the iDevices. The Mac App Store sells applications that are fully vetted by Apple. Other third-party sources that have trusted names, such as Adobe and Quicken, are also good sources for applications.

 TIP   Do your homework before downloading software from a third party. Search for the software on the Internet and read any reviews, blogs, and so on that refer to it.

If you are downloading a third-party application from the Internet, be sure that the application you are installing is actually from the reputable source it claims to be and not from a malicious source. The new Gatekeeper feature in Mountain Lion goes a long way in protecting you from installing potentially dangerous software that is masquerading as legitimate software. Learn more about the Gatekeeper feature in Chapter 29, "Maintaining and Securing Your Mac."

Installing Apps from the Mac App Store

To buy from the App Store, you just need to have your Apple ID set up with a credit card. To go to the App Store any time you are online, click the **App Store** button in the Dock. When you find an application you want to install, follow these steps:

1. Click **Store**, **Sign In**. Enter your ID information and click **Sign In**.

2. Click the button beside the application with the price in it or the word *Free* in it.

3. Click the **Install** button. The App Store downloads the application to Launchpad. While the application is downloading, a progress bar appears under the Launchpad icon in the Dock.

 NOTE If you lose your Internet connection during the download, the Mac App Store will restart the download when the connection is restored. You also can quit the Mac App Store during the middle of the download, and the download will restart the next time you launch the App Store.

After you have purchased an application or downloaded a free application, you can install it on all your Macs for no additional charge! To download software to another Mac, just launch the App Store from that Mac, sign in, and then click **Purchases** in the toolbar. Click the **Install** button beside any purchase you want to download to that Mac.

Installing Mac Applications from Third-Party Sources

The steps to install an application from a source other than the App Store vary, so I can't really outline the exact procedure for you. Generally, though, the software has a Setup Assistant that guides you through the process. The process is normally simplified to the point that all you have to do is drag an icon for the application to an icon for the Applications folder.

Getting the Most from the Mac App Store

You can shop for applications in the App Store in a couple of ways. You can browse through applications by clicking the **Featured** button or the **Top Charts** button in the toolbar. Featured applications include New and Noteworthy, What's Hot, and Staff Favorites. These are applications that Apple has selected to highlight. The Top Charts include Top Paid, Top Free, and Top Grossing. The applications in these categories are the ones that are popular with users.

You also can shop for applications in different categories. Click **Categories** in the toolbar and select one of the categories shown in Figure 12.6.

FIGURE 12.6

Click a category icon to view applications in the category.

If you know the name or something about the application you want, you can search for it instead of browsing through categories. Just type a key word or phrase in the Spotlight search box. The App Store supplies suggestions in a list under the search box. If one of the suggestions that appears is relevant, click it. The App Store displays the search results, and you can see whether the application you want is among the results.

Before deciding to purchase an application, you might want to learn more about it and read the reviews that buyers have posted about it. A typical information screen for an application has a description of the application and the cost at the top. Below the description are sample graphics of the application, and to the right of the graphics is information such as the released date, version number, size of the file, requirements, rating number that tells the age the application is appropriate for, and so on. Customer Ratings and Customer Reviews are below the sample graphics. You can sort the reviews (if there are any) by Most Helpful, Most Favorable, Most Critical, and Most Recent.

THE ABSOLUTE MINIMUM

- The Launchpad contains your applications, and it's probably the best place to go to launch applications that don't appear on the Dock.

- You can customize the Launchpad so that applications are grouped together in folders or on separate pages.

- You can quit an application without closing your work and resume right where you left off the next time you launch the application.

- The App Store is the safest source for obtaining applications.

IN THIS CHAPTER

- Looking at your first experience with Safari
- Assembling all your favorite websites in Top Sites
- Getting around on the Web and retracing your steps
- Making sure you can get back to a web page any time you want
- Creating a list of pages you want to read later
- Downloading files to the folder of your choice
- Passing links along to your friends via email, text messages, and tweets

13

USING SAFARI

Be honest. How much time do you spend on the Internet every day? It's probably a significant amount. After all, the Internet can keep you posted on the latest news, the weather, stock prices, how to get to Topeka, the price of gas at nearby gas stations, the name of the actress in *The Dragon Tattoo*, and on and on. Don't you owe it to yourself to make sure you are getting the most out of your Internet usage? This chapter should do just that—teach you how to use the application that opens the Web—Safari.

Launching Safari the First Time

Safari is the native OS X web browsing application. To launch Safari, click the icon that looks like a blue compass in the Dock. The first time you launch Safari, the Apple Start page opens. This is the default home page set in the Safari preferences.

If you would like to select a different page, click **Safari** in the menu bar, and then click **Preferences**, **General**. Click **Set to Current Page** and close the window.

Using Top Sites

If you have several favorite sites that you want to access quickly, you can use the Top Sites feature. To open Top Sites, click the **Top Sites** button in the Bookmarks bar (see Figure 13.1). Then click the site you want to go to. Initially, Top Sites has preselected sites, but as you browse the Web, your favorite sites take the place of the preselected sites.

Top Sites Button

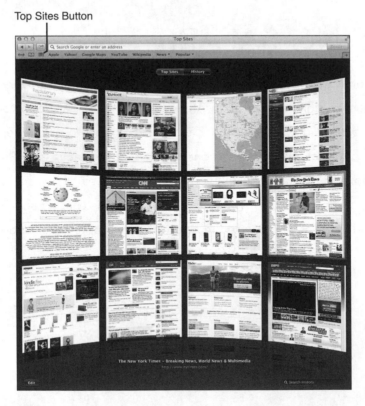

FIGURE 13.1

Apple's own website is the first preview in the first row of Top Sites.

If you really like using Top Sites, you can make it appear by default when you open a new window by following these steps:

1. Click **Safari** in the menu bar and click **Preferences**.

2. Click **General** if necessary.

3. Click the **New Windows Open With** pop-up button and click **Top Sites**.

4. Close the Preferences window.

Instead of letting Safari populate Top Sites for you over time, you can decide what sites you want to include. When you are on a page you want to add to Top Sites, just click **Bookmarks** in the menu bar. Then click **Add Bookmark** and select **Top Sites** from the pop-up menu.

To further customize Top Sites, follow these steps:

1. If necessary, click the **Top Sites** button to display Top Sites.

2. Click the **Edit** button at the bottom-left corner of the screen.

3. Choose **Small**, **Medium**, or **Large** to determine how many sites are displayed. Figure 13.2 shows the large previews.

4. To delete a site, click the **X** button in the upper-left corner of the site.

5. To keep a site from being replaced, click the button that looks like a stickpin on the site.

6. To add a site, click **File**, **New Window**. Go to the site, drag the icon in front of the website address to the Top Site window, and drop the icon where you want it.

> **NOTE**   Websites that don't have a proprietary icon use the generic icon of a globe.

7. Rearrange the sites by dragging them to different locations.

8. When you are finished customizing, click the **Done** button in the lower-left corner of the window.

FIGURE 13.2

Using the Large option makes the previews larger and easier to read.

Navigating the Web

Navigating the Web just means going from one page to another. You can simply click links to go to other pages, or you can go directly to a specific page by typing its web address in Safari's new *omnibar* at the top of the screen. (When typing a web address, you no longer have to type **http://www** at the beginning of the address. Just type the domain name, such as **apple.com**.)

Using the Omnibar

Mountain Lion's omnibar is an all-in-one-address-and-search bar. You can type either a web address or search phrase in this bar. Just click once in the bar to select all the current text in the bar and then begin typing your address or search words. Safari immediately displays a list of suggestions, and you can select one or finish typing and press **Return**.

TIP   Safari uses the Google search engine by default. You can change to a different search engine by clicking the magnifying glass in the Search text box.

If you want to search for a word or phrase on the current page, follow these steps:

1. Type the search text in the omnibar.

2. In the list of suggestions, select the option labeled **Find** ***<Search Phrase>*** **on This Page**. (It's always the last option.) Safari adds a new bar under the Bookmarks bar that has the familiar Spotlight search box with your search text in it, as shown in Figure 13.3.

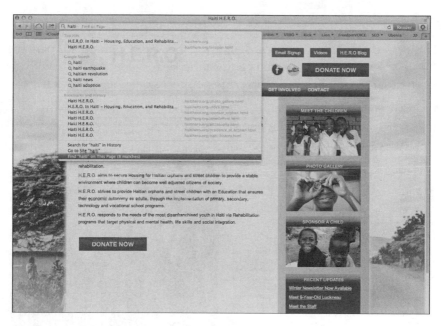

FIGURE 13.3

Safari lists suggestions to help you search.

3. Click the **Forward** and **Back** buttons to the left of the Spotlight search box to go to each occurrence of your search text. (If no occurrences are found, the bar says None on it.)

4. Click **Done** when you are finished.

Retracing Your Steps

Surfing the Internet takes you on a journey of intricate paths and tangents. It's not called the "Web" for nothing! Finding your way back to a page you saw 20 clicks ago could be time-consuming. Clicking the Back button 20 times would eventually get you there, but there are a couple of other, quicker ways to get back.

If you have a Magic Mouse or a Magic Trackpad, you can swipe to the right or left to go back or forward through your pages. Additionally, you can point to the Back button and hold down the mouse button to reveal a list of your last-visited pages. Click the one in the list you want to go back to if you recognize it. If you're not sure, just click one that you think it could be and then use the Back button one click at a time to try to find the page. If you don't find it by going back, try going forward one click at a time using the Forward button. Note that the Forward button also displays a list if you point to it and hold down the mouse button.

Using History

If you need to retrace your steps from another session in Safari, perhaps earlier in the day or on another day, you can use the History feature. Follow these steps to use History to go back to a web page you have previously visited:

1. Click **History** in the menu bar. The menu shows all the sites you've visited today, and it contains submenus for other recent dates, as shown in Figure 13.4.

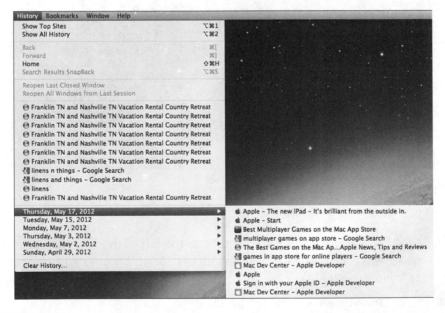

FIGURE 13.4

The History menu shows links for the current day and the last several dates.

2. Click a link for today or point to a submenu for another date and click a link on that menu, or click **Show All History** if you need to go back to an earlier date. If you click a link on the menu, the web page opens. If you click Show All History, your entire saved history is displayed, as shown in Figure 13.5.

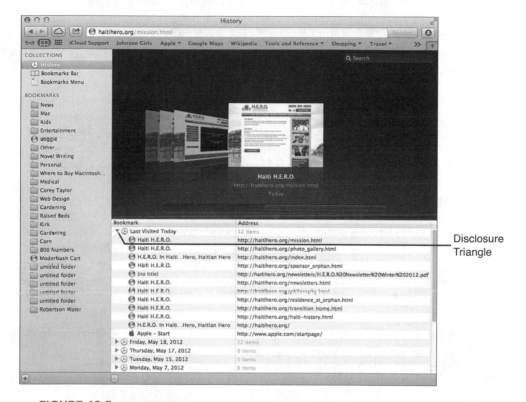

Disclosure Triangle

FIGURE 13.5

This window shows your complete browsing history as well as all bookmarks.

3. Click the disclosure triangles beside the relevant dates to reveal the links and click the link you think is correct. A preview of the web page is displayed in the Cover Flow view at the top of the screen.

4. When you find the correct link, double-click it.

 NOTE   Safari keeps web pages in your History list for one year by default, but you can change this time interval or even select to remove pages manually. To set this preference, open the General pane in Safari's Preferences window and click the **Remove History Items** pop-up button to make your selection.

Browsing in Tabs or Windows

By default, when you click a link to go to a new page, Safari opens that page in the current window. This is generally best because it eliminates having a bunch of windows open in Safari, but sometimes you might want to open a page in a new window—if you want to compare it to another page, for example. If this is the case, click **File** in the menu bar and then click **New Window**. By default, the new window opens to the home page. Then you can go to the web page you want by whatever means you need to use.

 TIP To control what is displayed when a new window opens, go to the General page of Safari Preferences and select one of the following for New Windows Open With: **Top Sites**, **Homepage**, **Empty Page**, **Same Page**, **Bookmarks**, or **Tabs for Bookmarks Bar**. Additionally, you can select a folder to open in tabs by clicking **Choose Tabs Folder**.

Another way to browse in Safari is to use a tab for each new page you want to go to. Working in a tabbed window is neat and efficient. You have only one window open, but you know exactly what else is open because each tab displays the web page's title. To open a new tab, press **Command-T** or click the **New Tab** button (the one on the right with the plus), shown in Figure 13.6. As soon as you open a second tab, the new Show All Tabs button appears to the right of the New Tab button.

FIGURE 13.6

The New Tab button moves up to appear at the right of the Bookmarks bar if the Tab bar is not visible.

By default, a new tab opens in Top Sites, and you can click one of your Top Sites to go there or enter a new web address for the tab. You can control what is displayed when a new tab opens by going to the General page of Safari Preferences and selecting an option for New Tabs Open With. Your choices are Top Sites, Homepage, Empty Page, Same Page, and Bookmarks.

When you close a Safari window, whether or not it has tabs open in it, the window just closes with no questions asked. If you really intended to close only one of the tabs, you can click **History**, **Reopen Last Closed Window** to get everything back again. To close a tab, point to the tab and click the **Close** button on the left side of the tab.

Using the Tab View

The Tab view, a new feature in Mountain Lion, displays each tab as a separate page in a continuous horizontal line that you can scroll left and right. To enter the Tab view, click the **Tab View** button that appears just to the right of the New Tab button (if you have more than one tab open). If you are using a trackpad, you also can pinch a tab to reveal all the open tabs.

Figure 13.7 shows the Tab view. Notice the dots at the bottom of the screen. There is one dot for each tab that you have open, and you can use these dots to navigate to the individual tabs or use typical scrolling gestures or the left and right arrow keys to navigate.

FIGURE 13.7

The new Tab view in Mountain Lion provides a navigation dot for each tab that is open.

To switch back to viewing only one tab at a time in the window, click **View**, **Show One Tab**. All tabs remain open but only the selected tab displays in the window. Additionally, if you click the New Tab button or choose **File**, **New Tab**, the view switches back to showing only one tab at a time in the window.

Synchronizing Tabs

Using iCloud technology, your Mac can display all the open tabs on your other qualifying devices—assuming you have your Mac as well as those devices set to synchronize Safari. The new iCloud button displays a list of the tabs currently open in Safari on your other devices, and all you have to do is select the tab you want to see. (To qualify, an iDevice must be running iOS6 and a Mac must be running Mountain Lion.)

For example, if you are viewing a web page on your iPhone, when you get home you can continue viewing it on your Mac by clicking the **iCloud** button on the Mac and selecting the tab under the iPhone category.

Getting a Better View of Web Pages

Sometimes web designers add content to web pages that you would like to zoom in on to get a better look. With the Smart Zoom feature, you can do just that. If you have a Magic Mouse, you can double-tap to zoom in or out. With a Magic Trackpad, you can pinch your fingers together to zoom in or spread them apart to zoom out. If a page has too many distractions on it, you can click the **Reader** button (if it's available) and strip the page down to a more readable form. The Reader button is not new in Mountain Lion, but it has been given more prominence in its new location outside the address field.

When available, the Reader button is blue, and it's gray when it's not available. Not all web pages trigger the Reader button; whether it's available depends on the HTML coding and the amount of text on the page. Figure 13.8 shows the Reader version of the web page shown in Figure 13.6.

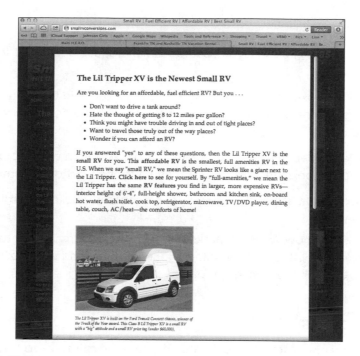

FIGURE 13.8

Use the Reader to display a page for printing.

Using Bookmarks

When you visit a web page that you think you might want to return to, it's a good idea to bookmark the page. Doing so eliminates the need to search for the page in your history. When you bookmark a page, you can tell Safari to store the bookmark in the Bookmarks menu, on the Bookmarks bar, or in a bookmark folder.

Bookmarking Web Pages

To bookmark the current page, click **Bookmarks** in the menu bar and then click **Add Bookmark**, or click the **Share** button and click **Add Bookmark**. Click the pop-up button and select **Bookmarks Bar** or **Bookmarks Menu**. Additionally, you can select any folder that is listed on the pop-up menu. By default, you have two folders to choose from—News and Popular—but you can create your own folders. You learn how to do that later in this chapter.

Using a Bookmark

To go to a web page that you have bookmarked, use one of the following methods:

- Click a bookmark on the Bookmarks bar. If you have too many bookmarks on the bar to be displayed, you may have to click the double arrow at the right end of the Bookmarks bar to reveal the bookmark you want.

- Click a folder name on the Bookmarks bar and then click the bookmark you want. (A bookmark folder has a triangle to the right of its name.)

- Click **Bookmarks** in the menu bar and click the bookmark on the menu that you want.

- Click the **Show All Bookmarks** button in the Bookmarks bar to view the bookmarks list. Select the folder in the left pane and then double-click the bookmark in the lower-right pane.

Creating Bookmark Folders

When bookmarks start to proliferate, it's more difficult to keep track of them. The best way to organize them is to create folders for them. After you create a folder, you can move existing bookmarks into it or just keep it on tap for future use.

To create a new folder for bookmarks, follow these steps:

1. Click **Bookmarks** in the menu bar.

2. Click **Add Bookmark Folder**. The bookmarks list window opens, as shown later in Figure 13.9. The new folder is displayed under the Bookmarks category in the left pane with its name (untitled folder) selected.

3. Type a name for the folder and press **Return**.

4. To move existing bookmarks into the new folder, select the current location of the bookmark you want to move. (For example, select **Bookmarks Bar** or **Bookmarks Menu** in the left pane.) Drag the bookmark (listed in the lower pane on the right) to the name of the new folder listed under Bookmarks in the pane on the left. Don't release the mouse button until you see an outline drawn around the folder name. This outline tells you that the bookmark will go inside the folder.

5. Close the bookmarks list window when finished.

Customizing the Bookmarks Bar

You can customize the Bookmarks bar in several ways:

- To rearrange the order of bookmarks and folders, drag an item to the left or right.

- To move a bookmark currently on the bar to a folder on the bar, drag the bookmark and drop it on top of the folder.

- To rename a bookmark or bookmark folder, right-click the item and click **Rename Bookmark** or **Rename Folder** (whichever is appropriate). Type a new name and press **Return**.

- To create a new folder on the Bookmarks bar, right-click the bar, click **New Folder**, type the name of the folder, and press **Return**.

- To delete a bookmark or a folder in the bar, right-click the bookmark or folder and click **Delete**.

Using the Reading List

The Reading List is a feature that was added in Lion. You can use it to store links to web pages that you want to read later. When not hidden, the Reading List is displayed on the far left side of the screen. To open and close the Reading List, click the **Reading List** button (the button with a pair of reading glasses).

Adding Pages to the Reading List

To add the web page you are currently viewing to the Reading List, click the **Share** button and click **Add to Reading List**. If the Reading List panel is visible, you also can click the **Add Page** button shown in Figure 13.9.

Another way to add a page to the Reading List is to Shift-click a link. In my opinion, this is a hidden time-saver that is underutilized. For example, it's perfect for a page such as the CNN home page. This page always has tons of links on it to different news stories. If you don't have time to read all the ones that look interesting, you can Shift-click all the links that you don't have time for and come back to them in the Reading List later.

FIGURE 13.9

Add pages to the Reading List that you want to be able to read later or over and over again.

Reading Pages in the Reading List

To read some of the pages in your Reading List, first display the list. Click the **All** or **Unread** buttons at the top of the panel to display all the items in your list or just the items you haven't read yet. Click the link to the page you want to read, and the page appears in the pane on the right.

Deleting Pages in the Reading List

After you read a page, if you no longer want to keep it in the list, you can delete it by clicking the **Close** button (**x**) in the upper-right corner of the item. (The button is displayed only when you hover the mouse over the item.) Additionally, you can delete all items in the list by clicking the **Clear All** button and clicking **Clear**.

Downloading and Viewing Files

When you click the link to download a file, the file jumps to the Download button in the upper-right corner of the window and begins downloading. A little progress bar is displayed in the button, but you can monitor the progress of the download more closely by clicking the **Download** button. Doing so opens the download window. When the file is finished downloading, the size of the file is displayed under its name, and the file opens if it is a *safe* file. (Safe files include movies, pictures, audio files, PDFs, text files, DMG files, and other archives as specified on the General tab of Safari preferences.)

To view a downloaded file that does not open automatically when you download it, go to the Downloads folder in the Finder and double-click the file. Safari saves all downloaded files in the Downloads folder by default. If you would prefer to have Safari save downloads in a different folder, open the General page of the Safari Preferences and specify the folder for **Save Downloaded File To**.

Sharing Web Content

Sharing a web page with a friend is even easier in Mountain Lion than in previous versions because there is a new Share button. The button has the following options: Add to Reading List, Add Bookmark, Email this Page, Message, Facebook, and Twitter.

You've already read about the first two options in this chapter, so they are not repeated here, but let's examine the other options:

- **Email This Page**—This option opens a new email message, and the content of the web page appears in the body of the email, as shown in Figure 13.10. If you prefer, you can click the **Send Web Content As** pop-up button and select **PDF** or **Link Only**. If you select PDF, the text of the page is converted to a PDF file and attached to the email, and a link is embedded in the body of the email. If you select Link Only, only a link is embedded in the body of the email. Whatever you choose for the way you want to send the web content is remembered and used the next time you share a web page by email.

- **Message**—This option creates a new message with a link to the web page in the text of the message.

- **Facebook**—This option creates a new post with a link to the web page.

- **Twitter**—This option creates a new tweet with a link to the web page.

FIGURE 13.10

You can send a web page in email as a page, PDF file, or link.

THE ABSOLUTE MINIMUM

- The new omnibar combines the old address box and search box into one box.

- The History feature saves a list of links to all the web pages you visit each day, and you can use the links to revisit the pages.

- To make returning to a web page at a later time easier, bookmark the web page or add it to your Reading List.

- Use the new Share button to share web pages in email, messages, Facebook, and tweets.

USING CONTACTS

To be more consistent with the iDevices, Mountain Lion has changed the name of the Address Book application to Contacts. Contacts is your repository for names, addresses, phone numbers, email addresses, and so on, and using iCloud, you can synchronize your contacts across all your devices so you always have the latest information. This chapter covers the basics of creating, editing, deleting, and archiving contacts. Additionally, it tells you how to customize the Contact template so it is better suited to your own use and how to create groups to better organize your contacts.

Exploring the Contacts Window

To open Contacts, click the **Contacts** icon in the Dock. Figure 14.1 shows the two-page display of the Contacts window. Notice that there are only two contacts—one for Apple and one for the user, Sarah Beasley, both of which were automatically created by Mountain Lion. In the two-page display, the page on the left shows a list of all contacts, and the page on the right shows the information for the contact currently selected in the left page.

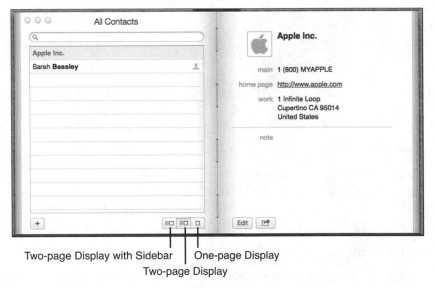

FIGURE 14.1

The three buttons at the bottom of the left page control the display of contacts.

Figure 14.2 shows the two-page layout with an added panel on the left page. This is Mountain Lion's new way of handling groups. The red ribbon bookmark and the corresponding Groups page used in Lion are both gone in Mountain Lion. Now, when you create new groups for your contacts, they are displayed in the Groups panel. In Figure 14.2, you can see that only one group is listed by default. This group is called All Contacts, and it is a master list of all your contacts.

Figure 14.3 shows the one-page layout. In this display mode, only the information for a single contact is displayed. To scroll through your contacts in this view, you use the buttons in the bottom-right corner.

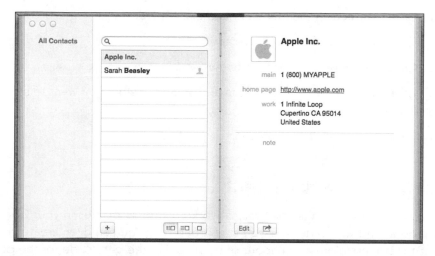

FIGURE 14.2

The sidebar on the left lists groups.

FIGURE 14.3

The one-page view includes all buttons at the bottom that are normally divided between the two pages in the two-page view.

By default, contacts are listed as <first name> <last name>, but they are sorted by last name. If you prefer, you can show the contacts as <last name>, <first name>. Additionally, you can sort your contacts by first name. To change the display order of the first and last name or to change the sort order, follow these steps:

1. Click **Contacts** in the menu bar and click **Preferences**.

2. Click the **General** tab, if necessary.

3. Click the option you want for **Show First Name**.

4. Click the **Sort By** pop-up button and select whether you want to sort by First Name or Last Name.

5. Close the Preferences window.

Creating a New Contact

Keeping all your friends, relatives, coworkers, and associates in your Contacts list will go a long way in helping you stay organized. You can even create contacts just for storing information about something like the gate code for the pool at the condo you are renting. To create a contact using the default contact template, follow these steps:

1. In any display mode, click the **Add** button. (It's the one with a plus on it.)

2. Begin by typing the first name and then tab to the next field and type the last name.

3. Tab to the Company field and type a company name if one is associated with the contact. If you want the contact to be listed (and therefore sorted) by company name instead of the individual's name, click the **Company** check box. If no company is associated with the contact, just tab to the next field.

4. If you don't want to enter a phone number, press **Tab** to go to the next field. If you have a phone number, type it in the field, click the pop-up button beside the phone number label to select the appropriate label, and press **Tab**.

5. Repeat step 4 until you have entered all the phone numbers you have for the contact. When you have no more phone numbers, press **Tab** to move to the next field.

6. If you don't have an email address, press **Tab** to go to the next field. If you have an email address, type it in the field, click the pop-up button to select the appropriate label, and press **Tab**.

7. Repeat step 6 until you have no more email addresses to add, and then press **Tab** to move to the next field.

8. Continue typing the text for each field and tabbing to the next field.

9. To add a field that doesn't appear on the form, such as the Birthday field, click **Card** in the menu bar, point to **Add Field**, and click the field you want to add.

10. If you have a photograph of the person you want to add, open Finder or iPhoto and drag the file to the photo box. Use the slider shown in Figure 14.4 to adjust the size of the picture. Drag the photo around in the box to position it. For a stylized effect, click the **Apply an Effect** button and click the effect you want. Click **Done** when finished.

Apply an Effect Button

FIGURE 14.4

To add a photo to your own card, you can use the Camera option to take a photo of yourself.

 TIP   Instead of using a photo for a contact, you can use one of the default graphics supplied by Mountain Lion. To use one of these graphics, double-click the photo box and click **Defaults**. Click the graphic you want and click the **Edit** button. Adjust the size and position or use a special effect and then click **Done**.

11. When finished, click the **Done** button to save the card and display it in final form. Fields that you left blank do not appear on the completed card.

 NOTE—If you have Facebook set up in Mountain Lion, your Facebook friends are automatically added to Contacts, including their profile photos and contact information. If a Facebook friend updates his or her photo or contact information it is also automatically passed through to your Contacts.

Dictating a Contact

Instead of typing the information for a contact, you can use the new Dictation tool in Mountain Lion that is accessible in many different applications. Before you can use the tool, however, you must enable it as described in Chapter 6, "Using and Controlling Your Hardware."

If you haven't enabled Dictation, the first time you try to use Dictation in any application, you will be presented with a dialog box asking whether you want to enable Dictation. Before you decide whether you want to use Dictation, read the privacy information that Apple provides for you by clicking the **About Dictation and Privacy** button. The words you dictate are actually sent to Apple to be converted into text. Additional personal information about you is also sent to Apple to "help the dictation feature understand you better and recognize what you say." Apple does not link this data to any other data it might have about you that you supplied to use other Apple services. If you are okay with the privacy issues, click **OK**, and then click **Enable Dictation**. The dictation pop-up opens.

 NOTE—The Dictation tool uses your internal microphone unless you have an external microphone attached that you have selected as your default input device.

After you have Dictation turned on, you can call it into action any time it is appropriate by pressing the FN key twice. So if you are using it to create a contact, you would click in each text field, such as the first name or last name field, and press **FN FN** to dictate that particular bit of information. This seems a little tedious to me, and I would probably use the Dictation tool only to enter a note about a contact.

After you press FN FN, you see a pop-up with a microphone icon. When the microphone turns purple and you hear a ding, begin speaking as distinctly as possible. You have 30 seconds. When you are finished speaking, click **Done** or press **Return**. The microphone icon is replaced by three purple, blinking dots and the Done button is replaced by the Cancel button. If you don't like what you have recorded, click **Cancel**. If you don't want to cancel, just wait for the Dictation pop-up to close and the text will be transcribed. To dictate more text, just press **FN FN** again.

If you are dictating complete sentences, you should also dictate the punctuation. For example, you could say, "Lives in gated community period," and the text would be transcribed as, "Lives in gated community." You also can dictate where a new paragraph should begin by saying, "New Paragraph." After the dictation is transcribed to text, you can add your own punctuation if needed, and, of course, you can edit the text just as you normally would.

Customizing the Contact Template

Each time you create a new contact, you use the default Contact template. You have lots of latitude when it comes to using the template. You are not strictly tied to the template. You can skip fields, add fields, and change field labels as you are using it.

If you find yourself making the same changes every time you add a new contact, you should consider customizing the template. If for no other reason, you should customize the template so it includes the birthday field. The Calendar application creates a birthday calendar for you automatically, but it takes the birthdate information from your contacts.

 NOTE Changes you make to the default template do not affect the existing fields on contacts that were created before the change. Any new fields you add will be available in existing contacts if you edit the contact.

To make changes to the template, follow these steps:

1. Click **Contacts** in the menu bar and then click **Preferences**.

2. Click the **Template** tab, if necessary. Figure 14.5 shows the default fields on the standard template.

FIGURE 14.5

Minus-sign buttons delete a field and plus-sign buttons add another field of the same type.

3. To add fields to the template, click the **Add Field** pop-up button and click the field you want to add. (Fields that already appear on the template have a check mark beside them on the pop-up menu.) The new field takes its assigned position on the form, and you cannot control where it goes.

4. To add more fields of a particular type, such as a Phone field, click the **Add** button (the green circle with the plus in it) beside the field. (Field types that do not have the Add button do not allow additional fields. The Birthday field is an example of this type of field.)

5. To remove a field, click the **Remove** button (the red circle with a minus in it) beside the field. You can delete all fields except First, Last, Company, and Note.

6. To change a field label, click the pop-up button beside the label and select the one you want from the menu; or select **Custom**, type the label you want to use, and click **OK**.

7. Close the window when finished.

 NOTE   You cannot change the formatting of the template in any way. For example, you can't change the fonts or colors used.

Working with Groups

As mentioned previously in this chapter, the All Contacts group is the master group. All your contacts are a part of this group, but you can create additional groups to help you organize your contacts or to make your life easier when sending out email messages. See Chapter 18, "Using Mail," for more information on using a group as an email distribution list.

A contact can be a member of multiple groups. For example, your boss can be in your Work group, your Christmas Card group, and your Marathon Runners group.

To create a group, click **File** in the menu bar and then click **New Group**. If not already displayed, the two-page view with the Groups panel opens, and your new group is listed in the sidebar, as shown in Figure 14.6. Type a name for the group and press **Return**. The new group moves into alphabetical order in the list; however, even if the name of the group would come before All Contacts in the alphabet, it is still listed below All Contacts.

 TIP   To rename a group, select the group in the Groups panel, press **Return**, type the new name, and press **Return** again.

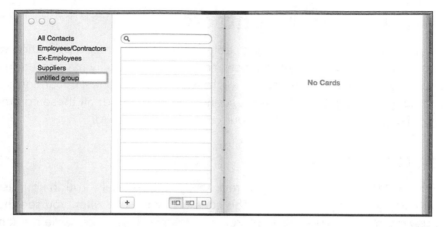

FIGURE 14.6

A new group is called Untitled Group until you name it.

Adding Contacts to a Group

To add contacts to a group, you can copy existing contacts or create new ones. To copy existing names, click the name of the group in the Groups panel that has a contact you want to copy. Scroll through the contacts until you see the one you want and then drag it to the name of the new group in the Groups panel. You can select multiple contacts to copy by Command-clicking them.

To create a new card in a group, click the group in the Groups panel and then follow the procedure for creating a contact outlined earlier in "Creating a New Contact." Adding a contact to a group adds the contact to the All Contacts group automatically.

When you have the Group sidebar displayed, you can see all the groups that a particular contact belongs to by Option-clicking the contact. All the groups that contain the contact are highlighted in the sidebar.

Deleting a Group

You can delete any group except the All Contacts group. To delete a group, select the group in the Groups panel and press the **Delete** key. When asked to confirm the deletion, click the **Delete** button. The contacts that were in the deleted group still remain in the All Contacts group.

Working with Your Contacts

On a day-to-day basis you are probably using your Contacts application to look up phone numbers or other information. You may occasionally have to edit a contact or delete one. In some cases, you might want to share one of your contacts with another person. In the following sections, you learn about all these common activities plus how to archive all your contacts as a backup.

Searching for a Contact

With the Magic Mouse or Magic Trackpad, you can scroll through your list of contacts by flicking up or down. The contacts fly by, but when you see the one you want, a quick tap stops the scrolling instantly. This is the same motion you use on an iPhone or iPad.

Another way to quickly go to a contact is to use the Spotlight search box. Click in the **Spotlight** search box and type any text that is stored anywhere in a contact. All contacts that contain the text will be found. They appear as a list if you are using the two-page display. If you are using the one-page display, use the **Next** and **Previous** buttons to go to each contact that meets the search criteria.

Editing a Contact

As people's information changes, you will need to edit their contacts to keep everything up-to-date. Fortunately, with iCloud, you don't have to make the change on every device or synchronize anything. This process all happens for you automatically when you edit a contact on any one of your iCloud-enabled devices.

 TIP Be sure to edit your own contact that Mountain Lion created for you so it has complete information. Other applications, such as Calendar, Message, and Mail, use information from your contact. To quickly go to your own contact, click **Card** on the menu bar and click **Go to My Card**.

To edit a contact, follow these steps:

1. Select **All Contacts** in the Groups panel or any group of which the contact is a member.

2. Select the contact you want to edit and click the **Edit** button.

3. Make the necessary changes and click **Done**. Any changes that you make to the contact appear in all groups to which the contact belongs.

Deleting a Contact

To delete a contact from all groups, select the **All Contacts** group, select the contact, and press the **Delete** key. When asked to confirm the deletion, make sure you have the correct contact selected and then click **Delete**. If you delete a contact by mistake, press **Command-Z** to get it back again.

If someone you placed in a group is no longer relative to the group (your boss dropped out of the marathon club, for example), you can remove the contact from just that particular group. To delete a contact from a particular group, select the group in the sidebar, select the card, and press the **Delete** key. When asked to confirm the deletion, click **Delete**. The contact is deleted only from the selected group. It still exists in All Contacts and any other group of which it is a member.

Sharing a Contact

To send a contact to someone else, you can share the contact via email or message. Click the **Share** button, as shown in Figure 14.7, and select **Email Card** or **Message Card**.

FIGURE 14.7

The Share button presents options for sending a vCard by email or by text message.

When you select Email Card, Contacts opens a new email message with a *vCard* attachment for the current contact. A **vCard** is a virtual business card. When the email recipient clicks the attachment, the card is imported automatically into the user's contact application.

By default, a vCard includes all the information you have stored for the contact. Before sending out a vCard, you might want to check the contact information to see whether there is anything you don't want to send out.

Additionally, you can set preferences for vCards so they do not include notes or photos. To change the preferences, click **Contacts**, **Preferences**, and click the **vCard** tab if necessary. Figure 14.8 shows the default preferences. You might want to enable the Private Me Card option so you can control what information you send out about yourself. When you enable this option, you can edit your own card and click check boxes beside the fields you want to be included in a vCard.

FIGURE 14.8

The default settings for vCard preferences are shown here.

Archiving Contacts

Creating an archive file for your contacts is a good way to back them up, especially if for some legitimate reason you are not using Time Machine. If you are not backing up with Time Machine, do yourself a favor and read more about it in Chapter 29, "Maintaining and Securing Your Mac." If you are using Time Machine, you don't need to archive to back up, but making an archive file of your contacts is a good way to move your contacts to another computer.

To archive contacts, follow these steps:

1. Click **File** in the menu bar and click **Export**.

2. Click **Contacts Archive**.

3. Type a different name for **Save As** if you don't want to use the name provided.

4. Select a location for **Where**, or click the down arrow to the right of the Save As field and select the desired location in the Finder.

5. Click **Save**.

Closing the Contacts Application

To close Contacts, press **Command-Q**, or right-click the **Contacts** icon in the Dock and click **Quit**. The Contacts application remembers the contact you have selected when you quit, and it displays that contact when you launch the application the next time.

You also can close Contacts by clicking the red **Close** button in the upper-left corner of the window. Many other applications can be closed in this same way, but not all. In some cases, clicking the Close button only closes the window, not the application.

THE ABSOLUTE MINIMUM

- The old Address Book application has changed its name to Contacts, and its interface has been given a facelift.

- You should consider customizing the Contacts template—if for nothing else to add the birthday field.

- Every contact you add to a group is also added to the master group called All Contacts.

- You can delete a contact from one of the groups you have created, but the contact will still be in the All Contacts group.

- Be sure to enable the Private Me Card option so you can decide what should be included on your own vCard.

- When you close the Contacts window, you are also quitting the Contacts application.

15

USING CALENDAR

Using the Calendar application, formerly called iCal, you can keep track of your schedule and even synchronize your events with your iPhone, iPad, iPod, and other Mac computers via the iCloud. This chapter not only covers the basic ins and outs of using the Calendar, but also tells you how to create recurring events, send meeting invitations, and create additional calendars.

Exploring and Navigating the Calendar Views

To open Calendar, click the **Calendar** icon in the Dock. (The Calendar icon on the Dock is a handy reference because it always displays the current month and date.) When the Calendar opens, it opens in the view that you were using when you last closed the application. Figures 15.1 through 15.4 show the four different views available in Calendar; they are Day, Week, Month, and Year.

The Day view, shown in Figure 15.1, displays a list of all your events for any date on the left side of the window. The right side of the window has a grid where you can create your new events for the day. The grid contains a line for every half hour, and every hour is labeled with the appropriate time on the left side. When you are viewing the current date, the current time is marked on the grid with a red indicator and gray line. You can use the buttons on the top right to go to the previous or next day (and use the Today button to return to the current date), or you can click a date on the mini-calendar to go directly to a specific date.

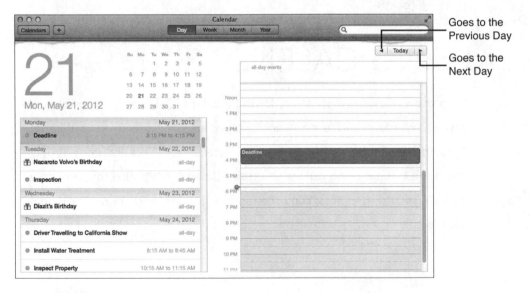

Goes to the Previous Day

Goes to the Next Day

FIGURE 15.1

The Day view shows the events for the selected day on the right and all future events on the left.

The default Week view shows seven days starting with Sunday, as shown in Figure 15.2. The time grid on the left is set up in half-hour increments as in the Day view. In this view, the scroll buttons go back or forward an entire week. This is the default setting, but you can change the buttons to scroll a day at a time by setting an option on the General page of the Calendar Preferences. Additionally, you can set preferences for which day to start your week and how many hours to show at a time on the grid.

Current Time   Goes to the Previous Week

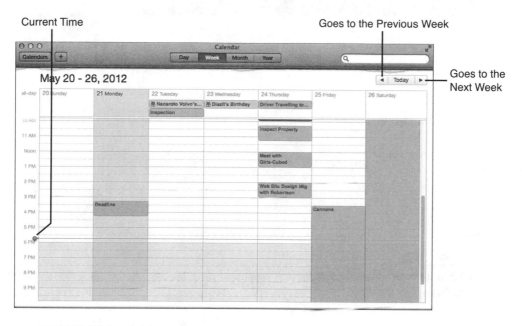

Goes to the Next Week

FIGURE 15.2

The Week view also marks the current time with a red indicator and gray line if you are viewing the current week.

In the Month view, the events for each day are displayed in the block for the appropriate date, as shown in Figure 15.3. By default, the start and end times do not display in this view, but you can at least display the start time by opening the General preferences for Calendar and clicking **Show Event Times**. In this view, the scroll buttons scroll forward and backward one month at a time.

The Year view shows your daily activities as a heat map. If you have lots of appointments scheduled for a single day, the day is colored dark red. Days with only one event are yellow. The shades in between denote the intensity of the day's schedule by the intensity of the color. To see the events scheduled on a particular day, click the date and a pop-up displays what's on the schedule for the day, as shown in Figure 15.4.

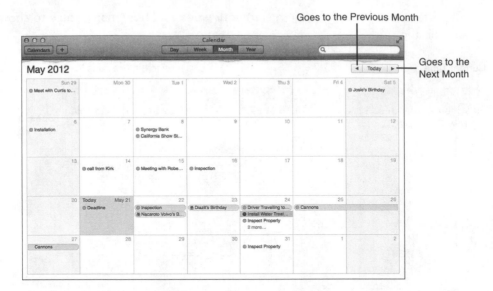

FIGURE 15.3

The Month view always shows five full weeks, so days before or after the current month are included in the view.

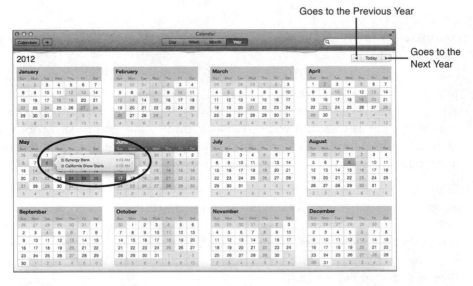

FIGURE 15.4

The Year view does not show individual events on the calendar. You must click a date to see them in a pop-up.

NOTE In addition to the navigation buttons provided in most calendar views, you can use swiping motions on a Magic Mouse or Magic Trackpad to scroll forward and back.

Clicking the **Calendars** button in the upper-left corner opens the Calendar List pane on the left, as shown in Figure 15.5. The Calendar List shows the default calendars that Mountain Lion creates for you—Home and Work—plus any other calendars that you create for yourself. Both the Home and Work calendars are checked by default, so events created in either calendar are visible in all views of the calendar on the screen. Onscreen, you can quickly tell the difference between an event for the Home calendar and one for the Work calendar because the events are color coded—blue for Work and green for Home. Calendars that you create yourself are also color-coded. If you are synchronizing calendars with iCloud, the word iCloud appears above the appropriate calendars in the Calendar List.

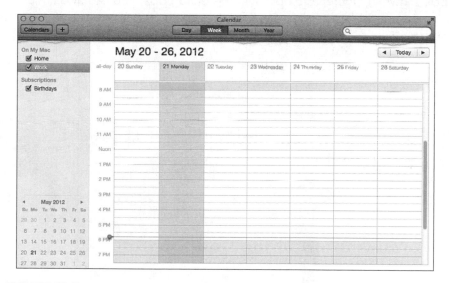

FIGURE 15.5

The two default calendars created for you by Mountain Lion are Home and Work.

Adding Events to the Calendar

An *event* is the name Apple gives to a single item you schedule on your calendar. Generally, an event has a start date and time and an end date and time unless it is an all-day event. An event that repeats on a regular basis is called a *recurring event*.

You can create new events in different views and in a few different ways. Here's a quick way to create events in the Day and Week views: select the appropriate calendar in the Calendar List and then double-click a specific time on a specific date. (Remember the space between two lines represents 30 minutes.) An event appears on the grid, and it is called New Event. The text of the name is selected, so whatever you type for the name of the event will automatically replace *New Event*. When you press **Return**, the event is created with a default duration of one hour.

 TIP If you want to create an event that has a duration other than one hour, you can drag from the start time to the end time instead of double-clicking to create the event.

To add any additional details to the event or to set an alert, you must edit the event. When you double-click the event and then click the **Edit** button, the dialog box shown in Figure 15.6 opens. In this dialog box, you can add a location, change the event to a different calendar, set an alert (more about this later), attach a file, add notes, and so on. When finished, click **Done**.

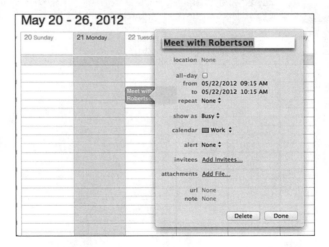

FIGURE 15.6

Set event details in this dialog box.

Creating an Event Using Quick Event

The Quick Event feature is a nifty little feature that creates an event for you from a typed description such as "Inspection at 8:15 am on Monday." To create an event using Quick Event, follow these steps:

1. Select the calendar in the Calendar List and then click the **Add** button. The Quick Event field appears. (See Figure 15.7.)

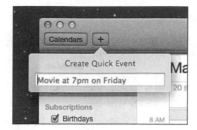

FIGURE 15.7

The Quick Event box gives you a hint about what to type.

2. Type a name, date, and start time. Additionally, you can type an end time for the event. For example, you can type **Inspection on Monday from 8:15 am-10:00 am.** (If you type only a start time, Calendar automatically sets the duration for one hour.)

3. Press **Return**. The dialog box with the event details opens.

4. Set other options as desired.

5. When finished, click the **Done** button.

Using Dictation

When creating or editing an event, you can use the Dictation feature to enter data in a text field, such as the Note field, instead of typing the data directly. If the note you are dictating is long, you might have to dictate several times because each dictation recording is only 30 seconds.

Additionally, you can use Dictation to create a Quick Event as described in the previous topic. For example, after you select the calendar and click the Add button, you can press **FN FN** to turn on the Dictation feature. After you see the microphone icon and hear a ding, dictate the name, date, and start time for the event. Click **Done** when finished.

NOTE Before using the Dictation tool, you must enable it. You can open the Dictation tab on the Dictation & Speech page of the System Preferences and click **On** for Diction, or you can press **FN FN** and respond to the question in the dialog box that opens. You might want to click the **About Dictation and Privacy** button before clicking **OK** to see exactly what information Apple must gather from you for you to use the tool. When finished reading the privacy information, click **Done**. If you decide you want to use the tool, click **OK**, and then click **Enable Dictation**.

Creating an All-Day Event

An all-day event has no start or end time; it simply lasts all day. In the Day view and Week view, an all-day event is listed at the top of the schedule.

The easiest way to create an all-day event is to use the Month view. Just double-click the date, type the name of the event, and press **Return**. Because you created the event in the Month view, it is automatically set to all-day for the duration. Of course, you can double-click the event to edit it just as you would any other event.

 NOTE You also can set an all-day event to extend over multiple days, such as to mark a vacation or business trip. Even if you set up an all-day event, you still can add other events for that day. So, for instance, you can mark an entire week as a business trip but still schedule individual meetings during the days of that trip.

Creating a Recurring Event

If you have an event that repeats on a predictable schedule, such as the first Monday of every month, you can specify the recurrence interval, and Calendar automatically adds the event to dates in the future. To create a recurring event, follow these steps:

1. Create an event using your preferred method.

2. Double-click the event, click the **Edit** button, and click the **Repeat** pop-up button.

3. Select a repeat time from the pop-up menu and click **Done**.

   Or

   Select Custom from the **Repeat** pop-up menu and select a **Frequency**. Specify the other criteria and click **OK**. If desired, specify an **End** option. Click **Done** to close the event.

Setting Event Alerts

Setting an event alert is like setting an alarm to go off to remind you of the event. By default, the Alert option is set to None for all new events, so you have to edit any new event you create if you want to set an alert. An alert can be an onscreen message (with or without sound), an email that you send to yourself, or a file that opens.

To set an alert, follow these steps:

1. Double-click the event and click **Edit**.

2. Click the **Alert** pop-up button.

3. Click the type of alert you want.

4. Supply additional information as needed (such as which email address to use or which file to open).

5. Click the pop-up button beside the time and specify a time for when the alert should occur.

6. Repeat steps 2 through 5 to set more alarms if you need them. For example, you can send yourself an email two days before the event and one day before the event. Then you could set a third alert to display a message with sound one hour before the event.

7. Click the **Done** button when finished.

 NOTE To set a preference for alerts, click Calendar, Preferences, and click the Alerts tab. Select an interval from the Events pop-up menu. Birthdays are automatically set with an alert even if you have None selected here.

Working with Events

As you are going about your business from day to day, you sometimes need to find an event you have scheduled. You may need to edit it or perhaps you are just looking for some information such as the name of the hotel you stayed in two years ago when you went to a convention. Sometimes you need to reschedule an event or cancel one. Read on to learn how.

Finding Events

If your schedule is really busy, or you have events scheduled for months in advance, you might need a little help finding a particular event. As always, when you are trying to find something, the Spotlight search is the feature you use. Follow these steps to use Spotlight to find an event:

1. In the Calendar List, check all calendars you want to search.

2. Type text that appears in the item you want to find. The Spotlight displays suggestions in a drop-down list, as shown in Figure 15.8.

3. Click any suggestion that is appropriate or just press **Return**. The results are displayed in a pane below the Spotlight, as shown in Figure 15.9.

4. Double-click an item in the results list to see the details of the event. If you need to edit the event, click the **Edit** button.

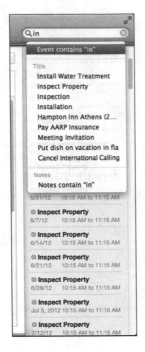

FIGURE 15.8

The suggestions at the top have the search phrase in the title of the event.

FIGURE 15.9

Scroll the list to see more events that contain the search text.

5. When finished, click the **Done** button.

6. To close the search results pane, click the **x** in the Spotlight field.

Editing Event Dates and Times

I've already discussed how to edit the details of an event, and you could certainly open an event and change the date or times that are already set for the event, but here are some quick ways to change an event's date or times.

- To move an event to a different date, switch to the Month view and drag the event to the new date.

- To change the start time, drag the event up or down in the Day or Week view. Note that the time changes in 15-minute increments.

- To change the end time, drag the bottom line of the event up or down in the Day or Week view.

Deleting Events

There is no point in deleting events after they are passed. You can keep events in your calendar forever. It's a good way to keep a record of your activities. To delete an event that has been canceled, use one of the following methods:

- Right-click the event and click **Cut**.
- Click the event to select it and press the **Delete** key on the keyboard.
- Select the event, click **Edit** in the menu bar, and click **Delete**.

 NOTE   If the event you are trying to delete is one in a series of recurring events, you have the options Cancel, Delete All Future Events, or Delete Only This Event.

To undo the deletion of an event, click **Edit** in the menu bar and click **Undo Delete Event**.

Inviting People to Events

If you want to invite people to an event, you can have Calendar send out an email to the people you want to attend. If any of the recipients also use Calendar, the event invitation can go straight to their calendars, depending on the preferences they have set.

To invite people to an event, create a new event or edit an existing event. Click **Add Invitees**. In the Add Invitees field, type the email addresses for all the desired attendees, separated by commas or returns. Click the **Send** button when you are finished.

Recipients can respond back to you with Maybe, Decline, or Accept. Refer to Chapter 18, "Using Mail," for more information about responding to meeting invitations.

If you make changes to the event, such as the start or end time, be sure to click the **Update** button so the recipients are sent a new email with the change.

Creating Additional Calendars

For most people, a Home and a Work calendar are sufficient, but suppose you also need to keep up with someone else's schedule—your middle-schooler perhaps. To create a new calendar, click **File** in the menu bar and click **New Calendar**. If you have several accounts set up, select the account under which the calendar should be created. Type a name for the new calendar and press **Return**. Calendar assigns a new color to the new calendar, and all events and reminders for that calendar use the assigned color. To select the color you want to use for a calendar instead of the arbitrary color Calendar assigns, right-click any calendar and click **Get Info**. Select the color in the color box to the right of the name, and then click **OK**.

One very useful type of calendar that Calendar creates for you automatically is a Birthday calendar. You don't have to do anything in Calendar because it is created and is displayed in the Calendar List by default. As discussed in Chapter 14, "Using Contacts," the calendar takes its information from the birthdays you have included for any of your contacts. You still have to do a little work on your own: you at least have to enter the birthdays in Contacts.

THE ABSOLUTE MINIMUM

- A fast way to add an event to a calendar is to use the Quick Event feature.

- Adding an event using the Month view creates an all-day event.

- Calendar automatically creates recurring events for you on all future dates based on the frequency you specify.

- You don't need to delete events after they have occurred. You may need to refer back to an event, and if you have difficulty locating it, you can use the Spotlight search feature to find it.

- Inviting people to an event sends an email with a response mechanism, so invitees can let you know whether or not they can attend.

IN THIS CHAPTER

- Creating a note with text, graphics, attached files, and links to websites
- Tearing a note off the legal pad and pinning it to your desktop
- Finding notes with a Spotlight search
- Editing and deleting notes
- Sending a note in email or a text message
- Creating your own hierarchy of folders for notes

16

USING NOTES

Notes used to be a part of Mail, but in Mountain Lion it's been given its own identity as a separate application. It corresponds to the Notes applications on the iDevices. I never really used the Notes feature when it was a part of Mail, and yet I used the Notes feature on my iPhone all the time. When Notes was a part of Mail, it was just too clunky to use, but now that it is an application, it is much more accessible and beneficial. Even in Lion, iCloud can synchronize your notes with your other iDevices, but in Mountain Lion, the interface is the same and the experience is more uniform.

Exploring the Notes Window

To launch Notes, click the **Notes** icon in the Dock, or click the **Launchpad** icon and click the icon there. Figure 16.1 shows what your Notes window looks like if you have created a few notes. The notes (and the date and time they were created) are displayed in the List area on the left. The complete text of the note selected on the left appears on the "legal pad" on the right.

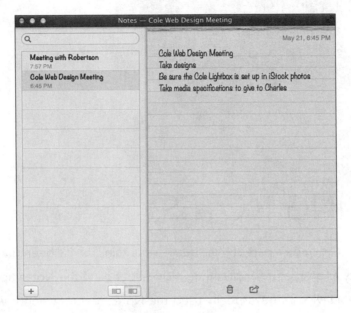

FIGURE 16.1

In the list of notes on the left, the first line of each note is displayed.

The Notes window has two views. In Figure 16.1, you see the view that is hiding the Folder list. If you click the button to view the Folder list, the window looks like the one in Figure 16.2.

 TIP To make the Folder list wider or narrower, drag the right border to the right or left.

The default folder in the Folder list is called Notes, as you can see in Figure 16.2. If you want, you can store all your notes in this folder, or you can create your own additional folders. See "Creating and Deleting Your Own Note Folders" later in this chapter for details.

Folder List

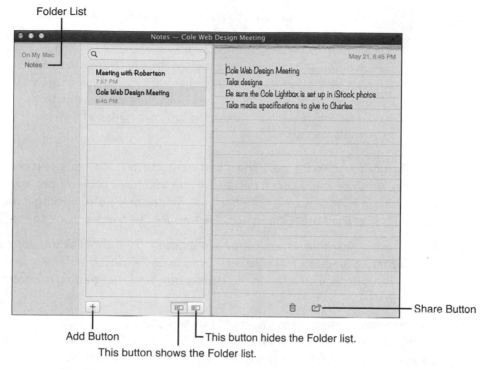

Share Button

Add Button

This button shows the Folder list.

This button hides the Folder list.

FIGURE 16.2

The "legal pad" shows the full text of the note selected in the list of notes.

Creating a Note

A note has no bells and whistles—no alerts, no due dates, no priority settings, and so on. You might think of a note as containing only text, but a note can have varied content, as explained in the following steps that show how to create a note:

1. If you have more than one folder, select the folder in the Folder list in which you want to store the note.

2. If there are no notes in the folder already, click on the blank yellow page. If there are notes in the folder, click the **Add** button.

3. Begin typing the note. Whatever you type on the first line becomes the title of the note and replaces the title New Note in the list. Alternatively, you can press **FN FN** and use the Dictation tool to dictate the note. After you see the microphone icon turn purple and hear a ding, dictate the note and then click **Done** when finished. (You can dictate in 30-second increments.)

NOTE If you haven't already turned on the Dictation tool, when you press **FN FN**, a dialog box opens asking whether you want to enable Dictation. You might want to click the **About Dictation and Privacy** button before clicking **OK** to see exactly what information Apple must gather from you for you to use the tool. When finished reading the privacy information, click **Done**. If you decide you want to use the tool, click **OK**, and then click **Enable Dictation**.

4. Press **Return** to go to the next line if you want to type or dictate text on the next line. Additionally, you can paste text that you have copied from any source, drag photos into the note from the Finder or iPhoto, or drag a file from the Finder into the note. (Dragging a file into a note creates a link to the file.)

5. You can even include a screen capture in a note. Just right-click the note and click **Capture Selection from Screen**. Drag over the portion of the screen you want to capture, as instructed in the dialog box, and the graphic is inserted in your note.

6. You can apply formatting to your notes by selecting text and using the format commands on the Format menu, as shown in Figure 16.3. Additionally, you can use keyboard shortcuts to format text. For example, you can select text and press **Command-I** to apply italic.

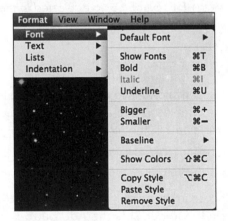

FIGURE 16.3

You can select a font and font style, align text, create bulleted or numbered lists, and indent text.

7. To check the spelling in your note, click **Edit**, **Spelling and Grammar**, **Show Spelling and Grammar**. Then you can interactively check and correct the spelling as the spell checker finds each word that is not in the spelling dictionary.

8. When you are finished with the note, just go on to something else. There is no command to save a note.

Pinning a Note to the Desktop

If you want to keep a note on your desktop in its own window, just double-click the note in the List area. Then drag the note by its title bar to the location on the desktop where you want to keep it. When a note is displayed in its own window, you can perform normal window operations on it, such as resize the window, maximize, minimize, and close it.

 NOTE If you close the Notes application, any notes that are open in their own windows remain open on your desktop.

Finding, Editing, and Deleting Notes

To find a note in any folder, click in the **Spotlight** search box and type a unique word or phrase that you remember is in the note. The list on the left displays only those notes that match your search text. When finished, click the **x** in the Spotlight search box.

To edit a note, select it in the list on the left and then click in the legal pad area and make any edits or format changes you want. If the note is open in a window, just click in the window and make the edits.

In addition to edits, there are some other interesting things you can do with the text in a note. You can select text, right-click it, and click **Look Up "<text>."** A pop-up displays some or all of the following, as appropriate: the definition of the text in the dictionary, synonyms for the text in the thesaurus, and the entry for the text in Wikipedia, as shown in Figure 16.4. Additionally, you can select a word or phrase and search for it on Google. Just right-click the selected text, click **Search with Google**, and click **Run Service**. When you find a web page that is appropriate, you might want to add a link to the web page in the note. Just drag the icon in front of the web address to the note. (Some websites have proprietary icons, and others just use the generic globe icon.)

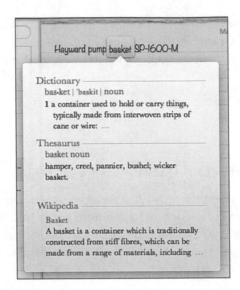

FIGURE 16.4

Looking up a word displays definitions from the built-in dictionary and from Wikipedia.

To delete a note, select it in the list on the left and then click the **trash can** icon at the bottom of the note. If you delete the note by mistake, click **Edit, Undo**.

Sharing a Note

You can share a note with another user via email or a text message. Select the note in the list on the left and then click the **Share** button (see Figure 16.2) at the bottom of the note. If you select Email, a new email message is created. The title of your note is the subject of the email, and the remainder of the note is in the body of the email. If you select Message, the entire note is in the message.

Creating and Deleting Your Own Note Folders

As mentioned earlier, you can store all your notes in the default folder called Notes, but if you need to organize your notes a little more, you would benefit from creating your own folders. To create a new folder, right-click the Folder list and click **New Folder**. A new folder called, you guessed it, New Folder appears in the Folder list. The name of the new folder is selected, so when you type the name you want to give the folder, the words *New Folder* are replaced. Press the **Return** key after typing the new folder's name. The new folder moves into alphabetical order in the list of folders but cannot move above the Notes folder.

TIP To rename a folder, right-click the folder in the Folder list and click **Rename Folder**. Type the new name and press the **Return** key.

You can create new notes in the new folder, or you can move existing notes into the folder. To move a note from one folder to another, first display the Folder list if it's hidden. Select the folder that has the note, and then drag the note from the sidebar and drop it on the folder in the Folder list where you want to move it.

If you are really a hierarchical kind of person, you can even create subfolders. To make a folder a subfolder of another folder, just drag the child folder in the Folder list and drop it on the parent folder. Make sure the parent folder turns blue before you release the mouse button when dropping the child folder.

To delete a folder that you have created, right-click the folder in the Folder list and click **Delete Folder**. Then click the **Delete Folder** button when you are asked whether you are sure you want to delete it. You cannot delete the default folders (Notes and All iCloud).

THE ABSOLUTE MINIMUM

- By default, all notes are stored in the Notes folder, but you can create your own folders to store notes.

- Pinning a note to the desktop is nothing more than opening the note in its own window.

- You can email a note in Mail or send a note in a text message using Messages.

USING REMINDERS

Reminders, in their pre–Mountain Lion existence, were part of iCal. In Mountain Lion, reminders have been pulled out of the Calendar and given their own application—one that is very much like the Reminders applications on the iDevices. That was the whole point, really, to bring the Reminders on a Mac in line with the iDevices. Reminders that you create on your Mac are synchronized with your other Macs and iDevices via iCloud, so no matter where you go, you always have your reminders with you.

The small Reminders application does a limited number of things. This makes it possible for me to tell you just about everything there is to know about reminders in this chapter—if not everything, then at least all the most important things.

Exploring the Reminder Window

To launch Reminders, click the **Reminders** icon in the Dock. The Reminders window opens, as shown in Figure 17.1.

Sidebar

Click this button to add a new Reminder list.
Click this button to show or hide a calendar
Click this button to show or hide the sidebar.

FIGURE 17.1

When creating reminders, you can use the calendar as a handy reference.

The sidebar on the left, which you can hide by clicking the first button at the bottom of the sidebar, is a list of all your Reminder folders. By default, you start with one list called Reminders.

The sidebar also displays a one-month calendar (which actually shows six weeks). You can scroll this calendar a month at a time using the scroll buttons in the top line of the calendar. To hide the calendar, click the second button at the bottom of the sidebar.

The pane on the right, which looks like a white legal pad, holds the actual list of reminders for a particular reminder list—one per line. When you start adding reminders, you will see that the left margin of the legal pad displays check boxes for each reminder. (You can see one in Figure 17.2.) To view only this pane, click the button to hide the sidebar.

Creating a Simple Reminder

To create a simple reminder, that is, one without any options, select the folder in the sidebar where the reminder should be stored and then click on the first blank line on the white page. As soon as you click on the line, the check box mentioned previously appears to the left side of the double red lines. (This is the box you can use to check the reminder off the list.) Type the text of the reminder, and you're done. See Figure 17.2. If you want to type another reminder right away, just press **Return** to go to the next line. You also can just click on the next line or click the plus button in the upper-right corner.

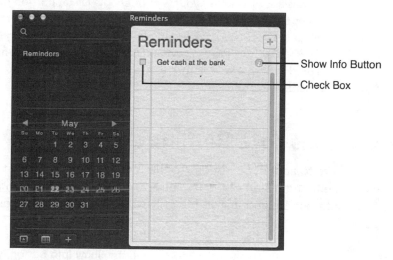

FIGURE 17.2

Each reminder occupies only one line.

When you are creating a reminder, some editing routines on the Edit menu are available to you, such as converting the case of text, checking spelling, and making substitutions. But seriously, do you want to use the Transformations command to change one word from lowercase to uppercase or go to the trouble to click **Edit**, **Spelling and Grammar**, **Show Spelling and Grammer** to check the spelling of one short line of text? Please add this reminder to your list: forget about it!

Dictating a Reminder

Using the new Dictation tool, you can dictate a reminder instead of typing it. To dictate a reminder, click the pointer on a new line in the appropriate reminder list and press **FN FN**. When you see the microphone icon turn purple and hear the ding, dictate the reminder. When finished, click **Done**. If the reminder takes more than 30 seconds to dictate, the microphone icon is replaced by three flashing purple dots and the Done button is replaced by the Cancel button. If you click Cancel, the dictation is discarded but if you just wait until the pop-up box closes, the dictation is transcribed. If you need to add more text, press **FN FN** again and dictate the additional text.

 NOTE If you haven't already turned on the Dictation tool in System Preferences as described in Chapter 6, "Using and Controlling Your Hardware," when you press FN FN, a dialog box opens asking whether you want to enable Dictation. You might want to click the **About Dictation and Privacy** button before clicking **OK** to see exactly what information Apple must gather from you to use the tool. When finished reading, click **Done**. If you decide you want to use the tool, click **OK**, and then click **Enable Dictation**.

Adding Options to a Reminder

If you would like to add some options to the reminder, click the *i* button that appears on the far right side of the reminder's box, as shown in Figure 17.2. This is the Show Info button, and it is visible only when you hover the mouse over the reminder.

 TIP As an alternative to clicking the Show Info button, you can right-click the reminder and click **Show Info**.

The options for a reminder are shown in Figure 17.3; they include the following: Remind Me, Repeat, End, and Priority. Additionally, there is a field in which you can type additional text for a note. Obviously, after you have set all the options, you should click **Done**. The options you have set are displayed as light gray text under the Reminder. You can see an example of this in Figure 17.3.

Setting an Alert for a Reminder

Although you do not see an option called Alert on the Information form, that's exactly what the On a Day and At a Location options are. Setting either one of these options triggers an alert displayed in the Notification Center. (The Notification Center is a new feature in Mountain Lion. For more details, see Chapter 7, "Personalizing the Desktop.")

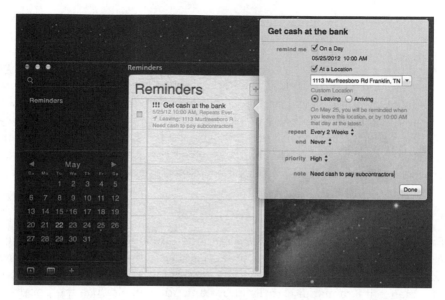

FIGURE 17.3

Notice that the High priority level of this reminder has three exclamation points.

When you click the On a Day option, the date defaults to the current date. The default time is rounded up to the nearest 15-minute mark. To set a different date, click the date, and then click the date you want on the pop-up calendar. To set a different time, click each part of the time (hours, minutes, am/pm) and type what you want.

 NOTE   If you set the On a Day option, the date on the mini-calendar displays a dot under the date.

When you click the At a Location option, a text box opens and you must enter a valid address, which Mountain Lion verifies. Instead of typing an address, you can enter a contact name. When you start typing the name of a contact, a list of contacts that match what you have started typing is displayed. You can select the one that is correct. (Only contacts that have addresses are included in the list.) After you specify the address, you have to click either **Leaving** or **Arriving**. Obviously, you are not going to carry your Mac around with you so the GPS feature in the Mac can monitor your location and send you an alert. The At a Location option is designed to take advantage of iCloud synchronization. When you set the reminder alert on your Mac, you are expecting the reminder to be synchronized with the iDevice that you *do* carry around with you, such as your iPhone or your iPad. The iDevice will send you the alert when its GPS detects the address.

Creating a Reminder That Repeats Automatically

A repeating reminder repeats at one of these regular intervals: Every Day, Every Week, Every 2 Weeks, Every Month, or Every Year. The interval is based on the date you set for On a Day; therefore, the Repeat option is not available unless you check the On a Day option. If you set the On a Day option for Monday, August 6, 2012, and set the Repeat option on Every Week, the reminder will repeat every Monday from August 6 until the End date, if you have specified one, or forever. So after you set a repeating reminder, this is what happens: when you mark the reminder as complete or when the reminder date passes, a new reminder is added to your list automatically.

Setting a Priority Level for a Reminder

Priority levels that you can set for a reminder are None, Low, Medium, and High. If you set a priority level, the reminder has one to three exclamation points (from Low to High) in front of it. The priority level is just a visual cue for you to see at a glance if a reminder is really important. You can also use the priority level indicators to help you identify the reminders that you might want to drag to the top of your list.

Marking Reminders off the List

I wish I could say that I make lists of reminders just for the satisfaction of checking items off the list, but, sadly, I really need to have my reminders; otherwise, I won't remember to do half the things I need to do. Still, it is satisfying when you can mark a reminder off your list, isn't it? All you have to do is click the check box beside the reminder. The first time you mark a reminder off your list, you will see a new folder called Completed has been created in the sidebar. That's where your checked-off reminder goes. If you check off one by mistake, you can open the Completed list and uncheck the item to return it to its original list.

 NOTE If a reminder has the On a Date option set, and the date or time has passed, the check box for the reminder turns pink as a visual cue that you are behind on your work!

Finding, Editing, and Deleting Reminders

If you are looking for all your reminders that have a due date of the current date, you can find them by clicking **View** in the menu bar and then clicking **Go to Today**. All reminders with the On a Day option set for the current date are displayed in the right pane.

Another way to find a specific reminder is to search for a word or phrase in the reminder. Unless this is your first rodeo, you probably know that you use the Spotlight search to find a reminder this way. Just type the text in the search box located above the sidebar, and all reminders that have the word or phrase will be displayed in the right pane, as shown in Figure 17.4. When finished, click the **x** in the Spotlight search box.

 NOTE The Spotlight search does not look for the search text in a reminder's note. You can use the Spotlight search box in the menu bar, however, and it will find reminders that have the search text in the note.

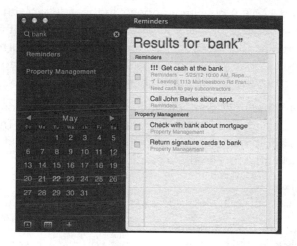

FIGURE 17.4

Search results are categorized by list.

After you find a reminder, if your purpose is to edit it, just click the reminder and make your changes. If you want to change options, click the **Show Info** button as described earlier in this chapter.

To delete a reminder, select it and press the **Delete** key. Sounds easy, right? But there's a catch. To select the reminder in the right pane, you must click a blank area anywhere in the reminder's box. Alternatively, you can right-click the reminder and click **Delete**. If you delete a reminder by mistake, you can get it back by pressing **Command-Z**.

Sorting Reminders

When the Reminders feature was a part of iCal, you could sort the reminders by various specifications, such as by Due Date, Priority, and so on. Now that Reminders is a separate application, the capability to sort is gone! Maybe it will reappear in a later update, but until it does, you will have to manually sort your reminders by dragging them into the order you want them.

Creating and Working with New Reminder Lists

To create a new Reminder list, click the Add button at the bottom of the sidebar (refer to Figure 17.1). A new item appears in the sidebar with the name New List. The name is selected, so when you type the name you want to use, the words *New List* are replaced. After you type the name, press **Return**. The new list appears in the sidebar at the bottom of the list. You can drag your Reminder lists into any order, but the Completed list cannot be moved.

If you view only the right pane of the Reminders window, you can navigate to other lists by clicking the dot at the bottom of the screen. (This is similar to navigating to additional pages in Launchpad.) Additionally, if you're using a Magic Mouse or trackpad, you can use a swiping motion.

Viewing Multiple Reminder Lists

If you want to see the reminders in the right pane for more than one list, Command-click each list in the sidebar that you want to see. The right pane will look something like the one in Figure 17.5.

 NOTE You cannot view the Completed list in conjunction with any other list.

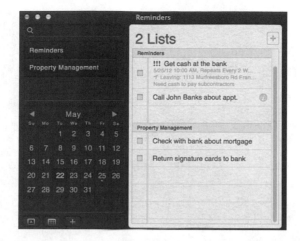

FIGURE 17.5

The number of lists you are displaying shows at the top of the right pane.

Moving a Reminder to Another List

Perhaps your purpose for creating another Reminder list is to break up an existing list. If this is the case, you will want to move reminders out of the old list and into the new list. This is how you do it: select the old list in the sidebar and then drag the reminder you want to move to the new list in the sidebar.

Deleting a List

Before you decide to delete a list, make sure you want to delete all the reminders in the list. Move any reminders you want to keep to another list before deleting. To delete a list, select it in the sidebar and press the **Delete** key. When asked whether you are sure you want to delete, click the **Delete** button. You cannot undo this action, so be sure you want to delete!

 NOTE   You can't delete or rename the Completed list.

THE ABSOLUTE MINIMUM

- Each reminder occupies one line in the list.

- You can set an alert for the reminder that alerts you on a particular date and time or when you are arriving or leaving a location.

- When you mark an item off your list, it is automatically removed and goes into the Completed list.

- You can create and delete additional lists, but you cannot delete or rename the Completed list.

18

USING MAIL

Statistics say that there are more than 1 billion email users worldwide, and you are undoubtedly one of them. It's probably safe to say that you already have a good grasp of email; you just need to get acquainted with Mail and learn exactly how to use it. That's what this chapter is all about: setting up your accounts, sending and receiving emails, replying to messages, forwarding messages, sending and receiving attachments, and so on.

Setting Up Mail Accounts

The Mail application enables you to set up accounts for all your email addresses. I highly recommend that you do so because having them all in one place eliminates having to log on to each web mail or corporate account separately. I hope one of your email accounts is a me.com address that is associated with an Apple ID. You will be able to synchronize that account across all your devices using iCloud.

Setting Up a New Account

You can set up your email accounts directly in the Mail application, or you can open the Mail, Contacts & Calendar page in System Preferences. To set up an email account using the System Preferences window, follow these steps:

1. Click **System Preferences** in the Dock or click **Launchpad** and click **System Preferences**. Then click **Mail, Contacts & Calendar**. The window shown in Figure 18.1 opens.

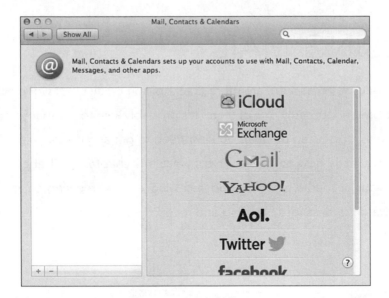

FIGURE 18.1

You can set up email accounts with iCloud, Microsoft Exchange, Gmail, and Yahoo!

2. Click the type of account you want to set up in the list on the right. If you don't see the kind of email you have, scroll down and click **Add Other Account**, click **Add a Mail Account** (if necessary), and click **Create**.

NOTE   You will need to select the Add Other Account option if you use your Internet service provider's email service or you have an email address through your own domain.

3. Enter the email address and password for the account you want to set up. (You also can change the default text for your Name.) Click **Set Up**.

4. The Mail account defaults to being used with Mail, and depending on the type of account, may also default to using Calendars & Reminder, Messages, and Notes. You can uncheck any of the defaults if you want. Then click **Add Account**. The new account is displayed in the list on the left.

5. To add another account, click the **Add an Account** button (the one with the plus), and repeat steps 2–4.

 NOTE   The first time you open Mail after setting up a new account, it can take a little while for all your existing email messages to populate the Mail application.

Upgrading Existing Accounts

If you upgraded to Mountain Lion and you already had all your email accounts set up in a previous version of Mac OS X, everything will still be set up for you in Mountain Lion. However, Mountain Lion has to upgrade your existing email accounts before you can use them. The first time you open the Mail application, it performs the short process to upgrade the messages for you.

Exploring the Mail Window

Now let's look at the Mail window. Aside from the typical window features (title bar, toolbar, borders, and so on), the Mail window has a Favorites bar under the toolbar, and it has three panes. (If you don't see three panes on your system, the Mailbox List, shown in Figure 18.2, is hidden. To open the Mailbox List pane, click the **Show** button in the Favorites bar.) The pane in the center is the Message List pane, and the pane on the right is the Message pane.

This button changes to the Show
button when the Mailbox List is hidden.

Mailbox List   Favorites Bar   Message Pane

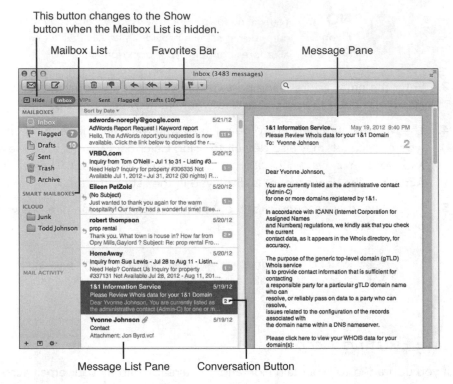

Message List Pane   Conversation Button

FIGURE 18.2

The Message pane displays the content of the email message that is selected in the Message List pane.

Using the Mailbox List

The Mailbox List contains these standard mailboxes: Inbox, VIPs, Flagged, Drafts, Sent, Trash, Archive, and Junk. Many of these mailboxes are not displayed by default, but they appear as soon as you use them. For example, the Junk mailbox does not appear in the Mailbox List until you mark an email as Junk. Additionally, the Mailbox List displays mailboxes for email services you have set up, such as Gmail, Smart Mailboxes (more about those later), mailboxes for iCloud, mailboxes that you create, and so on. (The mailboxes you set up for email services appear in the Inbox.)

Selecting a Mailbox in the list displays the messages that are in that mailbox in the List pane. For example, selecting the Sent mailbox in the Mailbox List pane displays all the email messages you have sent.

Using the Message List Pane

By looking at the list of emails in the Message List pane, you can see who sent the email, the subject of the email, the date or time the email was sent, and the first part of the body of the message.

 NOTE If the email arrived today, you see the time it was sent. If the email was sent yesterday, you see the word *Yesterday*. Emails sent prior to yesterday display the date they were sent.

The blue dot in front of the message tells you that you haven't opened it yet, and the brown text used for some emails tells you that the email has been automatically marked as Junk Mail.

You also can tell if the message is part of a group of emails that are about the same subject, otherwise known as a *conversation*. A button with the number of emails in the conversation is displayed just under the date or time, as shown in Figure 18.2. If you click the disclosure triangle in the button, you see the other email messages listed. (Sometimes the list of emails in a conversation is not really a conversation, but instead a list of emails you receive on a recurring basis that always have the same subject.) If you prefer not having messages grouped by conversation, which is the default, click **View** in the menu bar and then click **Organize by Conversation** to deselect this option.

Using the Message Pane

The Message pane displays the complete email message unless the message is considered Junk Mail. Then graphics in the message are not displayed. To see the graphics, you can click the **Load Images** or **Not Junk** button.

The header at the top of the message shows the email address of the sender on the first line, the subject on the second line, and the recipients on the third line. If a photo is included for the sender in your Contacts, the photo also appears on the right side of the header. You can view some additional information in the header, such as the number of attachments (if any), by clicking **Details** (located on the right under the date/time stamp).

When you move the mouse pointer over the line that divides the header from the body of the message, you can see four buttons. They are the Delete, Reply, Reply All, and Forward buttons, respectively. (These buttons also appear on the toolbar.)

Exploring the Favorites Bar

The Favorites bar contains names of your "favorite" mailboxes—in other words, the ones you use the most. Initially, it contains only Inbox, Sent, and Flagged, but you can add more mailboxes to it. If you add enough mailboxes to the bar, you can turn off the Mailbox List pane and never miss it. Doing so would give you more room on the screen for the other two panes. To add a mailbox to the Favorites bar, drag it from the Mailbox List and drop it in place on the Favorites bar.

To rearrange the favorites, drag them to different locations on the bar as you like. To delete a favorite, drag it off the bar.

 NOTE   If one of your favorites on the bar has a drop-down arrow, it means that the favorite contains more than one mailbox for you to select. For example, the Inbox has a drop-down arrow on the Favorites bar if you have set up several mail services because each service has its own mailbox and each mailbox is listed in the Inbox.

Using the Classic View

The Mail interface for Mountain Lion has not changed since Lion. Before Lion, however, the interface looked completely different. If you'd like to try the "classic" interface, shown in Figure 18.3, follow these steps:

1. Click **Mail** in the menu bar and click **Preferences**.

2. Click the **Viewing** tab, if necessary.

3. Click **Use Classic Layout** and close the preferences window.

In the classic layout, the pane on the right can be split horizontally into two panes so that the pane at the top displays a list of messages and the one at the bottom displays the content of the selected message. To split the pane, double-click the separator bar. It appears at the bottom of the window before the pane is split.

The classic layout offers the advantage of seeing columns of data about your emails, and you can even decide which columns you want to see. To add or remove columns, click **View** in the menu bar and then point to **Columns**. Click a column to select it or click a column that has a check mark beside it to remove the column from view. After you have all the columns you want, you can put them in the order you want by dragging the column headings to the desired locations.

Pane Separator

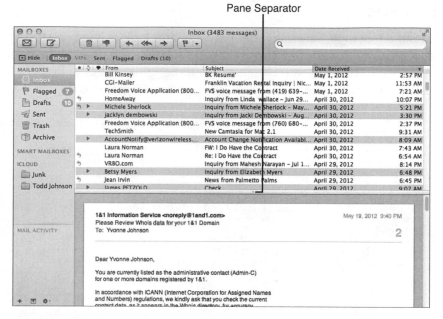

FIGURE 18.3

The classic layout still has the hideable Mailbox List and the Favorites bar.

 NOTE The remaining text and figures in this chapter assume that you are not using the classic layout.

Getting and Reading Email

By default, Mail checks your mail servers for all your accounts every five minutes and downloads any new mail that has come in to your hard drive. You can see the number of unread messages in each mailbox just to the right of the mailbox name in the Mailbox List. You can make Mail download new mail any time by clicking the **Get New Messages** button in the toolbar. Additionally, you can change the interval at which Mail checks the mail servers on the General page of the Mail Preferences.

 TIP If you are not sure what the buttons in the Mail toolbar are, you can turn on the names of the buttons. Click **View** in the menu bar and click **Customize Toolbar**. Select **Icon and Text** for the Show option, and then click **Done**.

Reading a Message

To read a message, select it in the List pane and look at it in the Message pane. If the message is part of a conversation, it looks like the one in Figure 18.4. If the message is a reply, you generally see the original message below the new message unless the sender has not included the original message in the reply.

 TIP Additionally, you can open a message in its own window by double-clicking it.

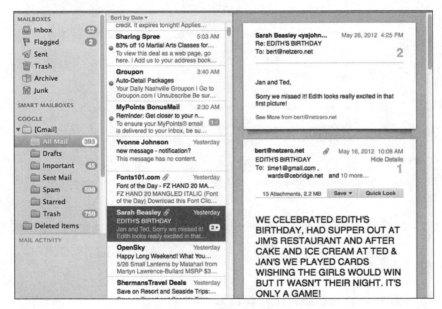

FIGURE 18.4

Each message in the conversation is numbered in the upper-right corner.

Handling Attachments

If you receive a message with a file attached, known as an *attachment*, the attachment information appears at the bottom of the header area, just above the dividing line, as shown in Figure 18.5. (Click **Details** if you do not see the information.)

To see the content of attachments without actually opening them, click the **Quick Look** button in the header. If you have more than one attachment, you can scroll through them using the Forward and Back buttons in the upper-left corner or the right- and left-arrow keys on the keyboard.

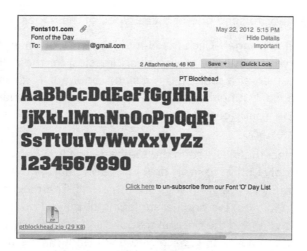

FIGURE 18.5

Mail displays the number of attachments and their combined total size in the header.

To save all attachments to the Downloads folder at one time, click the **Save** button. If you want to save only one of the attachments or save one or all the attachments in a different location, follow these steps:

1. Click and hold the pop-up button on the **Save** button until you see the pop-up menu.

2. Click the name of the file to save only one attachment or click **Save All** to save the attachments in a different location.

3. For a single file, specify the name for Save As, if you want to change it, and select the location. For all the attachments, select the location.

4. Click **Save**.

 TIP   If the attachment is a graphic file, you can click **Add to iPhoto** on the Save pop-up menu and import the files directly into iPhoto.

Some types of attachments, such as images or PDF files, show up in the body of the message. Often, people don't realize these are actually attachments. You can save them by right-clicking them and clicking **Save Attachment**.

Sending Messages and Replies

This section gives you the quick instructions for sending emails or replies, and then it looks at some of the finer points.

Follow these steps to send one of these types of messages:

- **New email message**—Click the **New Message** button in the toolbar. At a minimum, you must enter the email address(es) for the recipient(s) in the To box. You can enter a subject, but it's not required. You can type a message or attach a file, but neither of these is really required either. (Perhaps you just want to type a subject and that is message enough.) Click the **Send** button to send the message.

- **Reply**—Select the message in the Message List you want to reply to. Then click the **Reply** button to reply only to the original sender or click the **Reply All** button to reply to everyone who got the email. The recipient email addresses are entered for you, the original subject is displayed on the subject line with *Re:* in front of it, and the original text of the message appears in the body of the message below the space where you should type the reply. Type your message or attach a file, as desired, and click the **Send** button.

Filling Out Header Information

The information you fill out at the top of a new message or a reply is called the *header information.* Here's how to use each line of the header:

- **To address field**—This line contains the email address of the recipient(s). As you start typing a name or email address, the autocomplete feature completes the address for you if the recipient's name and email address are in your Contacts or if you have sent to the email address before. The completed address appears in a blue bubble, which separates the individual addresses. (You don't need to separate addresses with commas.) Type additional recipients in the To field if necessary. All recipients of your message are able to see all the addresses you include in this field and the Cc field.

- **Cc address field**—This Carbon Copy field contains more recipient email addresses. Autocomplete works in this field, too. All recipients of your message are able to see all the addresses you include in this field and the To field.

- **Bcc address field**—This Blind Carbon Copy field also contains recipient email addresses. By default, this field does not appear in the header. To add it to the header, click the pop-up button to the left of the Subject line and then click **Bcc Address Field**. Autocomplete works in this field also. Recipients listed in the To and Cc address fields cannot see recipients listed in the Bcc field, but Bcc recipients are able to see everyone you include in the To and Cc fields.

TIP To send an email to a distribution list, enter the name of a Group in your Contacts.

- **Reply-To address field**—This field also does not appear by default. To add it, click the pop-up button to the left of the Subject line and then click **Reply-To Address Field**. Select or type one of your other email addresses in this field if you do not want replies sent to the address that originates the message.

- **Subject field**—Use this field to briefly state the main thrust of the message.

Typing and Formatting the Message

Before you start to type your message, you should select the format. Mail gives you two different formats to use: plain text and rich text. Plain-text messages cannot use direct formatting (bold, italic, font color, and so on), stationery, embedded graphics, or anything else except plain text. Rich text can use all these and more. To select the format, click **Format** in the menu bar and then click **Make Plain Text** or **Make Rich Text**. (The menu option is a toggle.) The plain-text format has several advantages because of its "plainness." Any type of email service can read it, it's faster to send, and it uses less bandwidth. (Rich text can be used to mask security threats and malware; therefore, some mail services reject messages sent in rich text.)

NOTE If you are sending a reply to a message, it is usually a good idea to reply to the message using the same format that the message used. You can set a preference for this on the Composing page of the Mail Preferences.

Type the body of the message in the large white space below the header. Mail checks your spelling as you type, marking misspelled words with a dotted red underline. You can right-click a misspelled word to display a pop-up menu with suggestions for the word you meant to type. Click the correct word in the list to replace your mistake.

To add formatting to a rich-text document, click the **Show Format Bar** button (the one with an *A* on it). Use the tools on the bar to specify the font style, color, and size; add bold, italic, and underline; align text to the left, center, or right; create bulleted or numbered lists; and indent or outdent text.

Instead of typing a message, try dictating the message with Mountain Lion's new Dictation tool. In the body of the message, press **FN FN**. Wait until you see the microphone icon turn purple and you hear the ding, and then start dictating the message. When 30 seconds elapses, the recording stops. At this point, you can click **Cancel** to discard the dictation or simply wait about two seconds for the dictation to be transcribed. You can start another dictating session immediately if you were unable to finish the message in 30 seconds. Additionally, you can use the Dictation tool in any field where you would normally type text.

 NOTE   If you haven't already turned on the Dictation tool as explained in Chapter 6, "Using and Controlling Your Hardware," when you press FN FN, a dialog box opens asking whether you want to enable Dictation. You might want to click the **About Dictation and Privacy** button before clicking **OK** to see exactly what information Apple must gather from you in order for you to use the tool. When finished reading, click **Done**. If you decide you want to use the tool, click **OK**, and then click **Enable Dictation**.

While you are busy typing or dictating the email, Mail is continually saving your email in the Drafts folder. If the electricity goes out while you are in the middle of composing an email, when you turn your computer back on, the email message will be in the Drafts folder. You can open it, finish typing it, and send it. Of course, depending on the timing, some of the message might not be there if the electricity goes off after you have typed some text and before the next automatic save. Additionally, you can store an unfinished email in the Drafts folder yourself by closing the email and clicking **Save**.

Attaching Files

You can attach any type of file to an email, but be careful how large the file is. Most email servers accept files only under 5MB. If the file is too large, try compressing it first. (Select it in the Finder and click **Format**, **Compress "filename."**) If the file is still too large after compressing, you just have to find another way to send the file. You can use a free service such as You Send It or Dropbox.

To attach a text file to a new message or new reply, click in the body of the message (maybe at the end of the message under your name) and click the **Attach** button (the one with the paperclip on it). Select the file (or multiple files) in the Finder and click **Attach**. An icon for each attachment appears at the point of the cursor. The filename and size are displayed under each icon.

To attach a photo that is in iPhoto, use the iPhoto Browser. To display the browser, click the **Show or Hide Photo Browser** button on the right side of the toolbar. Scroll to the photo you want to attach and drag it into the body of the message. It comes in as a full-size photo, but you can right-click the photo and click **View as Icon**. (Any graphic file, such as a PDF or GIF file, is displayed in full size.)

TIP You also can send an attachment by right-clicking the file in the Finder and then clicking **Share**, **Email**. A new blank email message is created for you automatically with the file attached.

Sending the Message

When finished with a new message or reply, click the **Send** button (the button with the paper airplane on it). If you are online, the message goes out immediately. If you are offline, the message goes into the Outbox, where it sits until the next time you go online again. Then it is sent out automatically.

When a message or reply is sent, a copy of it goes into your Sent mailbox by default. Although you can delete sent messages immediately when you quit Mail, there's not much point in it, and keeping sent messages provides a good record for you. (See Figure 18.9 later in this chapter to see the Mailbox Behaviors tab where this option is set.)

Forwarding a Message

If you receive a message that you want to send on to someone else, select the message (or open it) and click the **Forward** button. Address the email and add a message (if you want). The subject of the message stays the same as it was when you received it, but it has *Fw:* at the beginning to identify it as a forwarded message. Click the **Send** button to send the message and file a copy in the Sent mailbox. Any attachments that the original message has also will be forwarded unless you remove them.

Finding Messages

If you are like my husband, you won't have any trouble finding a message because you have deleted practically every email message you have ever received. If you are like me and keep your email messages for years, you are going to need some help finding particular messages when you want to.

If you know approximately when you received a message, you might be able to find it by scrolling through the Message List pane, which is sorted by date by default. If you think you might be able to find it more easily if the messages were sorted by sender, you can do that by clicking the **Sort By** pop-up button at the top of the pane and clicking **From**. After selecting a criterion for sorting, you can open the menu again and select **Ascending** or **Descending**.

TIP If you are using the classic layout, you can sort on any column in the display by simply clicking the column heading. Click the column heading again to sort in the other direction.

If you still have no luck, it's time to use the Spotlight search feature. Using the Spotlight search enables you to type as many search words or phrases as needed. Additionally, you can save a Spotlight search if you think you will use it repeatedly. A saved search is actually called a *Smart Mailbox,* and it has its own category in the Mailbox List.

To search for messages, follow these steps:

1. Click the mailbox you want to search (Inbox, Sent, Trash, and so on).

2. Type the search phrase in the Spotlight search box. For example, you might type **cruise**. A pop-up menu appears with suggestions, as shown in Figure 18.6, and all emails that match in any way appear in the Message List pane. If you select a suggestion, the search field displays a search token, as shown in Figure 18.7, and the number of messages that match is usually reduced. If the search token has a pop-up button, you can click it to change the scope of the token. (It is not mandatory to select a suggestion.)

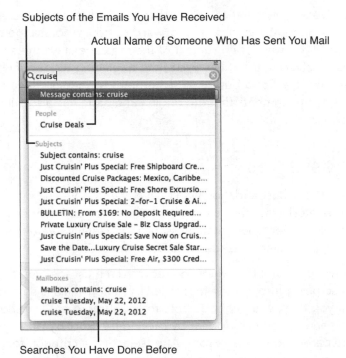

FIGURE 18.6

Suggestions provided are based on your actual emails.

Search Tokens

FIGURE 18.7

Narrow down your results by using as many criteria as you can.

3. Repeat step 2 as many times as needed. The number of messages that fit the criteria continues to dwindle as you get more and more specific.

4. To change the scope of the search, select **All** in the Favorites bar to search all Mailboxes or click a different mailbox.

5. To open a message that appears as a search result, double-click it.

6. When finished, click the **X** in the Spotlight search box.

To save a search that you have already performed (as just described), follow these steps:

1. Click **Save** in the Favorites bar (located on the far right side). The dialog box shown in Figure 18.8 opens.

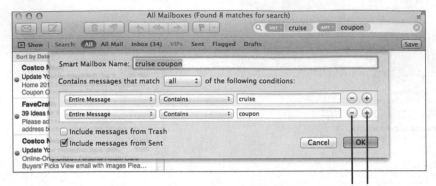

Remove This Criterion   Add Another Criterion

FIGURE 18.8

Change the default Smart Mailbox Name if you want to.

2. Type a name for the Smart Mailbox if you don't like the one that is supplied for you. This will be the name that appears in the Smart Mailbox category in the Mailbox List.

3. Make any changes you want in the criteria that are listed.

4. Delete an existing criterion by clicking the **Remove** button beside it (the button with the minus).

5. Add another criterion by clicking an **Add** button (the button with the plus). The new fields are displayed on the line under the line with the Add button that you clicked. Specify the options for the new criterion.

6. If you want the results of your search to include messages in the Trash or Sent mailboxes, check the appropriate option.

7. Click **OK** when all conditions are defined. The Smart Mailbox appears in the Mailbox List under the default Smart Mailbox called Today, and you can click it at any time to see the latest content.

Deleting Messages

To delete a message, select the message and click the **Delete** button. (To select multiple messages, you can Command-click each message.) The deleted messages go into the Trash mailbox, where they stay for a month and then are permanently deleted. If you don't want messages to be automatically deleted in a month, follow these steps:

1. Click **Mail** in the menu bar and then click **Preferences**.

2. Click **Accounts**, if necessary.

3. If you have more than one account, select the account you want to change in the list on the left.

4. Click the **Mailbox Behaviors** tab, shown in Figure 18.9.

FIGURE 18.9

The Mailbox Behaviors tab controls storage and deletion of messages.

5. Click the pop-up button for the **Permanently Erase Deleted Messages When** option and select another option.

6. Close the window when finished.

To delete an entire conversation, delete the most recent message in the conversation. (The Organize by Conversation option must be selected for this to work, of course.)

Dealing with Junk Mail

When you first start using Mail, Mail flags certain messages as junk, based on whether the sender is in your Contacts, if you have sent mail to the sender recently, or if the email is addressed to just your email address and not your full name. These messages appear in the Inbox with brown text and an icon of a brown bag of mail. If Mail flags a message that is not junk, you should select it or open it and click the Not Junk button so Mail knows not to mark a message from this sender the next time.

After Mail learns what is and isn't junk, you can tell it to start putting the junk mail messages in the Junk mailbox as soon as the messages come in so they are not mixed in with your regular mail in the Inbox. To set this option, follow these steps:

1. Click **Mail** in the menu bar and then click **Preferences**.

2. Click **Junk Mail** and click **Move It to the Junk Mailbox**.

3. Click **Move** when the dialog box opens asking whether you want to move all messages marked as junk now.

4. Close the window when finished.

 TIP   After Mail starts putting junk mail directly into the Junk mailbox, you should monitor the Junk mailbox for mail that you need to mark as Not Junk.

Creating Mailboxes

Even with all the emails I keep, I have never felt the need to create a hierarchical structure to organize them. It's just too easy to find a message, so why go to the trouble? For those who prefer a little more structure, Mail does provide you with the ability to store your messages in a more organized fashion. You can create your own mailboxes, calling them whatever you like, and then drag messages from the Inbox to the new mailboxes.

To create a new mailbox, click **Mailbox** in the menu bar and then click **New Mailbox**. Select the location, name it, and click **OK**. Although it's not within the scope of this book, I do want to tell you that you can create rules that automatically move messages into particular mailboxes for you so you don't have to find and drag them manually.

Another type of mailbox you can have is a VIP mailbox. Mail creates it for you automatically. All you have to do is identify the VIP. To do that, you open an email from someone who is very important to you and point to the sender's email address in the header of the message. A star appears in front of the email address, and you just click the star. The first time you create a VIP, a new category called VIPs appears in the Mailbox List, and the Sender's name appears under the new category. Any time you get an email from a VIP, the email goes into the Inbox and also appears in the VIP's mailbox.

Because you wouldn't want to miss an email from a VIP, you might want to have the Notification Center notify you when an email comes in. To set up a notification for a VIP, follow these steps:

1. Click **Mail** in the menu bar and then click **Preferences**.

2. Click **General**, if necessary.

3. Click the pop-up button for **New Message Notifications** and select **VIPs**. Selecting this option means you will not receive notifications for any other email messages.

4. Close the window when finished.

THE ABSOLUTE MINIMUM

- Mail checks for messages every five minutes.

- Rich-text messages can include formatting and graphics.

- You can attach files to an email, but you should keep the size of the file under 5MB.

- You can save a Spotlight search and use it over and over again to find emails that meet specific criteria.

- Mail flags emails as junk mail based on certain rules, but you can train Mail to recognize messages that are not junk.

19

USING MESSAGES

Messages, as its name implies, is the Mac application that sends and receives messages. If you are familiar with previous versions of OS X, then I must tell you that it replaces iChat and provides a much easier-to-use interface. Using Messages is similar to sending a text message on your phone, but Messages uses the iMessage protocol instead of the SMS or MMS protocols used on mobile phones.

In this chapter, I show you how to get a conversation going on Messages as well as how to send files, photos, links to web pages, and contacts in messages. If you are a fan of text messaging on your cell phone, read on. You're going to love Messages.

Getting Acquainted with Messages

The Messages application gives you free, unlimited messaging between a Mac running Mountain Lion and all iDevices (iPhone, iPad, or iPod touch) running iOS 5. Using iCloud, Apple can synchronize your messages between all your devices. This means you can start a message conversation on any device and continue the conversation on any of your other devices. Typing messages on my iPhone is a little annoying to me, so I love being able to type a message using my Mac's full-size keyboard!

Figure 19.1 shows the Messages window. The sidebar on the left shows a list of your conversations. Any messages you have not read yet have a blue bullet in front of them.

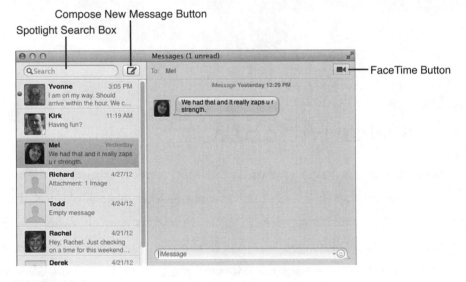

FIGURE 19.1

The Messages window uses the familiar two-pane format.

The pane on the right shows the text of the conversation selected in the sidebar. The messages you send appear on the right in a blue bubble, and the replies appear on the left in white bubbles. You can change the look of conversations by right-clicking this pane and clicking either **Show as Boxes** or **Show as Compact**.

Setting Up Your Messages Account

The first time you launch Messages, you have to sign in with your Apple ID and password. After you sign in with the Apple ID, you also can add other types of accounts, such as AIM, Yahoo!, Google Talk, and Jabber. Follow these steps to set up additional accounts:

1. Click the **Messages** icon in the Dock.

2. Click **Messages** in the menu bar, and then click **Preferences**.

3. Click the **Accounts** tab (see Figure 19.2).

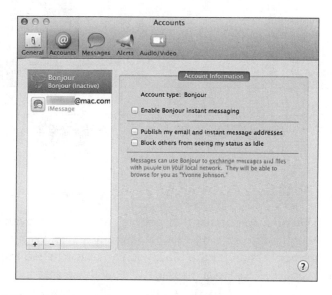

FIGURE 19.2

On this page, you can add additional email addresses where you can be reached for your Apple account.

4. Click the plus button at the bottom of the pane on the left. The Account Setup assistant opens. (See Figure 19.3.)

5. Select the account type, enter your username and password, and then click **Done**.

   NOTE   You cannot set up more than one Apple ID.

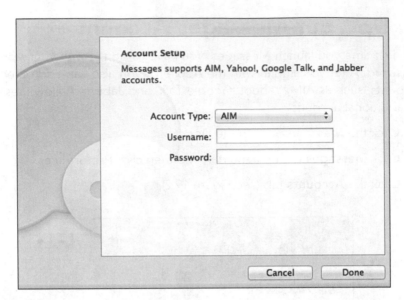

Account Setup

Messages supports AIM, Yahoo!, Google Talk, and Jabber accounts.

Account Type: AIM

Username:

Password:

Cancel   Done

FIGURE 19.3

The Account Setup assistant can set up an AIM, Yahoo!, Google Talk, or Jabber account for you.

Sending and Receiving Messages

Texting has become so popular that people can't resist it, even when they are driving, although doing so is now illegal in many states! With the introduction of the Messages application for the Mac, you can at least send messages safely from your desk or couch. To send a message, follow these steps:

1. Click the **Messages** icon in the Dock and then click the **Compose New Message** button. This starts a new message and places your text cursor in the To field.

2. Begin typing a recipient's name, handle, or phone number. As soon as you start to type, a list of your contacts is displayed, and you can select the recipient from the list or simply continue typing if the recipient is not in the list. Alternatively, you can click the Plus button to display all Contacts.

    NOTE   A handle is the name a user has given himself or herself. It's like a nickname or screen name.

3. To add another recipient, click the **Add** button on the far right side of the To field or press **Return** or type a **comma**. Then repeat step 2.

4. Repeat step 3 for each additional recipient.

NOTE Even if a person has a Mac or an iDevice, they might not have Messages enabled. In that case, the To name will appear in red at the top of the screen, and you'll get an error message if you try to send a message to the Apple ID or iPhone number.

5. Type your message in the iMessage box at the bottom of the window. Alternatively, you can press **FN FN** and then dictate your message after you see the microphone icon turn purple and hear the beep. You have 30 seconds. Click **Done** when finished dictating. Start again by pressing **FN FN** if you didn't have enough time to say everything you wanted to.

 NOTE If you haven't already turned on the Dictation tool in System Preferences as described in Chapter 6, "Using and Controlling Your Hardware," when you press **FN FN**, a dialog box opens asking whether you want to enable Dictation. You might want to click the **About Dictation and Privacy** button before clicking **OK** to see exactly what information Apple must gather from you for you to use the tool. When finished reading, click **Done**. If you decide you want to use the tool, click **OK**, and then click **Enable Dictation**.

6. To add a standard icon to your message, click in the text where you want the icon to appear and then click the smiley face on the right side of the iMessage box. Click the icon you want to add. (See Figure 19.4.)

FIGURE 19.4

Standard icons include variations of the smiley face as well as other icons. You also can insert icons by clicking Edit, Insert Smiley in the menu bar.

7. When finished, press **Return** to send the message.

When the message you sent has been delivered, you see a Delivered notification under your message bubble. If the message cannot be delivered for some reason, you see an exclamation mark in a red circle beside the bubble. To try sending the message again, click the circle and click **Try Again**.

When the recipient of your message sends a reply, you see the reply in the right pane of the Messages window. If the reply is on its way but is taking a little while to get to you, you will see a bubble with three dots in it from the recipient.

 TIP While you are sending messages back and forth, you can switch to FaceTime by clicking the **FaceTime** button. See Chapter 20, "Using FaceTime" for more information on FaceTime.

If you want to start a new conversation with someone, you can click the **Compose New Message** button. If you want to be lazy, like me, you can just continue from an old conversation. Select the recipient's name from the sidebar and type a new message in the iMessage text box.

Sending More Than Text in a Message

Using Messages, you can send photos, videos, documents, links to websites, and contacts. It's unlimited and free. Additionally, sending a file in Messages may be a good workaround for sending a file that is too large to include in an email as an attachment. You are limited to a file size of 100 MB, but that's still 20 times larger than you can send to most email accounts. Keep in mind, however, that you cannot use Messages on a Mac to send messages to the world at large. You are limited to other Mountain Lion Mac users and users of iDevices running iOS 5.

To send a text file, photo, video, audio file, or any other type of file in a message, click **Buddies**, **Send File**. When the Finder opens, navigate to the file in the Finder and double-click it. If the file is a photo or graphic file, you see a thumbnail of it in the iMessage box. Other types of files appear encapsulated in a blue bubble in the iMessage box.

Another way to send a file in Messages is to initiate the message from the Finder. Just right-click the file in the Finder and click **Share**, **Message**. A new message opens on the desktop. Enter the recipient's name, handle, or phone number; add any text you want; and click the **Send** button. Even if Messages is not open, the message you initiate from Finder is added to the sidebar of the Messages window.

To send a link from a web page, open the web page and drag the icon that precedes the web page address (in the omnibar) to the iMessage field in your message. Similarly, to add a contact, open Contacts and drag the contact to the iMessage box.

Deleting Conversations

If your list of conversations is starting to get too long, you might want to delete some of the conversations. To delete a conversation, hover the mouse over the conversation in the sidebar that you want to delete. Click the **Close** button that appears on the right side and then click **Delete** when the confirmation dialog box opens. Deleting a conversation cannot be undone.

Searching for Messages

If you seldom delete conversations, you might need to use the Spotlight search box to help you find a particular conversation. To search for a conversation, enter a name, handle, phone number, or even part of the text of the message in the Spotlight search box located at the top of the sidebar. All conversations that match your search text appear in the sidebar. Click the **Close** button in the Spotlight search box when finished.

THE ABSOLUTE MINIMUM

- You can send messages to other Mac users on Mountain Lion; iDevice users with iOS 5; and users of instant message services such as Google Talk, Jabber, AIM, and Yahoo! And sending messages is completely free and unlimited.

- You can set up multiple accounts in Messages, but Messages puts all your accounts in one list to make your life easier.

- You can send text as well as files, hyperlinks, and contacts in a message.

USING FACETIME

The FaceTime application for Mac makes video calls over WiFi to other Macs, iPads, iPods, and iPhones. Use it to keep in touch with friends and family who are far away or just around the corner. It's a simple little application to use, but what a great way to communicate! Don't be left behind. Read this chapter to get up to speed on FaceTime and get in on the action.

Getting Acquainted with FaceTime

The FaceTime window, shown in Figure 20.1, uses two panes. The pane on the left uses the Mac's built-in camera to take live video of you. The pane on the right displays your Favorites, Recents, or Contacts. You click the corresponding button at the bottom of the screen to choose. You can select a person to call from any of these three lists.

FIGURE 20.1

Click a button at the bottom of the right pane to see additional lists.

If you click Favorites, you see a list of your favorite people to call using FaceTime. You populate the Favorites list yourself, and I tell you how later in this chapter. If you click the Recents button, you see a list of your most recent FaceTime calls, as shown in Figure 20.2, or if you click the Missed button at the top, you see a list of missed calls. If you click the Contacts button, you see a list of your contacts, as shown in Figure 20.3. In Figure 20.3, notice the Groups button at the top. This button displays all the groups you have defined in Contacts. You can select a different group of contacts by clicking this button and selecting the group you want.

FIGURE 20.2

Click the Clear button to delete all calls in the list, or click the Missed button to see a list of calls you missed.

FIGURE 20.3

The same contacts you have in the Contacts application are displayed in FaceTime.

Setting Up the FaceTime Application

Because FaceTime relies on your Apple ID to function, the first time you launch FaceTime, you must sign in and receive validation. Follow these steps to activate FaceTime:

1. Click the **FaceTime** icon in the Dock.

2. Enter your Apple ID username and password and click **Sign In**.

3. Enter the email address that people will use to call you (if it does not already appear in the Address box).

4. Click **Next**. The system verifies the address and then displays all your Contacts so you are ready to use FaceTime.

Making a Call

You can make a FaceTime call only to people listed in your Contacts and then to only those who have an Apple ID and the proper equipment: an Intel-based Mac, an iPad 2 or later, an iPhone 4 or later, or the fourth-generation iPod touch or later.

If you don't have a contact for the person you want to call, you can add a contact directly in FaceTime. Click the **Contacts** button at the bottom of the right pane, and then click the **Add** button (the one with the plus). Enter the new information in the fields and click **Done**. Figure 20.4 shows you the information fields available in FaceTime. If you want to enter more information about the person, you can edit the new contact in the Contacts application.

FIGURE 20.4

Enter only an iPhone number in the Mobile field.

If the person you want to call has a contact card in Contacts already but doesn't have an email address or mobile phone number that you can use, you also can edit the contact from within FaceTime. Select the contact in the list and click the **Edit** button (at the top-right corner of the window). Add the information and click **Done**.

To make a video call, follow these steps:

1. Click the contact in the list to open it.

2. To call another Mac, iPad, or iPod touch, click the email address that is associated with the person's Apple ID or click the mobile phone number to call an iPhone.

 TIP As an alternative to steps 1 and 2, if the contact is someone you call frequently, click the **Recents** button and click the name in the list, or if the person is on your Favorites list, click the **Favorites** button and click the name there.

3. If the user you are calling accepts the call, the call goes through and your window changes to a single pane. The video of the person you called fills the pane, and your video shows in a smaller frame within the larger pane. Point to the bottom of the FaceTime window and click the **Full Screen** button to enlarge the window.

4. If the user you are calling declines the call or simply is not available, the call does not go through and a message appears at the top of the FaceTime window telling you that the user is not available for FaceTime. You can click the **Try Again** button to try to get through a second time or click **Cancel**.

> **TIP**   If you need to mute your microphone while you are on a call, point to the bottom of the screen with the mouse and click the **Mute** button. Click it again to turn the microphone back on. Note also that if you have more than one microphone attached to your Mac, you can select the one you want to use on the call by clicking **Video** in the menu bar and then clicking the option for the microphone you want to use.

5. To end a call that went through, point to the bottom of the FaceTime window with your mouse and click the **End** button.

Searching for Contacts

If you have a very long list of contacts, instead of scrolling to find the contact, you can search for it in the Spotlight search box. If you don't see the Spotlight search box, scroll the contacts all the way to the top. Begin typing either the first or last name. All contacts that match are displayed below the search box, and you can click the one you want to call. Of course, not all your contacts will be able to make and receive FaceTime calls.

Populating Your Favorites List

To add a contact to your Favorites list, click the contact to select it and then click **Add to Favorites**. If the contact has more than one way to be contacted—a mobile phone and two email addresses, for example—click the one you want to add. If you want to add all of them, you must add them individually by clicking the **Add to Favorites** button for each one. A blue star appears after the mobile phone number or email address in the user's contact. (This star does not show up in the Contacts application, only in FaceTime.)

To remove a user from the Favorites list, click the **Favorites** button at the bottom of the right pane and click **Edit** at the top of the pane. Click the **Remove** button in front of the contact you want to delete. Click **Done** when finished.

Receiving a FaceTime Call on the Mac

When someone calls you on FaceTime, your Mac rings (just like a phone) even if FaceTime is not open. (This is assuming that you have not turned off FaceTime as described in the next topic.) To take the call, you have to launch FaceTime if it is not open and then click **Accept** or **Decline**. If you don't launch FaceTime and the call continues to ring, the caller will eventually see the notice that you are not available and end the call. The next time you launch FaceTime, you will have a missed call added to your list.

Turning FaceTime Off and On

If you don't want to be bothered with FaceTime calls for a period of time, you can turn off FaceTime and then turn it back on again when you want to. To turn off FaceTime, click **FaceTime** in the menu bar and then click **Turn FaceTime Off**. Your FaceTime window displays an Off button, as shown in Figure 20.5. If you close FaceTime while it is turned off, the next time you launch FaceTime, the window still looks like Figure 20.5. To turn FaceTime back on, click the **Off** button in the right pane and then click **Done**.

FIGURE 20.5

Click the Off button to turn FaceTime back on.

THE ABSOLUTE MINIMUM

- To use FaceTime, you must activate it the first time you use it by signing in with your Apple ID.

- FaceTime can make calls to a phone number or an email associated with an Apple ID.

- Additions and edits that you make to Contacts in FaceTime "flow through" to the Contacts application.

- If you don't want to be disturbed, you can turn off FaceTime.

IN THIS CHAPTER

- Configuring TextEdit so it works like a proper word processing application
- Examining Autosave, Versions, and Documents in the Cloud
- Navigating, editing, and formatting a document
- Creating tables

USING TEXTEDIT

TextEdit is Mountain Lion's built-in word processing application. Not just a little "plain-text" editor any more, it has enough features to handle most of your word processing needs. Be that as it may, if you do very much word processing, you probably use Pages or Microsoft Word instead of TextEdit.

When outlining this book, I decided that I couldn't devote as many pages to TextEdit as I would like to. So in this chapter, I cover a lot of information in a few pages by stripping out the "small talk" and listing the steps of as many features as I can.

Even if you don't intend to use TextEdit as your word processor, you should still read the sections titled "Examining Autosave and Versions," "Using Versions," and "Saving Documents in the Cloud." These features work the same way in other Apple apps such as Preview, Pages, Numbers, and Keynote.

Launching TextEdit

To launch TextEdit, click the **Launchpad** icon in the Dock and click the **TextEdit** icon. If you are *not* synchronizing Documents & Data in iCloud, by default, each time you launch TextEdit, it creates a new document. If you *are* using iCloud for your documents, when you launch TextEdit, it presents you with the dialog box shown in Figure 21.1. From this dialog box, you can choose to open an existing document on iCloud or your hard drive or create a new document that will be saved to either location.

FIGURE 21.1

You can select iCloud or On My Mac as the destination for your document.

 TIP When the dialog box in Figure 21.1 is open, you can organize your data in iCloud by dragging one document on top of another to create a folder.

Setting TextEdit Preferences

Before you begin creating documents in earnest, you need to set some preferences so that TextEdit works like a proper word processing application. Follow these steps to set the preferences for new documents using my recommendations:

1. Click **TextEdit** in the menu bar and click **Preferences**.

2. On the New Document pane, check the option **Wrap to Page** so that text wraps within your margins and not to the size of the window.

3. Under **Options**, check the boxes for the following:

    *   **Data Detectors**—Turns on a pop-up menu for dates, addresses, and phone numbers that allows you to manipulate the data in various ways, such as add a phone number to an existing contact

    *   **Smart Quotes**—Converts straight quotes to curly quotes

    *   **Smart Dashes**—Converts two hyphens to an em dash
    *   **Smart Links**—Converts a web address to a clickable link

4. Close the window. The changes do not affect a document that is open, but the next new document you create will use the new preferences.

Notice that Correct Spelling Automatically and Check Spelling As You Type are the default settings in the New Document preferences. For more on this topic, see "Correcting Misspelled Words," later in this chapter.

Creating and Saving Documents

After you have launched TextEdit, you can create a new document at any time by clicking **File** in the menu bar and clicking **New**. Every new document is called Untitled until you save it and give it a name. To save a file, click **File** in the menu bar and click **Save**. Type a name for the document, select the desired storage location, and click **Save**. The new name of the document appears in the title bar at the top of the window.

Examining Autosave and Versions

After you save a file the first time, you never have to save it again unless you want to. TextEdit saves the file for you about every hour while you are working on it (more often if you are making significant changes) and saves it one last time when you close the file. If you want to be prompted to save your changes before you close a file, you can set the option Ask To Keep Changes When Closing Documents on the General page of System Preferences. TextEdit also saves the file if you don't close it but close the app instead.

Each time TextEdit saves the file for you, it saves the file as a version within the document. Of course, you still can save manually at any time as well by clicking **File** in the menu bar and then clicking **Save**. Additionally, you can revert to the last saved version by clicking **File**, **Revert to**, **Last Saved**, **Revert**.

 NOTE   When you email a TextEdit file, only the most current version is sent.

Using Versions

The versions that Autosave creates for you are available for you to use as needed. For example, you can restore a previous version or save a version as a new document. To access the versions of a document, follow these steps:

1. Click the document name in the title bar and click **Browse All Versions**. An interface that is similar to Time Machine opens, as shown in Figure 21.2. Your current version is on the left and the previous versions are stacked on the right with the oldest version at the bottom of the stack.

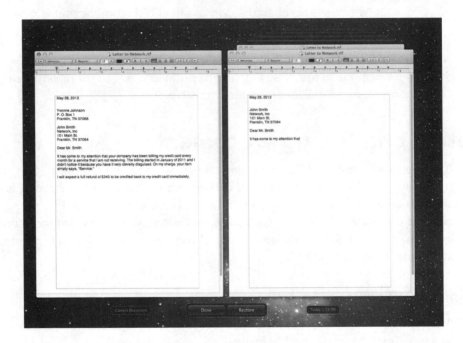

FIGURE 21.2

You might be familiar with the Versions interface if you have used Time Machine.

2. Click the title bar of a previous version to bring it to the top so you can see it. Alternatively, you can click a date on the timeline on the right side of the screen.

3. At this point, you might do one of several things. You could simply read something that was in the version, or you could restore the currently selected version, copy something from it, save it as a new document, or even delete it.

    *   To simply peruse the document, use the scroll bars or arrow keys if necessary and click **Done** when finished.

- To restore the version, click **Restore**. You are returned to the application window, and the document version you restored is the current version.

- To copy text, select the text, press **Command-C**, and then click **Done**.

- To save the version as a new document, press the **Option** key. Click the **Restore a Copy** button while pressing the **Option** key. A new document opens in a new window. The name of the new document is the same as the original document with the word *copy* appended to the end (after the extension). Click **File** in the menu bar and click **Save**. Give the file an appropriate name, navigate to the save location, and click **Save**.

- To delete the version, click the document title, click **Delete This Version**, and then click **Delete** in the warning dialog box. Then click **Done**.

 NOTE   TextEdit deletes some of the hourly versions that it saves to make browsing the versions a little easier. Each hourly version that it keeps, it keeps for 24 hours. Then versions are available on a daily basis until they are a month old, when they are then available on a weekly basis.

Saving a Duplicate of the File

The old Save As command was replaced by the Duplicate command in Lion, and this change caused quite a stir among users. Mountain Lion has improved the Duplicate command and given you a new keyboard shortcut that saves a file to a new name and a new location. To save a duplicate of a file in the same location, follow these steps:

1. Click **File** in the menu bar and click **Duplicate**. A new document is created, and the name of the document in the title bar is selected.

2. Type the new name for the duplicate and press **Return**. The file is saved with the new name in the same folder as the original file.

 TIP   If you want to save a file with a different name to a different location, press **Command-Shift-Option-S**.

Saving Documents in the Cloud

When you create a new document, you can select **iCloud** in the dialog box that you saw earlier in Figure 21.1. When you save the file, it automatically saves to iCloud. If you open a file on your hard drive and want to save it to iCloud, click

File in the menu bar and click **Move To**. Select **iCloud** if it is not selected by default and click **Move**. You also can use this command to move an open file from iCloud back to your hard drive.

Locking a Document

If you want to protect a document from being accidentally edited, you can lock it so that no additional changes can be made. To lock the document, click the document's name in the title bar and click **Lock**. If you try to make a change to a locked document, a confirmation dialog box opens asking whether you want to unlock or duplicate the document.

Resuming Your Work

If you want to resume your work every time you relaunch TextEdit, click the **System Preferences** icon in the Dock and click the **General** icon. Uncheck the option **Close Windows When Quitting an Application** and close the window.

 NOTE   Remember that this preference affects all applications, not just TextEdit.

After you choose this setting, if you leave a file open and quit TextEdit, the next time you launch TextEdit, the file opens automatically, and everything is just as you left it. Even the text insertion point is in the same location. If you had any inspectors open when you quit, such as the Fonts window, they also open and return to the same position on the screen where you last placed them.

Boiling It Down

Okay. Now I am really going to start boiling it down for you. The next three sections cover the three basic tasks you perform in word processing: navigating in the document, editing, and formatting. To be thorough, I would normally include a section on printing, but that is so universal that I'm hoping you don't need any instruction on that.

In these next three sections, you won't find a great deal of extra information due to space limitations. I don't define features or explain all the nuances of every option. If there is something you don't understand, you might have to do some more research on your own. For the most part, however, I think you will have no difficulty.

Navigating

To edit text, you must position the I-beam-shaped insertion point (text cursor) in the right place. You can click the mouse to position the I-beam or use any of the keystrokes listed in Table 21.1.

TABLE 21.1 Navigation Techniques

To Move To	Press
The beginning or end of a line	Command-Home or Command-End
The top or bottom of the document	Command-Up Arrow or Command-Down Arrow
The beginning or end of a word	Option-Left Arrow or Option-Right Arrow
Up or down one line	Up Arrow or Down Arrow

Another way to navigate in a document is to use the Find command. To find all occurrences of some particular text, you type the search text in the Spotlight field. To open the Spotlight bar, click **Edit** in the menu bar and then click **Find, Find**. After you type the search text, TextEdit highlights all the occurrences for you inline. Use the Next and Previous buttons in the bar to go to each one. Click **Done** when finished.

Editing Text

Editing text refers to inserting text; deleting text; and copying, cutting, and pasting text. When you make changes to a document, the word *Edited* appears to the right of the document title. When you see this word, you know that the Versions feature has not saved the changes yet.

Table 21.2 lists some of the most common editing commands and shortcuts. Any time you make a change to text, you can undo the change by pressing **Command-Z**. After you undo a change, if you want it back again, press **Shift-Command-Z**.

TABLE 21.2 Editing Techniques

To	Do This
Insert text	Click the cursor where the new text should go and type the text.
Delete the character to the left of the text cursor	Press **Delete**.
Delete the character to the right of the text cursor	Press **Fn-Delete** or the **Delete** key with the "x" on it if your keyboard has it.
Delete a complete word	Double-click the word and press **Delete**.
Delete a line up to the insertion point	Press **Command-Delete**.
Delete a complete paragraph	Triple-click any line in the paragraph and press **Delete**.
Delete a section of text	Drag the cursor through the text and press **Delete**.
Copy text	Drag the cursor through the text and click **Edit**, **Copy** or press **Command-C**.
Cut text	Drag the cursor through the text and click **Edit**, **Cut** or press **Command-X**.
Paste text	Click the cursor in the new location and click **Edit**, **Paste** or press **Command-V**.

Finding and Replacing Text

If you need to find a particular string of characters throughout a document and replace them with something else (for example, you want to find "Pucket's" and replace all occurrences with "Puckett's Grocery"), you can use the Find and Replace feature. Follow these steps:

1. Click **Edit** in the menu bar and then click **Find**, **Find and Replace**. The Spotlight bar opens just below the ruler at the top of the screen.

2. Type the text you want to find in the Find field.

3. Click the **Replace** check box and type the replacement text in the Replace field.

4. Click **All**.

 TIP If you don't want to change all occurrences of the text, click the **Next** button to skip the occurrence and go to the next occurrence. Click **Replace** or click **Next** again and repeat this action for each occurrence.

5. Click **Done** in the Spotlight bar when finished.

Inserting Symbols and Other Special Characters

To insert special characters, such as a copyright mark or the symbol for British pounds, follow these steps:

1. Position the insertion point where the special character should be inserted.

2. Click **Edit** in the menu bar and click **Special Characters**. The Characters Inspector opens.

3. Select the category from the sidebar and scroll the middle pane to see all the possible characters.

4. Click the character in the middle pane that you want to insert. Check the lower-right corner of the window to see whether a Font Variation or Related Symbol would be better.

5. Double-click the character you want to insert. The character appears in the document at the location of the insertion point.

6. Close the Characters inspector when finished.

Correcting Misspelled Words

As you type, TextEdit corrects some of your typographical or spelling errors for you and underlines those it cannot correct with a dotted red line. To correct an underlined word, right-click it and click the correct spelling in the list that appears at the top of the shortcut menu.

If you want to correct all misspellings at once, just wait until you have finished typing the document and then start the spell checker by clicking **Edit** in the menu bar. Then click **Spelling and Grammar**, **Show Spelling and Grammar**. This opens TextEdit's full-blown spell checker. We won't spend any time on this feature. Spell checkers work almost universally the same on all platforms, and I'm sure you've used one before or can figure it out on your own.

Formatting

Formatting occurs on three levels: the document level (setting paper size, margins, and tabs and inserting page breaks), the paragraph level (setting alignment, indents, spacing, numbering, bullets), and the character level (setting the font, size, color, and applying emphasis).

Setting the Paper Size

The default paper size is US Letter (8.5 inches by 11 inches). To change the paper size, click **File** in the menu bar and then click **Page Setup**. Click the pop-up button for **Paper Size** and select the size you want. Then click **OK**.

Setting Margins

By default, TextEdit uses one-inch margins all the way around. If you can't be happy with those margins, there is a little-known way to change them, but it is really clunky! To change the top, bottom, left, or right margin of the current document, follow these steps:

1. Create a new document. Save it and then close the document.

2. Click **File** in the menu bar, click **Open**, and select the document you just saved and closed.

3. Select the option **Ignore Rich Text Commands** at the bottom of the dialog box. (If you are using iCloud, click **Options** and then click the **Ignore Rich Text Commands** check box.)

4. Click **Open**.

5. Find the following text: `\margl1440\margr1440`. These are the Rich Text Commands for the left and right margins, respectively. (The codes for top and bottom margins are `margt` and `margb`, respectively.) The value 1440 equals one inch.

6. Change the value of 1440 to the value you want for each margin. If you changed all margins to half an inch, the code would look like this:

   `\margl720\margr720\margt720\margb720`

7. Save the document and close it. Reopen the document (but do not select Ignore Rich Text Commands this time) and type the document.

Setting Tabs

By default, TextEdit places a left tab every half inch on the ruler. To remove a default tab, drag the tab icon off the ruler. To set a tab, click the pointer on the ruler where you want the tab. TextEdit sets a left tab. To change to a different type of tab, double-click the tab repeatedly to cycle through the tabs (right tab, center tab, decimal tab, and finally back to the left tab). To change the location of a tab, drag it to the desired location on the ruler.

Inserting Page Breaks

TextEdit inserts a page break automatically when the page fills up. To insert a page break yourself, position the text cursor where you want the break. Click **Edit** in the menu bar and then click **Insert**, **Page Break**.

Setting Paragraph Alignment

To align a paragraph so it is flush left (left margin straight, right margin ragged), centered (all lines centered), justified (left and right margins straight), or flush right (left margin ragged, right margin straight), click anywhere in the paragraph, and then click the appropriate button on the Formatting toolbar. (See Figure 21.3.) If you start a new paragraph by pressing Return in the middle of the paragraph or at the end of the paragraph, the new paragraph will have the same alignment (as well as all the other paragraph characteristics).

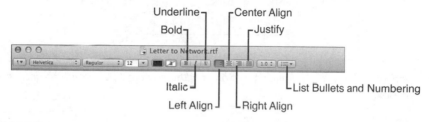

FIGURE 21.3

The Formatting toolbar has tools for formatting characters and paragraphs.

Setting Paragraph Indents

You can indent or outdent the first line of a paragraph, or you can indent the entire paragraph. To set indents, you use the ruler. The symbol at the far left of the ruler controls both the first line and the paragraph indents because it is actually two symbols that are set at the same location. If you drag the triangle symbol to the right, you indent the entire paragraph except for the first line. At this point, the first line is outdented. If you drag the "T" symbol to the right of the triangle symbol, you indent the first line. By dragging both symbols to the same location on the ruler, you indent the whole paragraph.

Setting Paragraph Spacing

Spacing options include line height multiple (single space, double space, and so on), line height, interline spacing, and paragraph spacing (space before and after paragraphs). To set spacing options in an existing paragraph, click anywhere in the paragraph, click **Format** in the menu bar, and then click **Text**, **Spacing**. The dialog box shown in Figure 21.4 opens. Set all the options that you want and click **OK**.

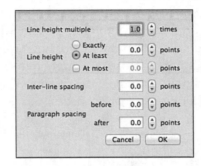

FIGURE 21.4

You can set all paragraph spacing options for the selected paragraph at one time in this dialog box.

Numbering or Bulleting Paragraphs

To create a numbered or bulleted list, follow these steps:

1. Select the paragraphs to be numbered or bulleted and click the **List Bullets and Numbering** button on the Formatting toolbar.

2. Select the bullet or numbering style you want.

Adding Emphasis to Characters

To add bold, italic, or underline to characters, select the text and then click the appropriate button in the Formatting toolbar. (See Figure 21.3.) You also can use the keyboard shortcuts: **Command-B** for bold, **Command-I** for italic, and **Command-U** for underline.

To change the character color, select the text and click the button for color in the toolbar; it's the one right after the font size. Select the color from the color palette displayed in the pop-up.

Changing the Font and Size

Each new document you create in TextEdit uses the default font specified in the New Document preferences. (See Figure 21.1.) To change the font, select the text and click the **Font** pop-up button in the Formatting toolbar. Then click the font you want. To change the font size, select the text, and click the **Font Size** pop-up button in the Formatting toolbar. Then click the size you want.

Creating a Table

For the final topic in this chapter, let's look at creating a table—one of the features that most people who do heavy word processing can't live without. To create a table, follow these steps:

1. Click **Format** in the menu bar and click **Table**. A table is inserted at the position of the insertion point, and the Table Inspector opens.

2. To change the number of rows or columns, increase or decrease the numbers in the Rows and Columns boxes in the Table Inspector.

3. To set options for individual cells (with or without data in them), select the cell(s) and do any of the following in the Table Inspector:

   - Click the appropriate buttons for **Alignment**.

   - Specify the size of the cell border and specify the color of the border. (Click the shaded box to the right of the **Cell Border** control and select the color from the Colors Inspector.)

   - Select the Cell Background (**None** or **Color Fill**). If you select Color Fill, click the box to the right of the Cell Background control and select the color from the Color inspector.

4. As you type the data in the table, move to the next or previous cell by pressing the **Tab** and **Shift-Tab** keys. Leave the Table Inspector open while you work so you can continue formatting cells as you go.

THE ABSOLUTE MINIMUM

- Be sure to set the preference for Wrap to Page to make TextEdit work like a regular word processing application.

- After you save a document the first time, you never have to save it again because TextEdit does the job for you.

- Use the Formatting toolbar to format paragraphs and characters.
- Leave the Table Inspector open as you are working on a table so you can format it easily.

IN THIS CHAPTER

- Selecting widgets for the Dashboard
- Downloading widgets from the Internet
- Organizing your widgets
- Creating your own Web Clip widgets

USING THE DASHBOARD

In this chapter, I explain how to select the widgets you want to use on the Dashboard, how to download more widgets from the Internet, and even how to create your own Web Clip widgets.

Waiting in the wings, just off-screen, is the Dashboard with its collection of little utilitarian apps called *widgets*. The initial selection of widgets is quite adequate, but the vast number and variety of widgets available for download from the Web is mind-blowing.

Exploring the Dashboard

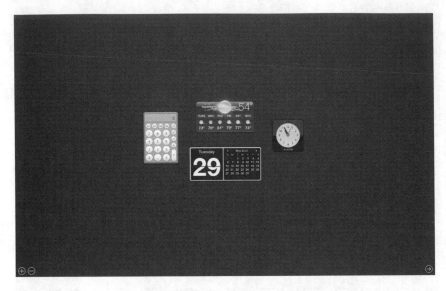

FIGURE 22.1

Only a few of the many widgets available appear on the Dashboard by default.

The Dashboard enables you to run a lot of mini-applications at once without cluttering up your Desktop with the added advantage that you can see many different items at a glance. For example, if you are traveling with a MacBook, you could have widgets open in the Dashboard to check your flight status, the local time, the weather, and the current currency exchange rate. These widgets would update automatically (if you were connected to WiFi, of course) with no effort on your part.

You don't need to launch the Dashboard because it is always there like a desktop. To view it, you can use a two-finger swipe (Magic Mouse) or a three- or four-finger swipe (Magic Trackpad) to bring it across your screen from the left. Of course, you can launch the Dashboard from the Launchpad instead of using the swiping gesture. When you are finished with the Dashboard, you can swipe it back to the left, press **Esc**, or click the right arrow in the lower-right corner.

Managing Widgets

The Dashboard comes with many widgets to choose from, and even more widgets are waiting for you to discover them on the Internet. To see the installed widgets that come with Dashboard, click the plus button in the lower-left corner of the Dashboard.

All installed widgets are displayed in a Launchpad-looking layout, as shown in Figure 22.2. When you download and install more widgets from the Internet, their icons join the ones you see in Figure 22.2. This screen doesn't have a name that I know of, but for the purposes of this book, I'm going to call it the *Widgetpad*.

FIGURE 22.2

This is what I call the Widgetpad, where all your installed widgets are accessible.

To add an installed widget to your Dashboard, click the corner of the Dashboard to open the Widgetpad; then click the widget you want. You can add more than one instance of the same widget. For example, you might want two weather widgets so you could monitor the weather in two locations.

To remove a widget from the Dashboard, click the minus button in the bottom-left corner to display a Close button on the upper-left corner of every widget. Click the **Close** button on each widget you want to remove. When you remove a widget, it closes on the Dashboard, but it's still available for use in the future in the Widgetpad.

You can arrange widgets on your Dashboard by dragging them. To drag a widget, just point to a spot at the top of the widget (as if it had a title bar) and drag it to the desired location on the screen.

Some widgets have an Info button (an italicized i) that you can click to enter additional information or preferences to customize the widget. Hover the mouse pointer over the widget to see the button, and then click it to flip the widget over to the back side where you can set the options. Click **Done** when finished.

Downloading and Installing Widgets

Lots of free widgets are available for download from the Apple website. To access these widgets, click the plus button in the lower-left corner and then click the **More Widgets** button. This button launches or switches to Safari and goes to the Apple Dashboard Widgets page.

Study the page for a while, and you will see multiple ways to find a widget that suits your needs. You can view categories, widgets that have just been added, the Top 50, staff recommendations, and so on. When you find a widget you want, click the **Download** button. After the widget is downloaded to your computer, click the **Install** button. The widget appears on the Widgetpad, but it doesn't go on your Dashboard automatically. To put the widget on the Dashboard, click the plus button in the lower-left corner of the Dashboard and then click the new widget.

 NOTE In some cases, you might need to open the Downloads folder and unzip the widget before installing it or, depending on your Security settings, you might have to manually override Gateway to install the widget. See Chapter 29, "Maintaining and Securing Your Mac."

Organizing and Finding Widgets on the Widgetpad

If you are a big fan of widgets, you might download tons of them, and then you would need to start organizing them on the Widgetpad. You can move widgets to different pages and also create folders for them. You use the same techniques that you use to organize the Launchpad. See Chapter 12, "Working with Applications."

To delete widgets on the Widgetpad, click the minus button in the lower-left corner, click the **Close** button on the widget you want to delete, and then click the **Delete** button in the confirmation dialog box. You cannot delete the default widgets, but you can delete any widgets you have installed from the Web.

The Widgetpad also has a Spotlight search box like the one in Launchpad. You can use this feature to find widgets for you by typing part of the widget's name in the search box.

Creating Your Own Web Clip Widget

If you go to a particular web page frequently to see the same thing, you can turn that portion of the web page into a widget. Then, instead of going to the web page, the information will always be available to you on your Dashboard.

NOTE   To be a good candidate for a Web Clip, the size and location of the area you want to clip should not change from day to day on the web page, but it's okay if the actual content of the area changes.

Follow these steps to create your own Web Clip:

1. Open Safari and navigate to the page that has the content you want.

2. Right-click the web page and click **Open in Dashboard**. The screen dims and a white rectangle appears. (See Figure 22.3.)

 TIP   If you don't see the Open in Dashboard option, you may have right-clicked a graphic. Right-click somewhere else on the page.

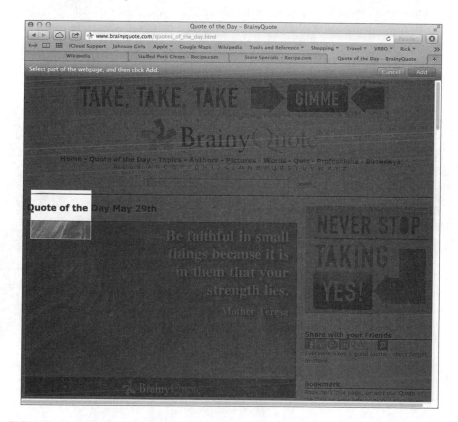

FIGURE 22.3

Move the white rectangle to the area of the web page you want to clip as a widget.

3. Move the cursor so that the white rectangle is over the information on the page that you want to clip.

4. If the rectangle does not automatically adjust to the correct size, drag the circular handles to adjust the size of the rectangle so it fits the size of the item you want to clip. (There is a minimum height and width, so you may not get a perfect fit.)

5. Click the **Add** button in the purple bar close to the top of the screen. The Dashboard opens and the clip starts loading. When finished loading, the clip opens on the Dashboard.

 CAUTION   The clip does not install on the Widgetpad, so if you delete the clip from the Dashboard, it's gone for good!

6. Drag the clip where you want to place it on the Dashboard.

 NOTE   If one day your Web Clip doesn't look right any more, the reason is probably because the web page has been redesigned. The area that you clipped has different content now.

THE ABSOLUTE MINIMUM

- Widgets are like apps for your iPhone.

- You can download additional widgets from the Web.

- You can organize all your widgets on pages and in folders on what I call the Widgetpad.

- When clipping a Web widget, be sure to select an item on the page that doesn't change in size or location.

USING PREVIEW

As its name implies, the Preview application is used primarily for looking at PDF documents. Preview can view most other graphic formats, such as JPG, TIF, PNG, and so on. Additionally, Preview can view Word files, Excel files, Pages files, and other types of files. If you are like most people, you will be surprised to learn that Preview can do much more than simply view a file.

Launching Preview

Preview opens automatically when you double-click certain types of files. But what happens if you actually launch Preview by clicking its icon in Launchpad or the Dock? The answer to that question depends on whether or not you are synchronizing Documents & Data in iCloud. If you are, it presents you with the dialog box shown in Figure 23.1. From this dialog box, you can choose to open an existing document on iCloud or your hard drive. If you are not synchronizing documents, when you launch Preview, no window opens. The only evidence you have that Preview is open is the menu bar.

FIGURE 23.1

Preview can open documents on iCloud or on your Mac.

Editing Files

In PDF and graphic files, Preview can actually make edits to the file. Preview has two sets of tools—one for PDF files and one for graphic files—because the file types are different and users treat them in different ways. For example, you don't search for text in a graphic file, and you don't use the Smart Lasso selection tool in a PDF file.

There are some editing tasks that Preview can perform in either type of file, however. These tasks include magnifying a portion of the page; drawing shapes, lines, and arrows; cropping and rotating a page; and sharing the file. In the following sections, we examine the editing tasks that are common to both PDF and graphic files.

Magnifying a Portion of a Page

The Magnifier feature works just like a magnifying glass. It enlarges the portion of the page under the Magnifier, as shown in Figure 23.2. To turn on the Magnifier, click **Tools** in the menu bar and click **Show Magnifier**. Move the "magnifying glass" around to different areas of the page as needed using the mouse. To turn off the Magnifier, go back to the **Tools** menu again and click **Hide Magnifier**.

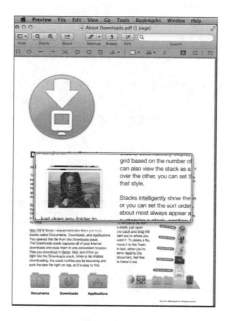

FIGURE 23.2

The Magnifier tool zooms in on a portion of a page.

If you want to zoom in on the entire page, use the Zoom tool with the plus in the toolbar, or if you have a Magic Mouse or Magic Trackpad, you can double-tap to zoom in. To zoom out, use the Zoom tool with the minus or double-tap again.

Drawing Shapes and Lines

Drawing tools are available for both PDF and graphic files. Shape tools include the Rectangle, Oval, Line, Arrow, Speech Bubble, and Thought Bubble buttons. To draw a shape, follow these steps:

1. If necessary, click the **Edit** button to display the Edit toolbar.

2. Click the button for the shape you want to draw.

3. Click the **Colors** button and select a color from the top of the menu for the line or outline.

4. If the shape is a rectangle, oval, or speech or thought bubble, click the **Colors** button again and select **No Fill**, or select **Fill Color** and then select a color.

5. Drag the cursor to draw the shape.

Press **Shift** after you start drawing to make a rectangle a perfect square, an oval a perfect circle, or a line or arrow perfectly horizontal or vertical. When you are finished drawing the shape, be sure to release the mouse button before you release the Shift key; otherwise, the shape will revert.

After drawing a line or arrow, you can set the thickness of the line by selecting the shape, clicking the pop-up button on the Line Width menu button, and clicking the thickness you want. You also can change an arrow to a double-headed arrow from this menu.

Adding Text

You can add your own text to PDF files and graphics by using the Text tool. When using the Text tool, you use the Font Inspector to select your font color, font styles, and font sizes. Here's how to use it:

1. If necessary, click the **Edit** button to display the Edit toolbar.

2. Click the **Text** button. Drag a box on the page where you want the text to appear, and type the text. Alternatively, you can just click on the page and start typing and the size of the text box adjusts to what you have typed.

3. Click the **Show Font** button and select a font and size from the Font Inspector.

4. In the Font Inspector, click the **Text Color** button to open the Color Inspector and select a color.

 NOTE   Text has no background color, so if you want a background color, you must draw a rectangle with a fill color and then place the text on top of the rectangle.

Cropping a Page

Cropping a page cuts away the area outside a selected portion of the page. When you crop a page in a PDF file, the cropped content is not really deleted. It's only hidden in Preview, and you might be able to see it in other applications. When you crop a graphic file, the content is actually deleted. To crop a page, click the

Selection tool and drag through the page outlining the portion of the page that you want to keep. Then click the **Crop** button.

Rotating a Page

Sometimes when people scan pages to a PDF file, they scan some of the pages upside down. Additionally, I'm sure you have lots of photographs that are turned sideways when they should be vertical. You can fix these problems by rotating the page. To rotate a page, simply click the **Rotate** button. The page turns counterclockwise 90 degrees each time you click the Rotate button. If you want to rotate in a clockwise direction, use the **Tools**, **Rotate Right** command from the menu bar.

 TIP If you are editing a graphic file, you also can flip the file vertically or horizontally. For example, you might want to flip a photo of a person's left profile if you are placing it on the left side of the page in a brochure. You wouldn't want the person to appear to be looking off the page. If you flip the photo horizontally, the person's profile changes to the right side. Now the person would be looking into the page. To flip a graphic, click **Tools** in the menu bar and click **Flip Horizontal** or **Flip Vertical**. Note that if you horizontally flip a photo that has text or a recognizable logo in it, the text or logo will obviously be reversed.

Sharing

To send a file that you have open in Preview, click the **Share** button. If the file is a PDF document, your choices are Email or Message. If the file is a graphic file, your choices also include Twitter and Flickr. Of course, you must have registered accounts to use these two options. Additionally, AirDrop is a choice for either type of file.

Viewing PDF Files

PDF files have become so well known by their three-letter extension that you might not even remember that PDF stands for Portable Document Format. It is a format created long ago by Adobe to solve the then-existing problem of the inability of applications to read each other's files. Because Adobe gave users the Adobe Reader application free (and still does), the PDF file became the standard format used for Web document downloads. Although a PDF is a "graphic" file, it is not graphic in the sense that a JPG file is graphic. Without my going into a lot of technical explanations, suffice it to say that the PDF document is constructed to deal with text, whereas a JPG file and other graphic formats are constructed to deal with photographs.

NOTE I don't mean to say that a PDF file cannot contain a photograph. The PDF file just does not handle a photograph in the same way a JPG file does.

Changing the View of a PDF File

Figure 23.3 shows a PDF file open in the Preview window. In the figure, the sidebar shows thumbnails of all the pages in the document. If you select a different view, the sidebar can show a Table of Contents or Highlights and Notes (if the document contains them). These choices are on the menu that is displayed when you click the **View** button. To return to a single-paned window, you select **Content Only** from the View menu. If you want to see all the pages at once in the single-pane view, you choose **Contact Sheet** from the View menu.

FIGURE 23.3

The Thumbnail view shows each page in the sidebar as a thumbnail.

Additionally, you can view the pages in a file in a continuous scroll, single pages, or two pages at a time. If you are viewing pages as single pages, a one-finger swipe on the Magic Mouse turns the page. (On a Magic Trackpad, you can configure either a two-finger or three-finger swipe for turning pages.)

In Figure 23.3, notice that the toolbar at the top displays the names under each button. This is not the default, but it will aid you in finding the buttons when I refer to them in the rest of this chapter.

TIP If you like the idea of seeing the button names, turn them on for yourself. Click **View** in the menu bar. Then click **Customize Toolbar** and select **Icon and Text** for the Show option. Click **Done** to close the dialog box.

Preview provides some features that you might find helpful when you are viewing a PDF file. You can search PDF documents, bookmark your place in the file, and select and copy text.

Searching in a PDF File

If you are looking for a word or phrase in a PDF document, you can use the Spotlight search feature to help you find it. Follow these steps to search for text in a PDF file:

1. Click in the Spotlight search field and type the text. The pages that contain the text and how many matches are found on each page are displayed in the sidebar, as shown in Figure 23.4. The current page on the right shows all the occurrences highlighted in yellow. Additionally, the bar that opens under the toolbar(s) has options for sorting and navigating to each occurrence.

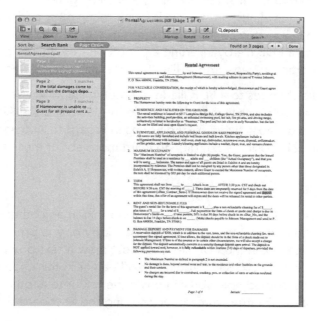

FIGURE 23.4

Sorting by Search Rank list the pages in the sidebar with the most occurrences first.

2. To sort the results, click the **Page Order** button or click the **Search Rank** button.

3. Click a page in the sidebar to display that page in the right pane.

4. Click the **Next** and **Previous** buttons, the buttons with the right- and left-pointing triangles, to go to each occurrence.

5. Click **Done** when finished.

Using Bookmarks in a PDF File

Go to the page you want to bookmark and click **Bookmarks** in the menu bar. Then click **Add Bookmark**. Type a name for the bookmark and click **Add**. The new bookmark becomes an option on the Bookmarks menu so you can later go back to the bookmarked page by selecting the bookmark from the menu.

Modifying PDF Files

Even though Preview is used most often to view files, it can perform some editing tasks that change the file. For example, you can highlight, underline, or strike through text; draw lines, arrows, circles, and rectangles; add a comment box; add text; add your signature; and crop and rotate pages. Additionally, you can actually add pages to a PDF file by inserting a page from a scanner, inserting a blank page, or inserting a page from a file. (See the Edit, Insert menu.)

As you make changes to a PDF file (or a graphic file, discussed later in this chapter), Preview saves versions of the file for you using the Autosave feature. Preview functions exactly as TextEdit does in regard to Autosave and Versions. See Chapter 21, "Using TextEdit," to learn more about these features.

Copying Text in a PDF File

Copying text in a PDF file is just like copying text in any other type of file. First, you select the text and then you click **Edit**, **Copy** or you press **Command-C**. To paste the text back in the PDF file, you must draw a text box with the Text tool and paste it in the box. See "Adding Text" earlier in this chapter. Additionally, after you have copied text, you can paste the text into another document by clicking the **Edit**, **Paste** command or pressing the keyboard shortcut **Command-V**.

 TIP If you follow the instructions to copy text and it just doesn't work, the text you are trying to copy is probably really a graphic and not text. You can't tell by looking at a PDF file how it was originally created and formatted.

Modifying Text in a PDF File

You can highlight text in a PDF file, underline it, or strike through it. To add any of these text attributes to text in a PDF file, follow these steps:

1. Drag the cursor through the text to select it.

2. Click the **Markup** button in the toolbar.

3. Select the color for a highlight or select either **Underline** or **Strikethrough**.

Although you cannot retype the text in a PDF document per se, there is a way that you can replace the text in a document—maybe—if you can match the background color, font, and font sized used in the document. This is much easier to do if the background is pure white or pure black. First, you must hide the text you want to replace by drawing a rectangle (or multiple rectangles) over the text. Use a color fill for the rectangles that matches the background. Then you add text as described in the topic "Adding Text" earlier in this chapter, positioning it over the existing text. The replacement text generally has to fit in approximately the same number of lines as the text it is replacing. (You will not have to resort to this technique for replacing text in a PDF file if you have the original document and the application that created it. You can just edit the original and save it again as a PDF file.)

Adding a Note to a PDF

Adding a note to a PDF file is not the same as adding a text box. You use a note to make comments on the file that can be read and later deleted when you want to clean up the file. To add a note to a page, follow these steps:

1. Click the **Edit** button in the toolbar. The Edit toolbar opens, as shown in Figure 23.5.

FIGURE 23.5

The Note button is circled.

2. Click the **Note** button and then click the **Color** button to choose a color for the note.

TIP You might want to use different colors as a way of coding your notes. For example, you could use one color for notes that point out critical errors and another color for notes that ask a question.

3. Click in the text in a location that is germane to your note. A colored note space opens in which you can type the note. The color of the space is determined by the color you select in step 2.

4. Type the text and click anywhere outside the note when finished. The typing space closes, and a small, colored note icon is displayed in the document.

To read or edit a note, just click the colored note icon. The note space opens. When you are finished reading or editing the note, click anywhere outside the note to close it. To delete a note, click it to select it and press the **Delete** key.

To view all your notes in the file, click the **View** button and click **Highlights and Notes**. Figure 23.6 shows you what the sidebar might look like.

FIGURE 23.6

No highlights are listed in this Highlights & Notes view simply because the document doesn't have any text highlighted.

Using a Signature in a PDF File

The signature feature takes a picture of a signature and stores it so it can be used over and over again in any PDF document. After you take a picture of a signature, it becomes available as an option on the Signature menu. You can have as many signatures on file as you need.

To take a picture of a signature, follow these steps:

1. For best results, sign your name using a fine-tip black ink pen on a piece of white paper. Make your signature a little smaller than you would write it on a check.

2. Click the **Edit** button, if necessary, to display the Edit toolbar.

3. Click the **Signature** button and click the option to create the signature from your camera. The Signature Capture dialog box opens, and you see yourself in the picture box. The option to save the signature after you quit Preview is checked.

4. Hold the paper up in front of the camera so your signature rests on the blue line. This is the tricky part! Try to keep the paper as still as possible and try not to tilt the paper at an angle to the camera lens.

5. When the signature is lined up on the blue line and the signature shows in the Preview box, click **Accept**. The signature is saved, and you can access it any time.

6. To add signatures for other people, repeat these steps.

 TIP You can store multiple versions of your own signature or your initials because every time you sign something, it's slightly different. This is helpful for forms where you need to sign or initial in various places so it's not as obvious that you signed digitally.

To add a signature to a PDF file, follow these steps:

1. Click the **Signature** button and select the signature you want to insert in the document.

2. Click in the location where you want the signature to appear. If you click on a line, Preview will attempt to size the signature to fit the line. Sometimes you need to click and drag to place the signature.

THE ABSOLUTE MINIMUM

- Preview views several different types of file but can edit PDF files and most graphic file formats, such as JPG, GIF, PNG, and TIF.

- You can use Preview to crop and rotate photographs.

- You can search for text in a PDF, add comments, bookmark pages to return to them, and even add your signature.

24

USING THE GAME CENTER

It's difficult to pin down the number of people who play computer and online games every day, but a brief review of existing statistics will convince you that there are hundreds of millions of people worldwide. These statistics include people who are just playing a game of solitaire on their computers as well as those who are playing multiplayer games.

You've always been able to play games on a Mac, but before Mountain Lion, only iPad or iPhone users had Game Center. With the introduction of this new app in Mountain Lion, Mac users have one more point of continuity with their iDevices. If you are not already familiar with Game Center, this chapter shows you how to get started, download games, add friends, and generally have some fun.

Getting Started with the Game Center

Before we really get started, let's get one thing straight. The Game Center is not a repository for all your games. So if you have downloaded some games from the App Store previous to installing Mountain Lion, those games do not show up in the Game Center. To play one of those games, you still have to launch it from the Launchpad (or the Dock if you have placed the game's icon on the Dock). After launching the game, it might subsequently show up in Game Center (if it has been updated for Game Center). Only specific games work with Game Center—those that are listed in the App Store's Game Center section.

 CAUTION Don't purchase iOS games (for the iPhone and iPad) and expect to play them on the Mac.

To use the Game Center on the Mac, you can use your existing Game Center account if you have one or set up a new account if you don't have one. You also can see all the Game Center games you've played, start a new game, send friend requests, check leaderboards, and compare your achievements with your friends.

Launching Game Center and Signing In

To launch Game Center, click the **Launchpad** icon in the Dock and then click the **Game Center** icon. If you entered your Apple ID when you first installed Mountain Lion, or if you subsequently supplied your Apple ID to the Mac when setting up other applications, your Apple ID appears automatically on the initial Game Center screen. If you have never supplied your Apple ID to the Mac, the Game Center looks like the one in Figure 24.1.

If you don't see your Apple ID, enter it. Then type your password and click **Sign In**. If you already have an account set up with Game Center through one of your other devices, the Game Center displays your nickname at the top. If you don't have a Game Center account, the message shown in Figure 24.2 appears when you click **Sign In**. Click **Continue**. Agree to the terms of the agreement, complete your profile information, and click **Done**.

 NOTE After you type your password or complete the setup of a new account, you are officially signed in. You don't need to sign out each time you quit using the Game Center. You will continue to be signed in and can use Game Center any time by just launching it.

FIGURE 24.1

The Me tab is all about you—your name, nickname, status, photo, and so on.

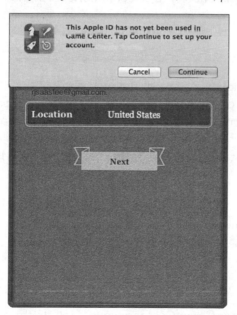

FIGURE 24.2

To use Game Center, you must have a profile set up.

Adding or Changing Your Photo

If you want to add or change your photo on the Me tab, just follow these steps:

1. Click the **Change Photo** banner.

 NOTE The Change Photo banner acts just like a regular button, but the graphic looks like a banner instead of a button.

2. You can click **Defaults** or **Recent** and select a photo, or you can select **Camera** and click the shutter button. After taking a photo with the camera, you can resize the photo, move it around in the frame, or click the **Special Effects** button and select an effect.

 NOTE Every time you select a different photo for yourself, Game Center stores the photo in the Recents category. This enables you to easily change your profile photo from time to time by selecting different photos from this category.

3. Click **Done**. The photo you selected appears in the photo frame on the Me tab.

Setting Your Status

Your Status is simply a statement that you enter in the Status banner. This statement shows on your Me tab. Because it also appears above your name on the Friends tabs of your friends' Game Center application windows, you could use the status to let your friends know whether you are available for a game challenge. To change your status, click the **Status** banner on the Me tab, type the text, and press **Return**.

 NOTE Some people just use the Status to further describe themselves or make a statement that has nothing to do with their game-playing availability.

Changing or Viewing Your Game Center Account

The settings in your Game Center account include the following:

- Your nickname
- Whether you allow friends to invite you to play
- Whether your profile information is public or private

- The email address(es) your friends can use to find you to invite you to play
- Your location

To change or view these settings, click the account banner on the Me tab and then click **View Account**. (You may be prompted to enter your Apple ID password.) Scroll the Game Center Account window to view all the information and click **Cancel** when finished, or if you have made changes, click **Save**.

 TIP You also can sign out of Game Center when you click the account banner.

Acquiring Games

Before you can play any games, you need to have some! The first time you click the Games tab after installing Mountain Lion, you see the screen shown in Figure 24.3. Click the **App Store** banner to go to the section of the App Store that contains all the Game Center games and download the ones you want.

 TIP Another way to get to the App Store to acquire games is to click a game icon on your Me page.

FIGURE 24.3

After you download your first game from the App Store, you will not see this screen again.

After you download your first game, when you open the Games tab, it contains the three categories (Game Recommendations, OS X Games, and iOS Games) shown in Figure 24.4.

FIGURE 24.4

The Games tab looks like this after you download at least one game.

The steps to download a game are different after you have downloaded your first game. To download more games, follow these steps:

1. Click the **Games** tab.

2. Click the **Game Recommendations** bar at the top. The Game Recommendations page opens.

3. Click the game you want. A page opens for the game.

4. Click the price banner for the game. The App Store opens.

5. Click the price of the game to download it. (Sign in with your Apple ID, if prompted.) After the download is complete, the new game appears on the Games tab in the OS X category.

Playing Games

As mentioned earlier, regular games downloaded from the App Store do not appear in Game Center, but you can still play them just as you did before. Any iOS games you have downloaded are displayed in their own category, as shown in Figure 24.4. You can see the leaderboards and your achievements for any of your games listed on the Games tab, but you can play only the OS X games. The iOS games can't be played from the Mac.

NOTE If you have downloaded the same game for OS X and for iOS, your stats are still kept separately.

To start playing one of your games that you can play by yourself, follow these steps:

1. Click the **Games** tab and click the game you want to play (in the OS X category). A new page is displayed for that game showing your achievements. While on this page, you also can see stats for the game, friend and global leaderboards, and which of your friends have the same game (if you have added friends).

TIP Also while on this page, if you want to tell a friend about the game, you can send an email to your friend by clicking the **Tell A Friend** banner.

2. If you decide against playing the game and want to return to all your games, click the **Back** button in the upper-left corner.

3. To play the game, click the **Play Game** banner. Play the game as many times as you want, and when you are finished, close the game application window.

TIP To see your achievements and compare them to your friends, click the **Games** tab and click the game. Click **Leaderboards, Achievements,** or **Players.**

As an example of how to play a multiplayer game, use the Chess game, which is now integrated in Game Center. To play Chess against a live opponent, follow these steps:

1. Click the **Games** tab and click **Chess**.

2. Click **Play Game**.

3. Click **Game** in the menu bar and click **New**.

4. Click the **Players** pop-up button, click **GameCenter Match**, and click **Start**.

5. Click **Play Now** to let Game Center find a match for you, or click **Invite a Friend**. Then click the friend you want to invite and click **Next**. An invitation is prepared for the friend that says, "Want to play Chess?" You can edit or add to the message. Click **Send**. If your friend accepts the invitation, when ready, click **Play Now**.

NOTE Of course, you must have some friends to invite. Learn how to add friends in the next section.

Adding Friends

If you want to play multiplayer games with your friends or just keep up with what they are playing and track their achievements, you can add your friends to the Game Center. To add a friend, follow these steps:

1. Click the **Requests** tab.

NOTE If anyone has sent you a friend request, you see it on this tab and can accept or ignore it. Additionally, a number in parentheses in the Requests tab alerts you to the fact that you have one or more requests waiting.

2. Click the **Add Friends** banner.

3. Type the person's nickname if you know it or the email address.

4. Edit the message if you want.

5. Click **Send**. Your friend gets an alert in the Notification Center. If the person accepts your invitation to be friends, you are listed as a friend, and information about the games you play, your points, and any friends you have in common all become available to your friend, as shown in Figure 24.5. Additionally, you see the same information about your friend on your own Friends tab.

NOTE After you have friends on your Friends tab, you can unfriend them on this tab if you want to stop playing games with them.

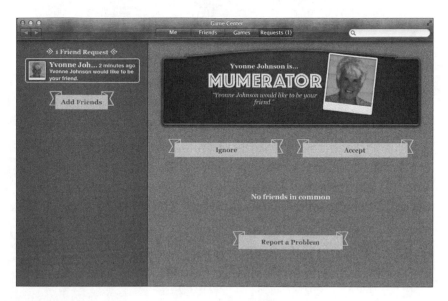

FIGURE 24.5

The Requests screen shows the friend request you have received and enables you to make your own requests.

THE ABSOLUTE MINIMUM

- You can't do anything in Game Center until you sign in.

- You can play only Game Center games in the Game Center.

- You can add friends to the Game Center, and then you will know what games they are playing and can see their achievements.

- You also can play multiplayer games with your Game Center friends or with other players that Game Center finds for you.

IN THIS CHAPTER

- Playing DVD movies and short videos
- Recording and editing short videos
- Making instructional videos of computer applications
- Sharing videos on many of the major video websites, including YouTube, Vimeo, and Flickr

25

USING VIDEO APPLICATIONS

Mountain Lion has you covered on viewing full-length movies as well as short videos. With QuickTime Player, you can create and edit your own short videos. This chapter tells you how.

Using DVD Player

When you are ready to watch a DVD on your Mac, just pop it into the SuperDrive and, by default, Mountain Lion launches the application called DVD Player. The DVD begins playing automatically in Full Screen mode. To use the DVD controls for fast forwarding, adjusting volume, and so on, you can display the controls in Full Screen mode by pointing to the bottom of the screen, or you can click the **Exit Full Screen** button and use the full onscreen remote control shown in Figure 25.1. When you are finished, click the eject button in the onscreen controls and then close DVD Player.

FIGURE 25.1

The onscreen DVD remote control has all the controls of a real DVD remote control.

TIP If you don't want the DVD Player to start playing the movie immediately when you insert the DVD, open **System Preferences**, click **CDs & DVDs**, and select **Ignore** for When You Insert a Video DVD.

Using QuickTime Player

QuickTime Player is a video player, but not one that plays DVDs. You use QuickTime Player to view short videos such as movie trailers on the Apple website. QuickTime Player can also record movies, record audio only, record action on your screen, and do some video editing, such as splitting, adding, and trimming clips.

TIP If you want to do more serious editing, you should use iMovie (at a minimum) or look into more advanced video editing applications.

Playing a Video on QuickTime Player

QuickTime Player reads videos in these formats: QuickTime Movie (.mov), MPEG-4 (.mp4 and .m4v), MPEG-1, 3GPP, 3GPP2, AVI, and DV, and you can download plug-ins for additional formats. To play a video of the type QuickTime Player can read, double-click the file. QuickTime Player opens automatically with the file loaded and ready to play. Click the **Play** button to start the video. (You may have to mouse over the video window to see the Play button in the controls at the bottom of the screen.) When you finish watching the video, click the red **Close** button in the upper-left corner of the application window to close the file.

 NOTE   Even short videos that QuickTime Player can open may not play if they use a compression/decompression format that QuickTime Player cannot process.

Recording with QuickTime Player

QuickTime Player enables you to record a video using only your built-in camera and microphone. You also can connect external cameras and microphones if you want. In addition to recording movies with audio, you can record audio only and capture your screen actions.

Recording a Movie

To record a movie with audio and video, follow these steps:

1. Click **File** in the menu bar and then click **New Movie Recording**. The Movie Recording window opens, and the built-in camera shows you or whoever is in front of it.

2. Click the pop-up button on the right to set options as shown in Figure 25.2.

FIGURE 25.2

Select options for Camera, Microphone, and Quality from this menu.

3. Test the sound level by speaking and observing the level in the onscreen control. Adjust the volume as needed using the slider to the left of the red button.

4. When you are ready to record, click the red **Record** button. The number of elapsing seconds and the corresponding size of the file that is being created are displayed in the control at the bottom of the screen.

5. When you are finished, click the black **Stop Recording** button. (If you don't see it, mouse over the bottom of the screen.) The movie appears in the QuickTime Player window. To play the movie, click the **Play** button.

6. To save the movie, click the **Close** button in the video window. A dialog box opens asking whether you want to save the changes.

7. Type a name for the video in the **Save As** field. Select a location for **Where,** select a format that is suitable for your target device, and click the **Save** button.

Recording an Audio File

An audio file has no video component; it is purely a sound file. You can record an audio file of your spoken voice, music, and so on. To record an audio file, follow these steps:

1. Click **File** in the menu bar and then click **New Audio Recording**. The tiny Audio Recording window opens.

2. Click the pop-up button on the right to select the microphone or specify the quality.

3. Test the sound level by speaking and observing the level in the onscreen control. Adjust the volume as needed using the slider under the red Record button.

4. Click the red **Record** button and begin speaking. The number of elapsing seconds and the corresponding size of the file that is being created are displayed in the control at the bottom of the screen.

5. When you are finished, click the black **Stop Recording** button.

6. To save the audio file, click the **Close** button in the audio window. A dialog box opens asking whether you want to save the changes.

7. Type a name for the file in the **Save As** field. Select a location for **Where** and click the **Save** button.

Recording the Screen

Making a recording of the screen is a great way to create an instructional video about something on your Mac. To record action on your computer screen, follow these steps:

1. Click **File** in the menu bar and then click **New Screen Recording**. The Screen Recording window opens.

2. Click the pop-up button on the right to set options, as shown in Figure 25.3.

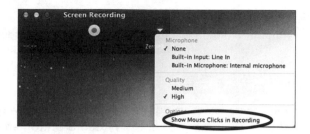

FIGURE 25.3

Show Mouse Clicks in Recording adds a circle around the mouse pointer when it is clicked.

3. Test the sound level by speaking and observing the level in the onscreen control. Adjust the volume as needed by using the slider under the red Record button.

4. Click the red **Record** button, and QuickTime Player prompts you with "Click to record the full screen. Drag to record part of the screen."

5. Click anywhere on the screen to record the full screen or drag the mouse cursor over a section of the screen such as a window. The number of elapsing seconds and the corresponding size of the file that is being created are displayed in the control at the bottom of the screen.

6. Perform the computer operations you want to record. For example, click **Finder** in the Dock and navigate to a folder; open a second Finder window and navigate to a different folder; and then drag a file from one window to the other.

7. When you are finished, click the black **Stop Recording** button. The movie appears in the QuickTime Player.

8. To save the recording, click the **Close** button in the video window. A dialog box opens asking whether you want to save the changes.

9. Type a name for the recording in the **Save As** field. Select a location for **Where**, select a format that is suitable for your target device, and click the **Save** button.

Editing Movies with QuickTime Player

Although QuickTime Player is not nearly as robust as the professional Final Cut Pro X application, it enables you to split your movies into clips, rearrange the clips, insert clips from other videos, or insert complete video files.

NOTE The steps in this section for trimming and splitting movies are the same for movies and screen recordings.

Trimming a Movie

When making your own movies using the built-in camera, always record some "dead time" between the time you click the Record button and start the action. Likewise, allow some dead time after the action stops and before you click the Stop Record button. This allows you to trim these motions at the beginning and end of your video without cutting off any of the real action.

 NOTE You also can trim an audio recording, but you cannot split it.

To trim the beginning and end of a movie, follow these steps:

1. Open the movie file in QuickTime Player.

2. Click **Edit** in the menu bar and click **Trim**. A trimming control opens at the bottom of the screen.

3. If you want to trim the beginning, click the **Play** button on the far left and then click the **Pause** button when you get to the location where you want the movie to actually start. Make a "visual note" of this location and then drag the yellow handle at the beginning of the clip to the location, as shown in Figure 25.4. As you drag, the number of seconds you are going to eliminate is displayed above the yellow handle.

FIGURE 25.4

The movie is displayed as separate frames. Use the yellow handles on both ends of the movie to trim the beginning or the end of the movie.

4. To locate the place where you want to trim off the end of the movie, click the **Play** button again, and when the movie reaches the position where you want to trim it, click the **Pause** button so you can see the approximate location. Drag the yellow handle on the right to the approximate location.

5. Click the **Play** button again to play the entire section between the two trim handles to be sure you have what you want.

6. Adjust the handles if necessary and then click the **Trim** button.

7. If this is the only change you want to make to the movie, click the red **Close** button to save the changes.

8. Type a name for the file in **Save As**, select a location for **Where**, select a format that is suitable for your target device, and click **Save**.

Splitting a Movie into Clips

Splitting a movie cuts a movie into two pieces, or *clips*. After you split a movie, you can select one of the pieces you split and split it. So basically, you can cut a movie into as many pieces as you want. Perhaps your question is "Why would I cut a movie at all?" One reason is to cut out a piece in the middle of the movie that you don't want.

To split a movie into clips, follow these steps:

1. Open the movie file in QuickTime Player.

2. Click **View** in the menu bar and click **Show Clips**.

3. Click the movie frames to select the entire clip. The movie is outlined in yellow.

4. Click the **Play** button and then click the **Pause** button when you get to the location where you want to split the movie.

5. Click **Edit** in the menu bar and click **Split Clip**. The movie is divided into two clips and both are selected, as shown in Figure 25.5.

FIGURE 25.5

Each clip is selected, as evidenced by the yellow border around both clips. (This figure intended for mature audiences only.)

6. At this point you could do any of the following:

- Select a clip and perform the normal steps to trim the beginning or the end.

- Select one of the clips and repeat the steps to split it.

- Select a clip and delete it by pressing the **Delete** key.

- Drag a clip before or after the other clip to rearrange them.

- Open the Finder, drag a movie file to the QuickTime movie, and drop it between the two clips.

- Open another movie in QuickTime Player, split it into clips, and drag one of the clips from that movie to the one you are currently working on.

7. When you are finished, click **Done**.

8. To save the file, click the red **Close** button. Type a name for the file in **Save As**, select a location for **Where**, select a format that is suitable for your target device, and click **Save**.

Sharing QuickTime Files

You can share files in Email, Message, Facebook, YouTube, Vimeo, and Flickr. To share a video, open it and then click the **Share** button that appears on the far right side of the onscreen controls.

THE ABSOLUTE MINIMUM

- The DVD Player application plays full movies on DVD, whereas QuickTime Player is used for short videos such as movie trailers.

- QuickTime Player can record videos, audio, and screen recordings.

- QuickTime Player has some video editing capabilities, such as trimming and splitting clips.

- You can share QuickTime Player files in Email, Message, Facebook, YouTube, Vimeo, and Flickr.

26

USING iTUNES

iTunes is a media storage and media player application. It can store and play music, movies, TV shows, educational courses, and podcasts. Additionally, it can play radio programming for live streaming radio stations. iTunes is also a repository for books and apps that run on your iPod, iPhone, or iPad. This chapter looks at the features of iTunes you can use on your Mac.

Exploring the iTunes Window

When you open iTunes the first time, you have to agree to the License Agreement. After you do that, the iTunes window opens but is soon obscured by the Welcome to iTunes video tutorial window. You can watch all the videos to get an overview of how iTunes works or just close the window and go back to it later by clicking **Help** in the menu bar and clicking **iTunes Tutorials**.

If you close the tutorial window, you see that the design of the iTunes window is similar in function to that of the Finder window. The left pane is comparable to the Finder sidebar but in iTunes it is called the Source pane, not the sidebar. It lists categories of media sources. The pane to the right normally lists all the media stored in iTunes for the selected library, but when you first start using iTunes, this pane displays introductory information and links to more information or tutorials about the particular library. After you have stored media in a library, the iTunes window looks like Figure 26.1.

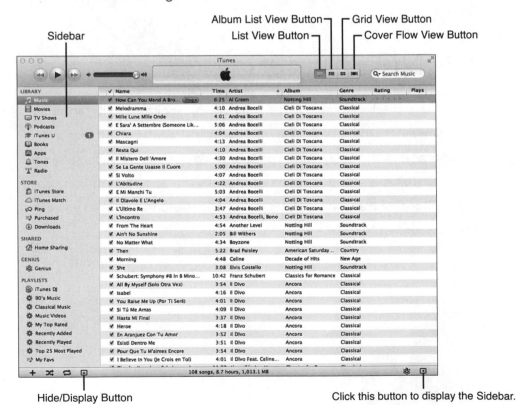

FIGURE 26.1

The iTunes Sidebar that displays Ping activity is not visible in this figure.

Another pane that is displayed on the far right—this one *is* called the *Sidebar* in iTunes—shows your activities in Apple's social network for music called Ping. You can hide and display the Sidebar using the button shown in Figure 26.1.

TIP Getting started with Ping is easy. Just click **Ping** in the left pane, sign in with your Apple ID, and fill out some profile information.

Using the View buttons in the toolbar, you can display media items in a list, as albums with a columnar list, as a grid of albums or tiles, or in the familiar Cover Flow view that is also used in the Finder. Figure 26.1 shows the Music library (selected in the left pane) in the List view. Figures 26.2 through 26.4 show each of the other three views. The view button in use is circled in each figure.

FIGURE 26.2

This view shows the cover art with a list.

FIGURE 26.3

This view shows only the cover art.

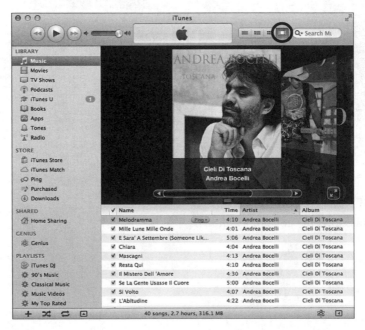

FIGURE 26.4

This is the Cover Flow view.

Listening to a Music CD

We long ago entered the age of downloadable music, and record stores have closed left and right because of it. Many people do still purchase physical CDs, however. If you have a CD that you want to play, you can play it with iTunes and have the advantage of skipping those tracks you really don't like.

To listen to a music CD, follow these steps:

1. Insert the CD in your optical drive. If it is not already open, iTunes opens automatically due to the preference set in the CDs & DVDs pane of System Preferences. I wish I could say the CD starts playing immediately, but it doesn't. You may have to clear a flurry of dialog boxes. The first thing iTunes does (if you are connected to the Internet) is look up the CD in the Gracenote Media Database.

2. If iTunes finds multiple entries for the CD in the Gracenote Media Database, a dialog box opens, listing all the entries found, and asks you to identify the CD. After you select the CD and click **OK**, another dialog box opens asking whether you want to import the CD.

3. I recommend you click **Do Not Ask Me Again** and then click **No**. Finally, you have access to the iTunes window. The CD is selected in the left pane under Devices, and the tracks on the CD are displayed in the right pane. Each one has a check mark beside it, meaning it is selected and will be included when you play the CD.

4. Uncheck the tracks you do not want to play.

5. Double-click the first track or any track to start playing the CD. iTunes plays the CD through to the end of the last track and stops.

6. If you click the **Repeat** button in the bottom-left corner before you play the first track in your list, iTunes plays all the tracks in your list in a continuous loop. If you click the **Shuffle** button, iTunes plays your tracks in random order.

7. Use the controls at the top of the window to adjust the volume, pause and start the CD, and so on.

 TIP To hide the iTunes window and show only a small set of controls, click the green **Zoom** button in the upper-left corner. Alternatively, you can click **Window**, **Switch to Mini Player** or press **Shift-Command-M**.

Using Visualizer

For your viewing pleasure, try the Visualizer. Random screen art pulses and changes color to the beat and intensity of the music. You can choose from six different Visualizers. To turn on the Visualizer, click **View** in the menu bar. Then click **View Visualizer** and click the one you want. To turn it off, click **View**, **Hide Visualizer**.

 TIP   The Visualizer is also good for hypnotizing small children.

Adding Music to the Library

You can add music to your iTune's library in several ways: purchase albums or single tracks from the iTunes store, download the free Single of the Week from the iTunes store, download music from other sources on the Internet, or import your own CDs. Storing your music in the iTune's library enables you to access your music on all your devices via the iCloud. For more information on setting up iTunes for the iCloud, see Chapter 5, "Using iCloud."

Importing Music

Instead of inserting a CD to play it, you can import the CD's tracks in the iTunes Music library on your hard drive. When you import a CD, if you are connected to the Internet, iTunes can find and supply data for the tracks. Otherwise, the tracks will simply be listed as Track 01, Track 02, and so on. To import music from a CD, follow these steps:

1. Insert the CD in the optical drive.

2. If the song names for the CD cannot be found online, a dialog box asks whether you still want to import the songs. When you import the tracks, they appear as Track 01, Track 02, and so on, but you can add the names yourself. Click **Yes** to import and then skip to step 4.

3. If multiple CDs found in the Gracenote Media Database match the one you are trying to import, a dialog box opens asking you to identify the CD. After you select the correct CD, click **OK**.

4. A dialog box opens (if you have not already checked Do Not Ask Me Again) asking whether you want to import the CD. Click **Yes**. If the dialog box does not appear, click the **Import CD** button in the lower-right corner of the window. The first track begins importing.

5. While the first track is importing, you can uncheck any tracks you do not want to import. If you didn't want the first track, you can delete it later.

6. A dialog box asking you to send information to the Gracenote Media Database may open. You can check **Do Not Ask Me Again** in this box if you want and then click either **Don't Send** or **Send**.

7. To stop the import at any time during the process, click the **Stop Importing** button.

8. When the import is finished, a tone sounds to alert you. Click **Music** in the left pane to see your newly imported tracks.

9. If you did not get the message referred to in step 2, and the track names were still imported as Track 01, Track 02, and so on, make sure you are on the Internet, select the tracks, and click **Advanced** in the menu bar. Click **Get CD Track Names**. Click **OK** to confirm you want to get information for multiple tracks. If no information is available for the tracks, you can supply the information yourself.

> **TIP** To enter track information, switch to the List view (for convenience). Click the track to select it and then click the name. Type the name of the track and press **Tab**. Type the name of the artist and press **Tab**. Type the name of the album and press **Tab**. Begin typing the genre, and iTunes supplies it for you. Press **Return**.

10. In the pane on the left, click the **Eject** button beside the name of the CD (under the Devices category) to eject the CD.

If you import a track you don't want, you can select the track and press the **Delete** key. A confirmation dialog box opens (unless you have previously selected Do Not Ask Me Again). Click **Delete Song** and then click **Move to Trash**.

> **TIP** If you want to import quite a few CDs in succession, first open the iTunes Preferences and click the **General** tab if necessary. Select **Import CD and Eject** for When You Insert a CD. Now you can simply insert one CD after another. ITunes will automatically import all the tracks on the CD and then eject it when finished.

Downloading Music from the iTunes Store

You can download music to iTunes from many different sources on the Internet. Obviously, this book can't cover the steps for all of them, so let's just look at the steps you use to download music from the iTunes Store:

1. Click **iTunes Store** under the Store category in the left pane.

2. Using whatever method you want, find the song or album you want to download.

3. Listen to a preview if you want to.

4. To download, click the price of the song or album.

5. Enter your Apple ID (if you are not already signed in) or enter your iTunes ID if you use a different ID. Enter your password and click **Buy**.

6. When the confirmation dialog box opens, click **Buy**. The download starts. When it is finished, the song appears in your Music library.

Importing Cover Art

Three of the views in iTunes can display cover art if you have downloaded it: Album view, Grid view, and Cover Flow view. To download cover art, you must have an iTunes Store account set up. Follow these steps to download the cover art for your existing albums and for new albums you obtain later:

1. Click **Advanced** in the menu bar and click **Get Album Art**. A confirmation dialog box advises you that information about your songs with missing artwork will be sent to Apple.

2. Click **Get Album Artwork**. The artwork is downloaded to your computer. A message opens if there are albums for which the artwork could not be found. Click the disclosure arrow in the dialog box to see the names of the albums for which cover art could not be obtained. Click **OK** if you see this dialog box.

3. To see all the artwork, if necessary, click one of the view buttons that shows cover art.

Creating and Playing Playlists

A playlist is a group of songs gathered from your Music library. You can listen to a playlist on iTunes, burn it to a CD for use in a CD player, publish it to the iTunes Store, or gift it to a friend.

As you can see by looking back at Figure 26.1, iTunes provides some playlists for you initially, but you also can create your own. The iTunes DJ playlist is a live mix type of playlist. This means that each time you select it, iTunes chooses songs randomly from your Music library or a playlist that you specify. If you don't like the mix, click **Refresh**, and iTunes chooses songs again.

All other playlists that iTunes provides for you are *Smart Playlists*, meaning iTunes populates them with any music you have that meets the criteria set up for the playlists. So, for example, if you have tracks from an Andrea Bocelli album, the tracks will most likely show up in the Classical Music Smart Playlist.

 NOTE   A Smart Playlist has an icon that looks like a gear before its name. A user-created playlist has a musical note icon before its name.

To play a playlist, first select it in the left pane. Uncheck any tracks you don't want to hear. Click the **Shuffle** button to play the list randomly or click the **Repeat** button to play the list repeatedly. Then double-click the first track in the list you want to hear.

Creating a Playlist

You can add your own playlists to the Playlist category. For example, you can select your favorite rock-and-roll tracks from your Music library and name the playlist "Rock-n-Roll Favs." All the playlists you create are listed for you in the left pane under the Playlists category.

To create a playlist, follow these steps:

1. Click the **Add** (+) button in the lower-left corner of the window. A new playlist called *Untitled Playlist* appears at the bottom of the Playlists category in the left pane. The name is already selected for you.

2. Type a name for the list and press **Return**.

3. Drag songs from the Music library and drop them on the name of the new playlist. (You can do this at any time.)

4. Drag songs in the playlist to rearrange their order.

5. Select a song in the playlist that you have decided you don't want and press the **Delete** key. Click **Remove** to confirm. The song is deleted from the playlist but not the library.

 NOTE   You can't delete tracks listed in the default Smart Playlists.

Letting Genius Create a Playlist

The Genius feature makes playlists by evaluating the songs you have in your library and selecting songs that it views as similar or compatible. To do its work, the Genius must gather information from your computer about the music you have stored in iTunes and transmit it to Apple.

 CAUTION Although Apple stores your information anonymously, if you have privacy concerns about anything that is shared from your computer, you might not want to turn on the Genius feature.

To use the Genius feature, you have to turn it on. Here's how:

1. Click **Genius** under the Genius category in the left pane. (If you don't see Genius in the left pane, click **Store** in the menu bar, and then click **Turn on Genius**.)

2. Click the **Turn On Genius** button

3. Enter your Apple ID or iTunes ID and password and click **Continue**.

4. Check the box beside **I Have Read and Agree to These Terms and Conditions** and click **Agree**. Genius begins sending information about your media to Apple and, when finished, displays a message telling you that Genius has been successfully turned on.

If you have only a few songs in your Music library, Genius may not be able to find enough related songs to actually create a playlist. If you have plenty to choose from, follow these steps to create a playlist using Genius:

1. Select a song in your Music library.

2. Click the **Genius** button in the bottom-right corner of the screen. If you get the message that you might need to update your Genius Information, click **Update Genius**.

3. If Genius is able to create a playlist for you, the songs for the playlist are displayed, and a new bar appears above the tracks, as shown in Figure 26.5.

4. Select a different number of songs for **Limit To** in the bar and then click the **Refresh** button in the bar, if desired. You also can click the **Refresh** button if you don't like the songs Genius selected.

5. To save the Genius playlist, click the **Save Playlist** button in the bar. The playlist name is automatically named the same as the song you selected in step 1, and the playlist is listed in the Genius category. (You cannot change the name of the playlist.)

FIGURE 26.5

You might want to call this the Genius bar, but I think the Geniuses at the Genius Bar in the Apple stores would object.

In addition to creating playlists, the Genius feature can create Genius Mixes and even recommend media to you that it thinks you might like, again based on what you already have. You can see these recommendations directly on the iTunes Store home page. Just click **Recommendations for You** under the Quick Links.

Genius Mixes are a set of autogenerated mixes from the songs in your iTunes library. The mix can play continuously like a commercial-free radio station. The Genius Mixes are listed under the Genius category in the left pane.

Creating Your Own Smart Playlists

You may have your own criteria you want to use to create a smart list. For example, you might want to create a Smart Playlist for two of your favorite artists, but only their country songs. To create a Smart Playlist, follow these steps:

1. Click **File** in the menu bar, and then click **New Smart Playlist**. The dialog box shown in Figure 26.6 opens.

FIGURE 26.6

You can add as many rules as you need to define the Smart Playlist.

2. Create your first rule by selecting options from the pop-up lists and then specifying the criteria, such as the artist's name.

3. To add another rule, click the **Add** (+) button and specify the details. Repeat this step for as many rules as you want to add.

4. If you have more than one rule, select an option for **Match**. If you select **All**, each song must meet each one of your rules to be included. If you select **Any**, to be included, a song can meet any one of your rules even if it doesn't meet the other rules.

5. If you want to limit the playlist in some way, click the check box for **Limit To**, enter a number, select an option from the pop-up list (Items, Minutes, Hours, MB, GB), and specify the method.

6. Check the box for **Match Only Checked Items** if you want to include only those songs that have a check mark in front of them in the Music library. (The check mark means the song is selected.)

7. If you want to allow the playlist to update when you get new music that qualifies for inclusion in the playlist or delete music from your library, check the box for **Live Updating**.

Sharing a Playlist via the iTunes Store

If you have a playlist that you want to share with other users, you can share it by publishing it to the iTunes Store, but you must have an Apple ID to publish. To publish a playlist to the iTunes Store, follow these steps:

1. Select the playlist in the left pane.

2. Click **Store** in the menu bar and, then click **Share Playlist**, **Publish**. Only the songs in your playlist that are available at the iTunes Store are listed. The reason is that iTunes makes your playlist available for sale.

3. Enter your Apple ID (if you are not logged in to the iTunes Store already). Enter your password and click **Continue**.

4. Enter a title and description of the playlist.

5. Click **Publish**.

Burning a Music CD

If you want to put some of your music on a CD, you can burn a playlist to a disc. Before you try to burn the playlist, however, make sure it's not too large to fit on the disc. After you select a playlist, the total size of the list is displayed in the status bar. To burn a playlist to a disc, follow these steps:

1. Select the playlist in the left pane.

2. Make sure the check boxes for the tracks you want to include are selected.

3. Click **File** in the menu bar and click **Burn Playlist to Disc**. A dialog box opens.

4. Click the **Burn** button and insert a blank disc as instructed. The progress is displayed at the top of the window. When finished, the name of the disc, which is the same name as the playlist, is displayed under Devices in the left pane.

Listening to Radio

iTunes can access lots of live, streaming radio broadcasts. To listen to one, click **Radio** in the Library category in the left pane, click the disclosure triangle beside a stream, and double-click a radio station to connect to it. The Information box at the top lists the name of the radio station, name of the song, and artist. If your Information box has nothing but little lines in it, click the button on the left side of the box. To disconnect from the station, click the **Stop** button in the toolbar controls.

 NOTE You can listen to music while doing other things in iTunes (such as browsing the Store or creating playlists). Your music will be interrupted only if you click to listen to something else in the Store or your library.

Acquiring and Playing Movies and TV Shows

In the iTunes store, you can purchase or rent thousands of movies and TV shows (many of which are available in HD and SD). To find a show you want to download, browse the categories listed on the drop-down menus for Movies or TV Shows, or use the Spotlight search box to search for a particular title.

Before purchasing or renting a show, you can view a free preview. If the show is a movie, you can view the movie trailer. If the show is a TV episode, you can click the Play button that appears beside the title to see a preview.

If you purchase or rent a movie or TV show, it begins to download immediately after you click the Rent or Buy button, but you don't have to wait for the download to finish before you start watching it. Additionally, if you rent a show, you have 30 days to start watching it and then 48 hours to finish watching it if it's a TV show or 24 hours to finish watching it if it's a movie.

 TIP To watch a show in Full Screen, click the Full Screen button in the onscreen controls.

Acquiring and Playing Podcasts

A podcast is an audio or video recording that has multiple episodes released over time, similar to a TV series. Using iTunes, you can download a single episode or subscribe to the series, in which case, iTunes automatically downloads new episodes when they become available.

 NOTE You also can just listen to the podcast while you are online in the iTunes Store.

To select podcasts for downloading, follow these steps:

1. Click **Podcasts** in the left pane. (If you do not see Podcasts listed in the left pane, open the iTunes General Preferences and select **Podcasts** listed under the **Show** option and click **OK**.)

2. Click the **Podcast Directory** button in the lower-right corner of the window.

3. To download a single podcast, click **Free** to the right of the episode's name. Notice in the left pane that the Downloads item under the Store category has a revolving circle, which lets you know that the file is indeed downloading.

4. To get all episodes automatically as they are available, click **Subscribe Free**. A dialog box opens, and you must click **Subscribe** again.

5. When the podcast finishes downloading, click **Podcasts** in the Library category in the left pane to see the listing for the podcast. If you have subscribed to a series, click the disclosure triangle to display all the episodes.

To play a podcast, click **Podcasts** in the left pane, click the disclosure triangle for the podcast series in the right pane that you want to play, and double-click the episode you want to play.

To unsubscribe to a series of podcasts, click **Podcasts** in the left pane, click the podcast in the right pane, and click the **Unsubscribe** button. All the podcasts you have already downloaded will remain in your list, but you will receive no new ones.

Acquiring and Playing Courses from iTunes U

You will find the number and quality of educational courses available at iTunes U to be mind-blowing, and all the courses cost...nothing. Talk about a free education!

You can simply watch or listen to a lecture or course while you are online at the iTunes Store, or you can download it to your iTunes U library. (Some courses are purely audio, but many are videos.) To download a course or a series of courses, go to the iTunes Store and click **iTunes U** in the navigation bar. When you find the course you want, click **Free** to download a single course or click **Subscribe Free** to download a course series.

THE ABSOLUTE MINIMUM

- You can play a CD using iTunes, but importing the CD into the iTunes Music library makes it more convenient for you to play it at any time.

- You can create a playlist or a Smart Playlist to listen to, burn to a CD, or publish to iTunes.

- The iTunes Store has a wealth of free content in the area of podcasts and educational courses.

27

USING PHOTO BOOTH

Photo Booth is definitely an application made for fun, but you also can do some useful things with it. Find out about both the fun and the practical side of Photo Booth in this chapter.

Exploring the Photo Booth Window

The first time you open Photo Booth (on a new installation of Mountain Lion), it opens in Full Screen mode. If you don't use the Full Screen mode, the user interface is somewhat different. To avoid having to give two sets of instructions for the two different interfaces, we use the Full Screen mode for the rest of the chapter. When you are familiar with Photo Booth, you really won't have any trouble using either mode.

TIP Remember that you can exit Full Screen mode any time by pointing to the top of the screen and clicking the Full Screen button on the far right side of the menu bar.

In the Full Screen mode, a wood-grain panel at the bottom of the screen contains your controls, as shown in Figure 27.1. The dial on the left has three positions denoted by the icons above it. The position on the left is for a four-up photograph; the position in the middle is for a regular photograph; and the position on the right is for a movie.

FIGURE 27.1

The tray holds the pictures and videos you have taken.

Taking and Viewing Photos

Using the built-in camera, you can sit in front of your monitor and take a picture of yourself or video yourself. Even more people can get in on the action if you have a newer Mac with the built-in widescreen FaceTime HD camera.

Taking a Still Picture

To take a still picture of yourself, drag the dial (shown in Figure 27.1) to the middle or just click the icon in the middle above the dial. Click the red **Shutter** button. Three "red lights" illuminate and beep one at a time as the camera gets ready to take your picture. You might be tempted, but don't watch the buttons. Look at the small camera lens at the top of the screen. When the picture is taken, the flash goes off and you hear the sound that a reflex camera makes when it snaps a photo. Your picture shows up in the "tray" at the bottom of the screen.

TIP   To use natural lighting when you take a photo, press the **Shift** key when you click the **Shutter** button.

Taking a Four-Up Picture

To take four quick pictures in a row in Full Screen mode, drag the dial all the way to the left (or just click the icon on the left above the dial). After the three lights are illuminated, the camera snaps four pictures in quick succession. You barely have time to change your expression. The four photos are grouped together as one photo, and the composite photo shows up in the "tray" at the bottom of the screen just as a single photo does.

Viewing Photos

Use a swiping motion to scroll through the thumbnails in the tray at the bottom of the screen, or click a photo to select it and then use the left- or right-arrow keys on the keyboard to scroll.

When you click a thumbnail in the tray, the photo appears in the full pane. If the picture is a four-up photo, you see all four pictures in the viewing area, but you can click any one of the four photos to zoom in on it.

To view a slideshow of all your photos, point to the upper edge of the screen until you see the menu bar. Click **View**, **Start Slideshow**.

Click the **Play** button that appears below the viewing area. The slideshow plays in a continuous loop, and it does not include videos. To stop the slideshow, point to the black space under the viewing area to redisplay the controls and click the **Pause** button. Click the **X** button to exit.

Recording and Viewing Movies

To record a movie, drag the dial all the way to the right. (You also can just click the icon on the right above the dial.) When ready, click the red **Shutter** button. Wait for the three lights to illuminate and beep and then start the action. As you are recording, a time counter at the bottom-left corner shows the time that has elapsed. Click the **Stop** button when you are finished recording.

The movie appears as a thumbnail in the tray at the bottom along with the still photos. You can tell the difference between a photo and a video because a video displays its duration (minutes and seconds) in the bottom-right corner.

To view a movie, click the thumbnail. The movie begins playing immediately and will play to the end and stop. To play the movie again, move the pointer over the video to make the controls visible and click the **Play** button. To pause the movie, show the controls again and click the **Pause** button.

TIP After viewing a movie, you can return to picture-taking mode by clicking the **Shutter** button.

Trimming a Video

When you record a movie in Photo Booth, you always have some frames at the end of the movie that show you turning the video camera off. You may also have some frames at the beginning of the movie that you don't want. Fortunately, you don't have to use some other program to remove these frames because Photo Booth has a built-in editing feature that trims the beginning or end of a movie. To trim a movie, follow these steps:

1. Select the thumbnail of the movie in the bottom pane. The movie begins to play.

2. Move the mouse cursor over the movie to display the controls at the bottom of the picture. Click the **Trim** button on the right. The entire movie is displayed as a film clip, as shown in Figure 27.2.

FIGURE 27.2

The filmstrip has trim handles at the beginning and end.

3. Drag the yellow handles at the left or right to trim the beginning or the end of the clip.

4. Click the button on the right with the check mark.

Using Effects

The Photo Booth has some very special effects that you can use to make your photos and videos more "interesting," shall we say. Some of these effects are like special lenses you might put on a real professional-type camera, such as a fish-eye lens. Other effects are similar to film development processes, such as black-and-white or sepia tone. Most of the effects are just whacko stuff that I assume the Apple programmers came up with late at night after 48 hours of no sleep and 20 cups of coffee. Of course, these are the effects that are the most fun (and entertain children and adults alike for hours on end).

You select an effect before you take a photo or video by clicking the **Effects** button. There are five pages of effects you can scroll through using swiping gestures, by clicking the scrolling arrows, or just by clicking the dot for the page. The first three pages are all the effects. The fourth page of effects adds a background to the photo, and the fifth page is for user-supplied backgrounds.

Scroll through the pages until you find the one you want and then just click it. The Full Screen mode returns. Drag the dial to take a photo, four photos, or a video and then click the red **Shutter** button. If recording a video, click the **Stop** button when you are finished. If the special effect you select is a background, you are asked to step out of the frame until the background is detected. After the background is detected, step back into the frame and click the **Shutter** button.

 NOTE   Some backgrounds on page 4 are videos, so you must click the **Stop** button when finished.

When you want to turn off an effect, click **Effects** and click **Normal**; Normal is the "effect" in the middle on every page.

Deleting Items in Photo Booth

If you want to delete a photo or movie you have taken, just click it to select it. Then you see an **x** in the upper-left corner. To delete more than one item, **Command-click** the items to select them, and then press the **Delete** button. When you select multiple items, they do not display **x**'s in the corner.

Sharing Your Photos and Movies

Clicking the **Share** button in the lower-right corner displays the appropriate Share options for the item(s) selected. To share photos or videos, first select the items in the tray, click the **Share** button, click the Share option you want, and then follow the steps shown here for the corresponding Share option:

- **Email**—Enter an email address and, if desired, a message. Click the **Send** button.

- **Message**—Enter a name or phone number, type a message (if desired), and click **Send**.

- **Facebook**—Select options for Friends or Wall. Type text if desired, and click **Post**. You must have an account set up for Facebook before you can use this option.

- **Vimeo** (Videos only)—Enter a title for the movie, a description, tags, and check or uncheck **Make This Movie Personal**. Click **Publish**. You must have an account with Vimeo first, of course.

- **Twitter**—Enter a tweet message (if desired) and click **Send**. You also must have an account with Twitter before you can send a tweet.

- **Flickr** (Photos only)—Enter a title for the photo, a description, tags, and select an option from the Access pop-up menu. Click **Publish**. Again, you must first have an account before you can use Flickr.

- **Add to iPhoto**—iPhoto opens and imports the items into a single event.

- **Set Account Picture**—Your user account opens in System Preferences and the photo automatically replaces the picture you had before. Close the window.

- **Set Buddy Picture**—The Edit Picture dialog box opens in Messages with the new photo. Make edits as desired and click **Done**.

- **Change Twitter Profile Picture**—The photo is automatically updated in your profile and you hear a twitter. Nothing happens on the screen.

THE ABSOLUTE MINIMUM

- Just have some fun with Photo Booth!

- Take pictures of yourself to use for your user account photo, your Messages photo, and your Twitter profile photo.

- You can send photos and videos to iPhoto via the Share button.

- Share your photos in email, messages, and tweets. Upload photos or videos to Flickr or Vimeo.

28

IN THIS CHAPTER

- Creating new user accounts and enabling a Guest account
- Controlling how multiple users log in and out
- Changing a user account password
- Changing the account picture
- Deleting a user account

MANAGING USER ACCOUNTS

A user account on a computer comprises, among other things, a username; a password; the requirement to log in or not; a folder structure for exclusive use by the user on the account; a set of the user's preferences for how the computer operates; and the ability to set up email, contacts, calendars, and social networking accounts. If you are the only user on your computer, Mountain Lion set up your user account for you when you went through the initial steps to set up your computer. You answered a few questions, and Mountain Lion created your Home folder with its default subfolders and made you an administrator on the computer, which means you can do anything you want on the Mac. This chapter tells you exactly what those things are.

Creating a User Account

If yours is the only user account on your Mac, and you don't even log in with a password, you probably never even think about your user account. It's just there, and it works; you don't have to think about it. If you are *not* the only person who uses the computer, we're talking about a whole new ball game. Ideally, every user of your computer should have her own user account. This enables each user to customize the system and maintain her own separate and private files, emails, contacts, calendars, and so on. Because you have an administrator user account, you have the power to create new user accounts for other users. Table 28.1 explains the types of user accounts that an administrator on the system can create.

NOTE If you need to share your computer only occasionally with people who just want to get on the Internet or use your printer, you don't need to create a separate account for each person. Instead, you can let them use the Guest account that Mountain Lion created and enabled for you when it set up your administrator account. All you have to do is enable it.

TABLE 28.1 Types of User Accounts

Account Type	Privileges
Administrator	Can create, delete, and change user accounts; modify system settings; install software; and change the settings of other users.
Standard	Can change the settings in only his account. Cannot create user accounts or change locked system preferences. Cannot create folders outside his Home folder or the Shared folder.
Managed with Parental Controls	Has at least the Standard privileges, which can then be further limited by the settings made under Parental Controls.
Sharing Only	Has access to only shared folders. Access to a shared folder may be further limited to No Access, Read & Write, Read Only, or Write Only (Drop Box in Public folder).
Group	Includes multiple individual users. Enables an administrator to make global changes to permissions or sharing privileges for these individuals.

To set up another user account, follow these steps:

1. Click the **System Preferences** icon in the Dock or in Launchpad and click the **Users & Groups** icon in the System row. The Users & Groups page opens.

2. Click the padlock icon in the lower-left corner of the window.

3. Type your password and click **Unlock**. The padlock opens, allowing you to make changes. (See Figure 28.1.)

 NOTE As an administrator, you have a username and a password, even if you don't use it to log in. I hope you remember your password, because without it, you will be severely limited, not only in creating user accounts, but administering your computer as a whole. If you do not have an administrator account, you must enter the name and password of someone who does; otherwise, you can't go on.

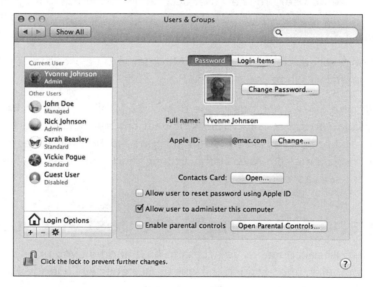

FIGURE 28.1

All user accounts on your system appear in the list on the left.

4. Click the **Add** (+) button. The form opens that you must complete to create a new account.

5. Select the type of account you want from the pop-up menu for New Account. Refer to Table 28.1 to help you make your decision.

6. Type a full name for the account. This will be the login name.

7. Type an account name. This will be the name of the user's Home folder and after it has been created, it is virtually impossible to change it. So choose wisely.

8. Type a password for the account and then type it again in the Verify field.

 NOTE Be sure to make a note of the full name and password to give to the user and keep a copy for yourself. Even though you are the administrator, you can't look up a password after it's been created. If the user forgets the password, you just have to create a new password for her.

9. Type a hint for the password if you want to, but don't make the hint obvious enough that someone could guess the password with a little research, such as "initials + birthday."

10. Click **Create User**. The new user account is added to the list in the sidebar, and it is selected. While it is selected, you can set the Apple ID, if the user has one, and specify additional options for the account.

11. When finished, close the window. Mountain Lion closes the padlock automatically when you close the Preferences window.

The first time a new user logs in, the desktop and all the System Preferences are set to the factory defaults regardless of what changes you've made to your own desktop and preferences in *your* user account. As the user makes changes to the system, the changes are saved in his account and do not affect your account or any other user's account.

Enabling and Disabling the Guest Account

The Guest user account has no access to anything that you or any other user does on the computer, and anything the guest user does while logged in is deleted or reset to the defaults when that user logs out.

 TIP If you want to make some files available to a Guest user, you can share a folder and then select the option in the Guest account to allow the guest to access shared folders. (To share a folder, open the Sharing preferences in System Preferences.)

Although Mountain Lion creates the Guest user account for you automatically, it doesn't enable the account by default. If you want to make it available for use on your computer, you have to enable it yourself. If you are an administrator on the system, follow these steps to enable or disable a Guest account:

1. Click the **System Preferences** icon in the Dock or Launchpad and click the **Users & Groups** icon in the System row.

2. Click the padlock icon in the lower-left corner of the window.

3. Type your password and click **Unlock**.

 NOTE   If you do not have an Administrator account, you must enter the name and password of an Administrator account.

4. Click **Guest User** in the sidebar.

5. To enable or disable the account, check or uncheck the option **Allow Guest to Log In to This Computer**.

6. To enable or disable Parental Controls, check or uncheck the **Enable Parental Controls** option. If you enable these controls, click the **Open Parental Controls** button to set the options you want.

 TIP   Remember that the parental controls will function for every guest that uses the Guest account. If you have a particular user in mind who needs parental controls, you should create an account specifically for that individual.

7. To enable or disable file sharing, check or uncheck the option **Allow Guests to Connect to Shared Folders**.

8. Close the window. Mountain Lion closes the padlock for you automatically.

When a guest logs in, he doesn't have to enter a password. When that guest logs out, he has to click **Delete Files & Log Out**. This is a reminder to the guest that every file he has added to the computer is deleted. Any changes that the user made to the desktop, system preferences, and so on, are reset to the original settings. In other words, Mountain Lion cleans house and gets everything ready for the next guest.

If you are logged in as a guest and you don't want to lose your files, you can save your files to a USB drive.

Setting Login Options

If you are the only user on your computer, you may like to turn on your computer and not have to log in. If the Automatic Login option is enabled for your account, this is exactly what happens. If you create additional user accounts or enable the Guest account, you should disable Automatic Login. Follow these steps to enable or disable Automatic Login:

1. Click the **System Preferences** icon in the Dock or Launchpad and click the **Users & Groups** icon in the System row.

2. Click the padlock icon in the lower-left corner of the window.

3. Type your password and click **Unlock**.

 NOTE If you do not have an Administrator account, you must enter the name and password of an Administrator account.

4. Click **Login Options**.

5. To disable automatic login, select **Off** from the **Automatic Login** pop-up menu. To enable it for your account, select your name from the **Automatic Login** pop-up menu.

6. Type your password and click **OK**.

7. When finished, close the window. Mountain Lion closes the padlock for you automatically.

Working with Multiple User Logins

If multiple users want to be logged in to the computer at the same time, each user must log in. When the Mac starts and displays the login screen, the first user can log in by clicking her account name, typing the password, and pressing **Return** or clicking the arrow in the password field. (If the user enters an incorrect password, the password box shakes back and forth and a hint appears, if there is one, after the third failure.) For the next user to be able to log in, the current user has to log out or switch places with the second user.

To log out, follow these steps:

1. Click the **Apple** menu and click the last option on the menu, **Log Out <_User Name_>** (where _User Name_ is the account name). An "Are You Sure" type dialog box opens.

2. Check or uncheck the box for **Reopen windows** when logging back in.

3. Click the **Log Out** button. The login screen opens so another user can log in.

CAUTION   Shutting down the computer when more than one user is logged in could cause other users to lose data. They should be allowed to log off before you shut down the system. Fortunately, Mountain Lion reminds you that other users are logged in when you attempt to shut down the computer. If you don't want to allow other users to log off before you shut down the computer, you can type an administrator name and password and click **Shut Down**.

To switch places with another user, you can use the feature called *Fast User Switching*. This feature allows all users to continue to be logged in, but only one user can be the active user at any one time. Using this feature can place more demands on the system resources, which, in turn, could cause your computer to slow down. This is true if all the logged-in users have lots of applications open. To quickly switch users, follow these steps:

1. Click the current username on the right side of the menu bar. A pop-up menu displays a list of all users on the system, and a check mark appears beside the names of all users who are currently logged in.

2. Click the name of the user account for the user who wants to log in. A login dialog box opens.

3. Type the password and press **Return** or click the right arrow in the password field. The desktop for the new user is displayed, but all the applications and files that the previous user was working with are still open and running (unseen) in the background.

Modifying a User Account

Two options in a standard or administrator user account that the user can change are the password and the user account picture. If you have a managed user account, you may or may not be able to change these two options.

Changing Your Password

As you probably know, security experts advise you to change your password frequently. Most people are not very faithful to this admonition, but for those who are, here are the steps to follow:

1. Click the **System Preferences** icon in the Dock or Launchpad and click the **Users & Groups** icon in the System row. Your account is selected by default.

2. Click **Change**.

3. Type your original password in the **Old Password** field.

4. In the **New Password** field, type a new password.

5. Type the password again in the **Verify** field.

6. If you want to (I recommend you do), type a hint to remind yourself regarding the password and then click **Change Password**.

7. Click **OK**.

8. Close the System Preference window when finished.

Changing the Account Picture

Your account picture may be a photo that you took of yourself using the built-in camera, or it could be one of the default icons. This is the photo or icon that shows up on the login screen.

To choose a new icon to represent you or take a new picture of yourself, follow these steps:

1. Click the **System Preferences** icon in the Dock or Launchpad and click the **Users & Groups** icon in the System row. Your account is selected by default.

2. Click the picture that currently represents your account.

3. Click a different picture in the library or click **Camera**. Click the shutter button. After the camera counts down from 3, it takes the photo. If you like the photo, click **Done**; otherwise, click **Cancel** and start with step 2 again.

 TIP Before clicking **Done**, you can use the slide to resize the photo and then drag it inside the frame to position it or click the **Effects** button and choose an effect.

4. Close the System Preference window when finished.

Deleting a User Account

When you need to delete a user account, you must decide what should happen to the data in the user's Home folder. There are a couple of ways to keep the data, or you can delete it completely.

To delete a user account, follow these steps:

1. Click the **System Preferences** icon in the Dock or Launchpad and click the **Users & Groups** icon in the System row. Your account is selected by default.

2. Click the padlock icon in the lower-left corner of the window.

3. Type your password and click **Unlock**.

 NOTE If you do not have an Administrator account, you must enter the name and password of an Administrator account.

4. Select the account you want to delete and click the **Delete** (-) button, located just above the padlock icon. The dialog box shown in Figure 28.2 opens.

FIGURE 28.2

This dialog box gives you options for handling user data in the Home folder.

5. If the user has data you want to save, select **Save the Home Folder in a Disk Image** or **Don't Change the Home Folder**. Otherwise, select **Delete the Home Folder**.

6. Click **OK**. Mountain Lion deletes the account, and when it is finished, the account name disappears from the sidebar.

7. When finished, close the window. Mountain Lion closes the padlock for you automatically.

THE ABSOLUTE MINIMUM

- If additional people use your computer, create a user account for each one and turn off Automatic Login so all users are required to log in.

- A user account allows each user to customize the system and maintain her own separate and private files, emails, contacts, and calendars without affecting any other user's account.

- You can delete a user account and still save the user data.

IN THIS CHAPTER

- Updating your applications
- Backing up and restoring data with Time Machine
- Using a firewall
- Setting security and privacy preferences

29

MAINTAINING AND SECURING YOUR MAC

This chapter covers issues that are vital to your Mac's health and well-being (as well as your own). In this chapter, I tell you how to back up and restore data, avoid malware with Mountain Lion's new Gatekeeper feature, and safely and privately surf the Web.

Maintaining Your Mac

Basically, there are only a couple of things you need to do to maintain your Mac. You need to keep the operating system software up-to-date, and you need to keep everything backed up. These two routines together provide coverage in the areas of prevention and damage control.

Getting Software Updates

After the release of a major version of any Mac application, Apple releases free updates that solve problems, add functionality, or address security issues. When an update for OS X or an Apple application is available, the App Store automatically downloads it and sends a notification to the Notification Center to let you know it is ready for you to install.

 TIP   Always install updates promptly.

To install an update, follow these steps:

1. Click the **App Store** icon in the Dock.

2. Although the App Store prompts you to sign in when necessary, you might as well go ahead and sign in as soon as you open the store. Click **Store** in the menu bar and then click **Sign In**, if necessary. Enter your Apple ID and password and click **Sign In**.

3. Click the **Updates** link at the top of the window.

4. Click **Update** beside the update that you want to install.

 TIP   You can check for software updates manually by clicking the **Apple** menu and clicking **Software Update**.

Backing Up Data with Time Machine

Before the Time Machine feature was introduced, you had to figure out how to back up your system and then remember to do it on a regular basis. With Time Machine, you click the mouse a few times, and your backup routine is basically on autopilot. You can literally set it and forget it.

 TIP   I recommend that you purchase a second hard drive to use with Time Machine. It should be at least 500GB or more (depending on the size of your hard drive), and it has to be formatted for a Mac.

To start using Time Machine, follow these steps:

1. Attach the hard drive to your Mac and click **Launchpad** in the Dock.

2. Type **Time** in the Spotlight search box and click the **Time Machine** icon.

3. Click **Time Machine Preferences**.

4. Click the padlock, if necessary, type your password, and click **Unlock**.

5. Slide the **Off** button to **On**.

6. Click **Select Backup Disk**, select the hard drive you connected in step 1, and click **Add Backup Disk**. The backup starts in two minutes.

7. Close the Preferences window.

The first backup includes everything on your hard drive: all data and preferences, all the other users' data and preferences, all applications, and the operating system. Depending on how much data is stored on the computer, this first backup can take awhile, but you can continue to work during the backup.

Going forward, as long as the drive is attached to the Mac, Time Machine checks your computer every hour and backs up the changes. It keeps multiple backups of your system, allowing you to restore from a particular date or time.

If you ever unplug the drive, Time Machine cannot perform its backups but will resume its backup procedure automatically when you plug it back in again. If you have to unplug the external hard drive often (to free up the port for another use, for example), consider buying the wireless Apple Time Capsule.

Restoring Data with Time Machine

Time Machine can restore single or multiple data files, entire folders, applications, or the entire system to the Finder. Additionally, it can restore an item to iPhoto, an entry to Contacts, or an item to Mail. In general, a file or item becomes unrecoverable (except perhaps by third-party software) if you delete it and then empty the Trash. If you are using Time Machine, however, the unrecoverable becomes recoverable.

Here's how you restore an item that has been "permanently" deleted:

1. Open the application to which you want to restore data: the Finder, iPhoto, Contacts, or Mail.

2. If you know the folder, album, mailbox and so on, where the item was stored, select it.

3. Open Time Machine from the Launchpad. The application appears to fly through space and then appears in Time Machine with windows of multiple backups behind it, as shown in Figure 29.1.

FIGURE 29.1

Use the hash marks on the right side of the desktop to select a particular date.

4. From this point, you have multiple ways to look for the item you want to restore: click one of the window title bars in the stack, click a date in the date line on the right, or click the flat arrow that is pointing away from you. If you do not know the exact location of the file, you can perform a search in the Spotlight search box.

 NOTE If the item you want to restore is a file in the Finder, select it and press the **spacebar** to view the content of the file to be sure it is the file you want.

5. When you find the item, select it and click **Restore** in the bottom-right corner of the screen. (If you have multiple items selected, click **Restore All**.) The application window appears to travel back to the present and makes a landing on the desktop with the item restored to its original location, and Time Machine closes.

Securing Your Mac

As in life, there are lots of "bad" people on the Internet. They are trying to connect to your computer or download malware (malicious software) to it so they can get your personal data or just wreak havoc. Apple provides multiple methods to ward off these attacks. To make sure your Mac is secure, you need to make appropriate settings for security in the System Preferences; make appropriate settings for security in Safari; use a firewall; and in some cases, encrypt your hard drive.

Setting System Security Preferences

Mountain Lion introduces a new security feature called *Gatekeeper*. New options added to the General page of Security & Privacy System Preferences control how Gatekeeper works on your system. Gatekeeper's job is to help you avoid malware.

To set preferences for security, follow these steps:

1. Click the **System Preferences** icon in the Dock or Launchpad and click the **Security & Privacy** icon in the first row.

2. Click **General**, if necessary. On this pane, shown in Figure 29.2, you have several options to protect your computer while you are working. If you work in an environment where you might have sensitive information on the screen that other people could see, check the box for **Require Password** and select a time interval for **After Sleep or Screen Saver Begins**. Additionally, you can check the box for **Show a Message When the Screen Is Locked**. Then click the **Set Lock Message** button, type a message, and click **OK**.

3. **Disable Automatic Login** is selected by default. If you have more than one user account on your Mac, you definitely need to keep this option disabled.

4. The options for **Allow Applications Downloaded From** are the new options associated with Gatekeeper. The most secure (and the most limiting) option is **Mac App Store**. If you select this option, you will not be able to download software from any other source. If you select **Mac App Store and Identified Developers**, you'll be able to download applications from other sources if the developer of the application has a certificate from Apple. If you select **Anywhere** (not recommended), you are very vulnerable to downloading an application that could be malware.

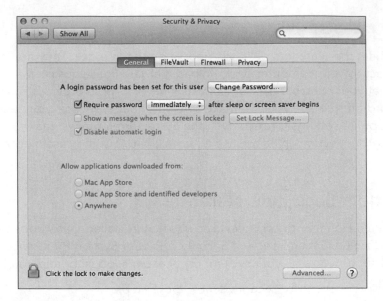

FIGURE 29.2

The General preferences contain the new Gatekeeper options.

 NOTE   Any developer can register with Apple and receive a certificate with no questions asked. Apple does not test the applications the developer creates, but it uses the certificate to track the developer on a daily basis. If a developer is found to be distributing malware, Apple immediately revokes the developer's certificate and adds it to a blacklist. Gatekeeper checks the blacklist server daily. If it finds a new blacklisted certificate, it will not allow any applications signed by that developer to run on your system.

Setting Safari Security Preferences

You probably don't need to change the default settings for Safari's security preferences, but you should at least know what they are. To view (or change) the security preferences, follow these steps:

1. Launch Safari.

2. Click **Safari** on the menu bar and then click **Preferences**.

3. Click the **Security** tab, if necessary. (See Figure 29.3.)

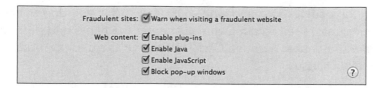

FIGURE 29.3

Security preferences for Safari warn you about fraudulent websites and control web content.

4. The **Warn When Visiting a Fraudulent Website** option is selected by default for **Fraudulent Sites**. Fraudulent sites often use various tricks to make their addresses appear to be the address of the site they are impersonating. When you have this option selected, Safari warns you when you land on one of these sites because it checks the site's certificate, which cannot be faked.

5. Each option for **Web Content** is selected by default. Plug-ins, Java, and JavaScript are all elements that websites may use to deliver content to you. If you disable any of these three options, a website may not function correctly. Most of the time you do not want to see pop-up windows, but occasionally a website may use a pop-up window for a legitimate reason. If necessary, when you need to use that site, you can deselect the **Block Pop-up Windows** option on this page.

6. Close the Preferences window when finished.

Using a Firewall

The Mac provides a firewall for you to block unwanted incoming connections from other computers on a network or the Internet. This option is turned on by default in Mountain Lion. If the firewall is turned off, your Mac accepts all incoming connections from other computers on networks or the Internet, which is not a good thing!

At some point you might need to turn off the firewall just long enough for something that is having trouble getting through to make the connection. As soon as the transaction is completed, you should turn the firewall back on immediately.

Follow these steps to turn the firewall off and on:

1. Click the **System Preferences** icon in the Dock or Launchpad and click the **Security & Privacy** icon in the first row.

2. Click the **Firewall** tab, if necessary.

3. Click the padlock icon and type your password. If you do not have an administrator user account, you must enter the name and password of an administrator user account. Click **Unlock** and the padlock opens, allowing you to make changes.

4. Click **Turn On Firewall** to turn on the firewall. Now the Mac allows only connections by software and services that have a signed, trusted certificate. Click **Turn Off Firewall** to turn off the firewall. Now any connection can get through.

5. Close the System Preferences window when finished. Mountain Lion locks the padlock for you automatically.

Encrypting a Drive

To keep all data on a drive from being seen or copied (without a password), you can encrypt the entire drive using FileVault. The encrypting and decrypting process is quite rapid and impacts the computer's performance very little. The initial encryption of a hard drive takes a little longer, but you can continue to work during the process.

To encrypt your data on the hard drive, follow these steps:

1. Click the **System Preferences** icon in the Dock or Launchpad and click the **Security & Privacy** icon in the first row.

2. Click the **FileVault** tab.

3. Click the padlock icon and type your password. If you do not have an administrator user account, you must enter the name and password of an administrator user account. Click **Unlock** and the padlock opens, allowing you to make changes.

4. Click **Turn On FileVault**. The list of users who have accounts on the Mac appears. Select each user who should be able to unlock the disk and click **Continue**.

5. You are given a recovery key that you can use to unlock the data if you forget your login password. Write down this key and keep it in a safe place. Click **Continue**.

6. In the next dialog box that appears, select **Store the Recovery Key with Apple** or select **Do Not Store the Recovery Key with Apple**. If you choose to store the key with Apple, you must then specify three security questions and give the answers to them. Click **Continue**.

7. Click **Restart** to restart your Mac. The encryption process will begin when it reboots. It's not too late to back out. You also can click **Cancel** at this point, but when the process starts, you can't stop it.

 TIP   To encrypt an external drive, open the Finder, right-click the drive in the sidebar, and click the **Encrypt** option.

Securing Your Privacy

Some features that provide you with real advantages also pose a degree of invasion of privacy. For example, the Mac's capability to send out GPS coordinates to applications enables those applications to give you information that is pertinent to you. It also gives an application private information about you that it could potentially use against you in some way. Mountain Lion gives you options to monitor and control these types of "double-edged" features in System Preferences and in Safari Preferences.

Securing Your Privacy on the Mac

To monitor and control applications that have requested information from your computer, follow these steps:

1. Click the **System Preferences** icon in the Dock or in Launchpad and click **Security & Privacy** in the top row.

2. Click **Privacy**, if necessary.

3. Select **Location Services** in the list on the left. Applications that have requested GPS coordinates are listed in the pane on the right.

4. If you want to allow location information to be given, check the **Enable Location Services** box and then check the boxes for the applications you want to receive the data. (Applications that have requested the information within the last 24 hours display an arrow symbol.)

5. To see what applications are trying to access your Contacts, Twitter, or other applications, select the desired application in the list on the left. Applications that want the information are listed in the pane on the right (if there are any). Check the boxes for each application you want to allow to receive the data.

6. To allow or disallow Apple to receive data from your computer for diagnostic and usage purposes, click **Diagnostics & Usage** in the list on the left. Check or uncheck the box for **Send Diagnostic & Usage Data to Apple**. (Note that this option is selected by default.)

7. Close the Preferences window when finished.

Securing Your Privacy on the Web

Many websites send data to be stored on your computer, such as cookies. They also keep a history of your surfing activities so they can serve relevant information (or advertising) to you. To monitor and control these website activities, follow these steps:

1. Launch Safari.

2. Click **Safari** on the menu bar and then click **Preferences**.

3. Click the **Privacy** tab, if necessary. (See Figure 29.4.)

FIGURE 29.4

Ninety websites are storing cookies or other data on this Mac.

4. Looking at the first option on the page, you can see how many websites are storing various kinds of data on your website. To see which websites have stored information on your computer and exactly what they have stored, click **Details**. Figure 29.5 shows the details for my Mac.

 TIP Instead of clicking Details, if you want to remove everything, click **Remove All Website Data**. Safari clears the information that websites have stored on your computer to track you online, including cookies, Flash plug-in data, as well as information from databases, local storage, and the application cache.

5. To remove a website's stored data, select the site and click **Remove**.

6. Click **Done** when finished.

These websites have stored data that can be used to track your browsing. Removing the data may reduce tracking, but may also log you out of websites or change website behavior.

- 2mdn.net
  Cache
- absurdlycool.com
  Cookies
- addthis.com
  Cache
- adobe.com
  Cookies, Local Storage
- allexperts.com
  Cookies
- amazon.com
  Cookies
- amazonaws.com
  Cache

Remove   Remove All   Done

FIGURE 29.5

Use the Spotlight search in this dialog box to find a particular website easily.

7. For the **Block Cookies** option, I recommend the default setting, **From Third Parties and Advertisers**. You cannot access some websites if you block cookies completely. By selecting the first option, you can go to a website that requires a cookie to accept you, but you block any third parties or advertisers on the website from also placing cookies on your computer.

8. The default setting for **Limit Website Access to Location Services** is **Prompt for Each Website Once Each Day**. With this option, you can allow or disallow the transmission of your location to a website when the prompt asking for your permission appears. If you use the website repeatedly throughout the day, you will be prompted only once.

9. The **Website Tracking** option is a new option in Mountain Lion. It's not enabled by default, but you can check the option if you don't want websites to follow your movements on the Web.

10. The **Web Search** option is also a new option in Mountain Lion, and it is not selected by default either. If you don't want search engines to make suggestions to you, select this option.

11. When finished, close the Preferences window.

THE ABSOLUTE MINIMUM

- You must install the latest updates to your applications to keep them running well and securely.

- If you delete an item and then empty the Trash, you can restore the item from Time Machine, assuming you didn't both create and permanently delete the item between Time Machine backups.

- The firewall is turned on by default, and you should leave it on!

- If you don't want websites to track your activities, you can turn off website tracking in Safari's Privacy preferences.

Index

Y

Z

   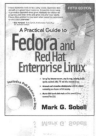  

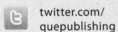

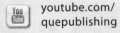
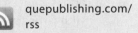

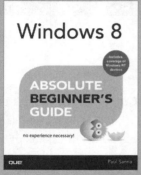
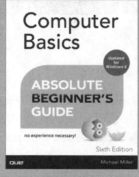

OS X
Mountain Lion

Covers all Mac desktop and notebook devices

ABSOLUTE BEGINNER'S GUIDE

No experience necessary!

Yvonne Johnson

FREE
Online Edition

Safari
Books Online

Your purchase of *OS X Mountain Lion Absolute Beginner's Guide* includes access to a free online edition for 45 days through the **Safari Books Online** subscription service. Nearly every Que book is available online through **Safari Books Online**, along with thousands of books and videos from publishers such as Addison-Wesley Professional, Cisco Press, Exam Cram, IBM Press, O'Reilly Media, Prentice Hall, Sams, and VMware Press.

Safari Books Online is a digital library providing searchable, on-demand access to thousands of technology, digital media, and professional development books and videos from leading publishers. With one monthly or yearly subscription price, you get unlimited access to learning tools and information on topics including mobile app and software development, tips and tricks on using your favorite gadgets, networking, project management, graphic design, and much more.

Activate your FREE Online Edition at
informit.com/safarifree

STEP 1: Enter the coupon code: JZVGXBI

STEP 2: New Safari users, complete the brief registration form.
Safari subscribers, just log in.

If you have difficulty registering on Safari or accessing the online edition,
please e-mail customer-service@safaribooksonline.com